ESPECIALLY FOR

....

FROM

....

DATE

....

Published by Barbour Publishing, Inc., 1810 Barbour Drive, Uhrichsville, Ohio 44683, www.barbourbooks.com

Our mission is to inspire the world with the life-changing message of the Bible.

Member of the
Evangelical Christian
Publishers Association

Printed in China.

001267 0722 HA

3-MINUTE

DAILY DEVOTIONS

FOR GIRLS

BARBOUR **kidz**

A Division of Barbour Publishing

INTRODUCTION

What a busy girl you are! You have so much going on—school, friends, sports, and family activities. There's not always time to sit and read, read, read. That's what makes this devotional so perfect for you! These short three-minute readings will give you all of the inspiration you need before heading out to school or to play. *And* you'll be learning a lot about yourself and God in a short time!

Here's what each power-packed devotion looks like:

Minute 1: Reflect on God's Word.

Minute 2: Read real-life application and encouragement.

Minute 3: Pray.

Of course, these devotions aren't supposed to take the place of regular Bible reading. They're just a fun jump start to help you form a habit of spending time with God every day. Here's a really cool idea: Why not share what you learn in this devotional with your school friends, family members, and even the girls you don't usually talk to? Everyone needs inspiration and encouragement, you know. So, girl, what are you waiting for? Let's dive in and discover how three minutes a day could change your entire life!

Your word is a lamp to guide my feet
and a light for my path.
PSALM 119:105 NLT

DAY 1

THE RACE

Do you not know that in a race all the runners run,
but only one gets the prize? Run in such a way as to get
the prize. Everyone who competes in the games goes into
strict training. They do it to get a crown that will not last,
but we do it to get a crown that will last forever.

1 CORINTHIANS 9:24–25 NIV

Have you ever trained for something—a race, or performance, or big game, or competition? When it gets close to the event, your thoughts and actions are consumed with preparing for it. You train as hard as you can so that you can do as well as you can, right? You should have the same diligence and self-discipline about your walk with God.

Maybe you've made some resolutions about how you want to live this year. It's very important that your resolutions include taking your walk with God more seriously. Commit to spending time in the Bible, praying, and memorizing scripture. Run the spiritual race this year like you want to win. Train yourself to be a better follower of God.

If you've ever won a prize, you know how good it feels to get that award. In life you are training to receive a crown in heaven that will never rust, never get lost, and never break. Keep your eyes focused on Christ and on the prize of an eternity in heaven with Him.

Lord, help me train well this year
so I can follow You more closely.

You, LORD, keep my lamp burning;
my God turns my darkness into light.

PSALM 18:28 NIV

Do you ever feel like the future seems dark? Or maybe something is happening in your life right now that makes you feel like you are lost in darkness and have no idea what's coming next. Imagine being out in the woods in the dark—isn't it so comforting to have a flashlight to turn on so that you can see what lies ahead? Similarly, when you put your trust in God, He will light your path and show you the way that you should go.

If you're confused about what you should be doing in some area of your life, ask God for advice and help. Ask Him to light the path in front of you so that you know the next step that you should take. Ask to be shown His will for your life.

A flashlight beam only lights up the area several feet in front of you. In the same way, God won't reveal to you your entire future. But He will show you the next step you should take. So seek Him and take the next step in faith, confident that you are never alone in the darkness. You have a Light by your side that is more magnificent and brighter than any other light in the universe.

Lord, thank You for lighting up the uncertain darkness around me. Thank You that I am never alone in the dark.

DAY 3

ETERNAL ROCK

*Trust in the Lord forever, for the Lord,
the Lord himself, is the Rock eternal.*

ISAIAH 26:4 NIV

Have you ever seen a mountain up close? Maybe you live near mountains or have visited an area that has them. They are so huge and impressive that they seem completely indestructible. It's easy to feel very small when standing at the base of a mountain.

When Isaiah, who wrote today's verse, says that God is your Rock, he isn't talking about a piece of gravel or a stone you can throw. He is saying that God is like one of those mountains. It is crazy to think that the mountains that you see today have been around from the beginning of the world. But God is even older than the mountains, and He will last infinitely longer than they will. You could never push down a mountain by leaning on it. In the same way, when you are feeling weak or afraid, you can lean on God and He will hold you up. He is stronger and even more indestructible than the biggest mountain.

Trust in God. He will always be there for you. He is stronger than anything and anyone on this earth, so He can give you strength and help you through anything you are struggling with. He is bigger than any problems you are having. Next time you are feeling weak or afraid, turn to your strong and eternal Rock.

Lord, You are my Rock. You will never be destroyed.
You are far stronger than anything on earth. You
will always be there for me when I call on You.

DAY 4

WHEN I AM AFRAID

When I am afraid, I put my trust in you. In God, whose word I praise—in God I trust and am not afraid. What can mere mortals do to me?

PSALM 56:3-4 NIV

There are a lot of things in this world that can cause us fear. Maybe you have fear about the future, your health, or the health of your family. Maybe you feel afraid when you're alone or have to do something outside of your comfort zone. Or maybe you're fearful when you hear the news about the things that are happening in the rest of the world.

Whenever you feel afraid, put your trust in God. Think about this—God created the world. He is the One who is in charge of what happens in your life and in the lives of everyone on this earth. He is all-powerful and all-knowing. And on top of all that, He loves you and will be right there with you through everything in your life. Even when there is no one else around, He is there with you. He will never leave you or forget about you. And He will always listen when you pray to Him. Can you think of anyone better to trust?

Thank You, Lord, for being the perfect One to trust. When I trust in You, I truly have nothing to fear because I know that You love me, You are in control of my life, and You will never leave me.

DAY 5

WORK HARD

Whatever you do, work at it with all your heart, as working for the Lord, not for human masters, since you know that you will receive an inheritance from the Lord as a reward. It is the Lord Christ you are serving.

COLOSSIANS 3:23–24 NIV

Whatever you do, you are supposed to work at it with all your heart. This means that you shouldn't do a bad job just so you can get it done. You shouldn't complain while working, but rather do the work assigned to you with a cheerful heart. It's not always easy to have a good attitude and good work ethic though, is it? Imagine if Jesus was the One who assigned you a paper in school. Or imagine if He was the One telling you to do your chores or clean up after yourself. Would your attitude about the work change? You would want to do your very best to please Him, wouldn't you?

In all of life, it *is* the Lord who you are serving. Even the small things that you do, like homework or cleaning the bathroom, can glorify God. So try to do everything with a willing attitude the first time you're asked. Bring glory to God by working in such a way that He is pleased. He cares about what you do. He watches over and delights in you. He notices when you do the small things well. So work wholeheartedly for Him.

Lord, forgive me when I have a bad attitude about the things I'm supposed to do. Help me remember that You are watching and that You are the One I am working for.

GOD'S WORD

"Keep this Book of the Law always on your lips; meditate on it day and night, so that you may be careful to do everything written in it. Then you will be prosperous and successful."

JOSHUA 1:8 NIV

In today's verse, God commands Joshua to make God's Word an essential part of his life. This command is also for you. God wants you to read the Bible, meditate on it, memorize it, and make it a daily part of your routine. You should know the Bible better than any other book, because it's through the Bible that you get to know God better and learn how to live in a way that pleases Him.

God also gives a promise in this verse. If you do spend time in God's Word, He promises that you will be prosperous and successful. This doesn't mean that spending time in God's Word is your ticket to being rich and famous. But you will be blessed and rewarded in ways that you may never have imagined. By reading and knowing the Bible, you will have a close relationship with God—you will know Him just like you know one of your best friends. Can you think of anything more successful than knowing the Creator of the universe as a close friend? So make the commitment now to spend time getting to know Him through His Word.

Lord, thank You that You have given me the Bible
as a way to get to know You better. Help me
be consistent and diligent in reading it.

DAY 7

REFUGE & STRENGTH

*God is our refuge and strength, an ever-present help in
trouble. Therefore we will not fear, though the earth give
way and the mountains fall into the heart of the sea.*

PSALM 46:1–2 NIV

Imagine what it would look like for the mountains to fall into
the ocean. That's a pretty scary image. But even if something
as frightening as that were to happen, today's verse tells you
that you have no reason to fear. Even if the whole earth would
change, you have no reason to fear. Why? Because God is your
refuge and your strength.

A refuge is somewhere that you can run to for safety—to escape
from something that is trying to harm you. God is your refuge, so
run to Him when you're scared, worried, or lonely. He will comfort
and protect you and give you the strength you need to continue.
He already knows how you're feeling, so there is no reason to hide
from Him. You can trust Him fully with any secrets or fears that you
have. Talk to Him and let Him be your refuge and strength.

The verse says that God is "an ever-present help in trouble."
What does that mean? It means that He is always right there for
you. You don't have to wait for Him to finish talking to someone
else. You don't have to worry that He doesn't hear you because
He's busy. He is always listening and always there to help as soon
as you call on Him.

Lord, thank You for being my refuge and
strength that I can run to at any time.

DAY 8

THE SAME

Jesus Christ is the same yesterday and today and forever.
HEBREWS 13:8 NIV

Why does it matter that Jesus has never and will never change? Think about your life. Have any circumstances changed recently? Maybe a friend or family member has changed and become someone different than you thought they were. Maybe you've noticed that you have changed. Chances are that something has changed in your life recently. Change can be scary. It can make the future seem very uncertain and dark. In this life, anything and anyone can change—*except* God.

God is the only One who has always and will always be the same. He loves you today, and He will love you through every day in your future. That will not change. He is the most powerful person in the universe. That will not change. He is in sovereign control of what happens in your life and the lives of those around you. That will not change. He has a plan and a purpose for you. That will not change.

In a world that is very uncertain and changeable, isn't it comforting to know that God will always be the same? You can trust Him fully because you can be absolutely certain that He will never go away and will never leave you or stop loving you.

Lord, thank You that You will never change. Some changes have been very hard in my life, but I know I can trust that You will be the same and will always be there for me through any changes that happen in my life in the future.

DAY 9

GREATER THAN, LESS THAN

"He must become greater; I must become less."
JOHN 3:30 NIV

Do you have the same attitude that John the Baptist had in today's verse? John was very aware of how great Jesus was and how small he was. He wanted nothing more than for Christ to be exalted more and more. Meanwhile, he wanted to become less. John was not concerned about his own glory or fame; he only wanted Jesus to be known and glorified.

We live in a world where people are obsessed with themselves. It seems that everyone craves notice and praise. Social media sites encourage people to post pictures and comments about themselves to attract attention and popularity. You may notice that you are being influenced by the world's self-centered attitude as well.

As a child of God, you are not called to promote and glorify yourself. Your life should be lived in such a way that you reflect and proclaim God's glory, not your own. Do the people around you think that God is great because of the way you live your life? Does your life revolve around God and others, or does it revolve around you? It's not easy to learn to honor God and others more than yourself. But we were created to live in a way that reflects God's glory and strives to lovingly serve others. When you live this way, you will find that you have so much more joy and peace because you are living for something greater than yourself.

Lord, I pray that You would become greater
in my life and that I would become less.

DAY 10

NO UNWHOLESOME WORD

*Do not let any unwholesome talk come out of your mouths,
but only what is helpful for building others up according
to their needs, that it may benefit those who listen.*

EPHESIANS 4:29 NIV

What is unwholesome talk? It's not just a swear word or rude talk—it's any talk that is not uplifting. The author of today's verse is telling you that you shouldn't gossip, shouldn't speak badly of someone else, or complain about a circumstance that you don't like. The words that come out of your mouth should be ones that build others up and that promote grace. You may be thinking that this verse gives an impossible command. Everyone seems to gossip and complain and say rude things under their breath. Just think about how much you will stand out as a good example of someone who follows God if you don't engage in these activities.

Not only will you stand out as a child of God, but you will have a happier, more fulfilling life too. Your thoughts will be so much freer if you rid yourself of all the negative comments that come up every day in your heart and mind. The people around you will flourish as well, as you begin to encourage rather than tear down, give grace rather than condemn. Pray for God's help in following the command from today's verse, and then watch as He transforms your thoughts and life.

Lord, forgive me for all the unwholesome words that
I have thought and spoken. Cleanse my heart and
mind now and help me to only speak words that
will benefit those who hear them.

FOR YOU

The LORD is with me; I will not be afraid.
What can mere mortals do to me?

PSALM 118:6 NIV

What is your view of God? Do you think that He is for you? Maybe at times, when things aren't going well, you think that He's against you. Or maybe you think He just doesn't really know you or care about you.

As Psalm 118 says, God is with you. He is *for* you. He is on your side. He desires the very best for you. He is working every day to make you more like Himself. He created you in His image and loves you in a way that you cannot possibly understand. He sent His only Son to die for the sins that you should have died for.

Really think about the fact that God is for you. If you don't already believe this, then it will radically change your life to start believing it now. Since He is for you, that means everything in your life is intended for your good and His glory. God will use even the worst circumstance in your life to draw you closer to Him. When you're going through a hard time, be encouraged that one day you will be able to look back and see how God used this circumstance for good. Remember as you go through your day today that the all-powerful God who created the universe is *on your side*. You truly do not have anything to fear.

Lord, help me recognize that You are with me and
for me. Thank You for loving me deeply and for
always working for my good and Your glory.

DAY 12

GOOD THOUGHTS

Finally, brothers and sisters, whatever is true, whatever is noble, whatever is right, whatever is pure, whatever is lovely, whatever is admirable—if anything is excellent or praiseworthy—think about such things.

PHILIPPIANS 4:8 NIV

Philippians 4:8 is a challenging verse. Do you only think about things that are true, noble, right, pure, lovely, admirable, excellent, and praiseworthy? Or are your thoughts filled with gossip, inappropriate language, rude words, and worthless things? With cell phones, computers, TV shows, and social media right at your fingertips all the time, you are most likely flooded with images and words that do not match the descriptions in this verse.

Be very careful what you let yourself watch, read, and dwell on. Those things will take root in your heart and mind and will begin to greatly influence your thoughts. Be wise about what you spend your time on. If you find that a particular show or website is making you think in ways that are not pleasing to God, cut that out of your life. It is much better for you to lose some entertainment than to let your mind be changed by things that are not true, right, and pure.

If your thoughts are focused on things that are not true and lovely, then very soon your words and actions will not be true and lovely either. So start now and work on focusing your thoughts on things that will point you to God—things that are described in this verse. See how that will change your life.

Lord, don't let me think about worthless things, but instead, may my thoughts please You.

DAY 13

GOD'S IMAGE

*So God created mankind in his own image, in the image of
God he created them; male and female he created them.*
GENESIS 1:27 NIV

Humans are created in God's image. This means that every human
has value and worth. So if someone is making you feel like you are
worthless or have no value, know that it is not true. You are highly
valuable to God. You're so valuable that He made you like Him, in
His image. Even more than that, He sent His Son to die for *you.*
He would not do that for someone that He did not deeply love
and care for. So don't listen to people who try to make you feel
unloved or unworthy.

Everyone who was created in God's image has worth. That means
the kid that no one wants to talk to at school is valuable to God.
That means the new family that just moved into the neighborhood
is valuable to God. That means someone that doesn't look or dress
or talk like you is valuable to God. If they are valuable to God, then
you should treat them as valuable too. If someone needs a friend,
reach out to them. Let them know that they have worth and value.
Don't participate in talk that hurts someone else. Instead, use your
words to build them up and love them as God would love them.

Lord, help me to always remember that I am valuable
and loved by You. Help me show Your
love to other people as well.

DAY 14

CONFIDENCE

*I lift up my eyes to the mountains—where does my help
come from? My help comes from the LORD, the Maker
of heaven and earth. He will not let your foot slip—he
who watches over you will not slumber; indeed, he who
watches over Israel will neither slumber nor sleep.*

PSALM 121:1–4 NIV

Where do you place your confidence? Do you place it in your own
skills, intelligence, or abilities? Do you place it in the status of your
family? Do you place it in your social standing or circle of friends?
Do you place it in the safety of your house or your neighborhood?

Your confidence should be placed solely in the Lord. He is the
One, the only One, who can keep you safe and give you help. The
earthly things that you place your trust in may someday fail you—so
place your trust in the Maker of heaven and earth. He will never fail
you, and He will forever guard and protect you.

He does not sleep or grow tired. Whenever you pray to Him, He
is alert and ready to help. He won't forget about you or get tired of
you praying to Him. In fact, He wants you to pray to Him all the time.
So bring your fears, joys, desires, disappointments, and requests to
Him. You won't catch Him at a bad time.

Place your confidence in Him. You will not be disappointed.

Lord, my help comes from You, not from anything else
on this earth. Forgive me when I put my confidence
in earthly things that cannot help or protect me.
Thank You for constantly watching over me.

CHILD OF GOD

See what great love the Father has lavished on us, that we
should be called children of God! And that is what we are!
1 JOHN 3:1 NIV

How do you think God sees you? Does He see you as a casual acquaintance? As someone that He knows from a distance? The truth is, He sees you as one of His children. You are part of His family. He loves you, protects you, cares for you, and wants the best for you.

This is amazing that you are called a child of God. He is the all-powerful God who created everything. He is completely self-sustaining and does not need anything from anyone. You are just a small speck in the whole scheme of eternity. You are one of billions of people on the earth. How is it possible that God would even notice you? And yet He has done more than merely notice you. He has adopted you into His family. What an amazing love that He would choose to take you and make you one of His own! Once you have accepted Christ into your life, you will never stop being one of God's children. It is a position and a heavenly status that you will hold into eternity. God will forever love and protect you as one of His family. Nothing can and nothing will change that.

Lord, I am amazed by the love that You have bestowed
on me by adopting me to be one of Your children. Thank
You that I am and always will be a part of Your family.

DAY 16

SAVE ME

But when he saw the wind, he was afraid and, beginning to sink, cried out, "Lord, save me!" Immediately Jesus reached out his hand and caught him. "You of little faith," he said, "why did you doubt?"

MATTHEW 14:30–31 NIV

In today's passage, Jesus was walking on water toward His disciples who were in a boat in the middle of a windy sea. Peter asked to come out to Jesus on the water. Jesus told him to come. So Peter started walking on the water toward Jesus. But when he saw the wind and the waves, he became afraid and started to sink.

Does this ever happen in your life—you get so overwhelmed by the difficult or frightening things in life that you start to feel like you're sinking under the waves of your struggles? Sometimes it is easy to lose faith during difficult times in life. You get so distracted by everything around you that you forget to keep your eyes focused on Jesus. But when this happens and you feel like you're sinking, call out for God to save you as Peter did. He will be there to reach out, pull you from the waves, and walk with you to safety. He will not leave you to drown in your struggles. So reach out to Him and have faith that He will save you.

Lord, keep me from getting distracted by all the overwhelming things in my life. May I keep my eyes focused on You and reach out to You in the difficult times of life.

OUTWARD APPEARANCE

*"The LORD does not look at the things people look at.
People look at the outward appearance,
but the LORD looks at the heart."*

1 SAMUEL 16:7 NIV

Self-image is a powerful thing. The way you think that you look can affect the way you live your life and the friends you make. It can also affect your perception of your self-worth. But your outward appearance does not matter to God. So if you find yourself wishing that you could be prettier or have clearer skin or a better smile, just remember—God does not look at those things. Your worth and value are not affected by your appearance. God does not choose how much to love you based on the way you look.

The same is true if you find yourself feeling prideful about the way you look. Remember, you can't get by on your looks when it comes to God. He pays attention to what's inside. He desires that your heart and mind be beautiful rather than your outward appearance.

Though some days it may not feel like it, God's opinion of you matters way more than anyone else's opinion. He is the One who is in charge of your life and your eternity. He is the all-powerful God of the universe—of course His opinion matters the most! And He is the One who will love you even on your worst days. The fact that God loves you makes you the most valuable thing on earth.

Lord, help me be more concerned about how my
heart is rather than how I look on the outside.

SEEK JUSTICE

"Learn to do right; seek justice. Defend the oppressed.
Take up the cause of the fatherless;
plead the case of the widow."

ISAIAH 1:17 NIV

Sometimes it is hard to stand up for what is right. Throughout history, we have many role models we can look to who stood against the odds for someone else's benefit. In January we celebrate one of those people—Martin Luther King Jr. He was a brave and courageous man who was not afraid or ashamed to speak out against the evil and injustice of his time. He was able to have amazing perseverance and courage because he knew that God backed him up. He knew that God hates injustice and oppression even more than he did. The Bible is filled with verses that talk about God's love for the orphan, the widow, and anyone who is oppressed, mistreated, or forgotten.

In this world, the rich, famous, strong, and beautiful are often the ones who we give our attention to. But that is not how God operates. He is not impressed by worldly standing. He doesn't look at skin color, bank accounts, or popularity. When Jesus was on earth, He reached out to the poor and outcast, condemned the prejudice of the well-to-do, and healed the sick and weak. As followers of God, we are called to do what is right, seek justice, and stand up for those who are oppressed and needy. . .even when it's unpopular.

Lord, You are a God of justice. Help me to always do right, seek justice, and stand up for the oppressed and needy.

DAY 19

SAVED FOREVER

"My sheep listen to my voice; I know them, and they follow me. I give them eternal life, and they shall never perish; no one will snatch them out of my hand."

JOHN 10:27–28 NIV

When you received Christ into your heart, you became one of His flock of sheep. He is your Good Shepherd. This means that He cares for you, protects you, leads you, and guides you. He knows you by name.

If you have prayed to receive Christ, you have already been given eternal life. You can have confidence that this life on earth is only the beginning. You will spend an eternity in unspeakable joy with your Good Shepherd in heaven. In today's verses, Jesus promises that you will never perish. You do not have to fear death. Death is only a doorway into the rest of your life. You will not perish—you will pass into glory.

Jesus also promises that no one will be able to snatch you out of His hand. There is no need to fear losing your salvation. There is nothing that you or anyone else can do to cause you to be separated from God. You will forever be part of His flock and His family. You don't have to live up to some standard in order to earn your salvation. He has freely given it. Be thankful that your future in heaven is already secured.

Lord, thank You that I am one of Your sheep. And thank You that absolutely nothing will ever be able to take me out of Your hand.

DAY 20

THE RISING SUN

Because of the LORD's great love we are not consumed, for his compassions never fail. They are new every morning; great is your faithfulness.

LAMENTATIONS 3:22–23 NIV

Do you ever doubt that the sun will come up in the morning? Of course not. You probably don't even think about whether the sun will rise because you just *know* that it will. It always has. Your trust in the rising of the sun is so complete that you don't have to waste any time thinking about it.

You can have the same attitude about God's love. It is just as (and even more) faithful than the rising of the sun. His love will never cease, and it will never fail you. It will never grow old or dim. You can put just as much trust in His love and faithfulness as you put in the rising of the sun.

Take a moment to think back through your life and consider all the times that you have witnessed God's love and faithfulness. It is good to remember and maybe even record those times so that if you ever go through a period in your life when you doubt God's love for you, you can look back on all the times that He has displayed how faithful He is. When the sun comes up in the morning, let it remind you that God's love is also shining on you fresh and new.

Lord, Your love is as faithful as the rising of
the sun. May I never doubt that You love me.

DAY 21

BOAST IN GOD

"Let not the wise boast of their wisdom or the strong boast of their strength or the rich boast of their riches, but let the one who boasts boast about this: that they have the understanding to know me, that I am the LORD, who exercises kindness, justice and righteousness on earth, for in these I delight," declares the LORD.
JEREMIAH 9:23–24 NIV

Let's look at today's verses in terms that might make more sense in your life: Don't be proud because you're good at sports. Don't be proud because you're pretty or popular. Don't be proud because of your good grades. Don't be proud because of your family's wealth. The verses are saying that, even though these are not bad things, they are not things you should be prideful about or base your self-worth on. Even though it's good to work hard, your earthly accomplishments are worthless compared to the incredible worth of knowing God.

Your greatest goal in life should be to know God. The thing that should cause you the most pride in life is the fact that you have the opportunity to know God. This is not an arrogant pride but rather a humble pride that causes you to be thankful that God allows you to know Him. How amazing would it be if your close walk with God was the thing that stood out about you the most? Work to be defined not by your athletic or intellectual abilities but by your relationship with your heavenly Father.

Lord, knowing You is more valuable than anything else on earth. Help me improve and strengthen our relationship.

DAY 22

HOLD MY HAND

*Yet I am always with you; you hold me by my
right hand. You guide me with your counsel,
and afterward you will take me into glory.*

PSALM 73:23–24 NIV

When you were younger, you probably were told to hold someone's hand when crossing the street or when walking through a busy area. Back then you held someone's hand for safety reasons. But even now that you're older, holding someone's hand is still comforting and gives you a sense of belonging. The author of Psalm 73 says that God has taken hold of his hand. He means that God's presence is as close and comforting to him as if he were actually holding His hand.

God is that close to you as well. He is there to hold your hand when you need extra courage, when you're feeling sad or lonely, or when you just need to be comforted. Holding hands is something you would only do with someone you're close to and belong to in some way. God offers to hold your hand because you belong to Him. He loves you and wants to be connected with you. Isn't that amazing? The God of the universe wants to be connected to *you* and walk through life with *you*.

He will never stop holding your hand. Even through death (when no one else can walk with you), God will be right there beside you and will welcome you home into heaven. So hold even tighter to His hand and know that He walks with you.

Lord, thank You that You are holding on to me tightly.

BE AN EXAMPLE

Don't let anyone look down on you because you are young, but set an example for the believers in speech, in conduct, in love, in faith and in purity.

1 TIMOTHY 4:12 NIV

Paul, who wrote today's verse, is encouraging Timothy to not let anyone look down on him because he's young. By saying this, he's not telling Timothy to ignore the advice or correction of those older than him. And he's certainly not saying that Timothy should arrogantly puff himself up with an "I'm better than you" attitude. Instead, Paul is encouraging Timothy to live in such a way that no one has anything negative to say about him. Challenge yourself to do the same.

Try to exemplify how a follower of Christ should act. Don't let your young age be an excuse to act immaturely or inappropriately. Instead, speak and love in such a way that you glorify God. Look for ways to serve. Immerse yourself in God's Word. Find people who need to be loved. Use your words to encourage instead of tear down. Glorify and acknowledge God in all that you do—whether it be homework, having fun with friends, or just relaxing. And don't give anyone a reason to think negatively of you or look down on you.

Lord, even though I'm young, help me be a good example of someone who follows You closely and brings You glory.

STRONG FOUNDATION

"They are like a man building a house, who dug down deep and laid the foundation on rock. When a flood came, the torrent struck that house but could not shake it, because it was well built."

LUKE 6:48 NIV

You have probably seen pictures or videos of houses that have been swept away by a flood. Or maybe you've experienced a flood in person. It's scary to see something that once stood so solid and strong get destroyed by a powerful wave. You do not want to be like one of those houses. You should have such a firm foundation that no amount of battering from waves can knock you down. It is inevitable that you will have struggles and storms in your life. Now is the time to start building a strong foundation to prepare for those hardships.

How do you build a solid foundation? Start by committing yourself to reading the Bible and praying every day. Set aside a time to do it and stick to it. Challenge yourself to memorize scripture and spend time meditating on it. Faithfully attend church and other events that get you in contact with God's Word and other believers. Work hard now to know God and place Him at the center of your life—then when trials come, you will not be shaken, because you will be grounded firmly on the unshakeable Rock of Christ. The only foundation that will survive the violent storms of life is one that is built on this Rock.

Lord, help me build a foundation now that will survive any future storm that life brings my way.

DAY 25

PRAISE HIM

*Let everything that has breath
praise the LORD. Praise the LORD.*

PSALM 150:6 NIV

Do you ever wonder why you should read the Bible? Or why you have to go to church? Or why God tells you to worship Him? Maybe you think that it's kind of arrogant of God to demand that you worship Him. You certainly aren't supposed to tell people to worship you, right? Well, God wants you to worship and praise Him because it is good for *you*.

Have you ever seen something so beautiful that it almost takes your breath away—like the Grand Canyon, a mountain range, a spectacular sunset, or an intricate flower? Think about that feeling you get after seeing something so beautiful. Don't you feel exhilarated and amazed? Maybe you want to share whatever you saw with someone else.

Does the mountain, sunset, or flower need you to look at it? Does it feel better because you thought it was beautiful? Of course not! It's the same way with God. He doesn't *need* your praise. He doesn't *need* you to go to church and learn more about Him by reading your Bible. He tells you to do these things because *you* will benefit from them. You will feel better and be more fulfilled when you worship and praise Him. He is a beautiful and awesome God who deserves your praise—so praise Him with gratitude for the opportunity to know Him and be loved by Him.

Lord, I praise You because You are beautiful, powerful, and glorious. I praise You because You have chosen to love me.

DAY 26

ON HIS HANDS

*"See, I have engraved you on the palms of
my hands; your walls are ever before me."*

ISAIAH 49:16 NIV

Do you ever write things on your hand with a pen? Why do you
do that? Probably because you don't want to forget whatever it is
you've written. You can't miss seeing something that's written on
your hand. It's right there in front of you, constantly reminding you
of what you wrote.

Today's verse says that God has engraved you on the palms of
His hands. He has put you in such a conspicuous place that He can't
possibly forget about you. No matter what He does, He is reminded
of you. The word *engrave* implies that something has been written
in a permanent manner. Unlike ink from a pen that will eventually
wash or rub off, you will never fade from God's attention. As you go
through your day, think about the fact that God is thinking of you
every single moment. The Almighty God loves you so much that
you are constantly on His mind. That realization just might change
how your day goes.

How wonderful would it be if your thoughts were constantly
turned to Him as well?

Lord, I am in awe that You think about me all the
time. Help me bring You to mind just as often.

PEACEFUL SLEEP

*In peace I will lie down and sleep, for you
alone, Lord, make me dwell in safety.*

PSALM 4:8 NIV

Do your thoughts ever keep you awake at night? Maybe you're worried about something in the future or something that you wish you had done differently in the past. Maybe you struggle to keep a fear from entering into your mind that prevents you from sleeping. But because you are a child of God, you can lie down and sleep in peace.

God offers you a peace that is unlike anything else on earth. If you are in Christ, you know that you are saved and will spend eternity in heaven. You know that in this life you are cared for by God. He loves you and will not let anyone take you from His hands. He will hold you up when you fall and comfort you in the dark times. You do not even have to fear death, because Christ has already conquered death and will walk with you through even that most feared experience. The all-powerful God is on your side and knows exactly what will happen in your future. If you can really grasp and believe these truths, you will recognize that you have no need to worry or fear. You will have a depth of peace that nothing can shake.

Lord, thank You that I can lie down and sleep in perfect
peace because of what You have done for me.

DAY 28

LIFE IS SHORT

*"Show me, LORD, my life's end and the number
of my days; let me know how fleeting my life is."*

PSALM 39:4 NIV

Today's verse brings up a somewhat uncomfortable truth: Life is short. Sometimes we try to ignore that fact or we just get so caught up in the everyday happenings of our life that we forget that we won't be here for very long. But the author of Psalm 39 is asking God to remind him of how short his life is. Why? So that he will live his life to the fullest without wasting the time he has been given.

You may think that you're too young to be thinking about the end of life on earth. And while you shouldn't obsess over those thoughts, ask God to reveal how precious each day is. Ask Him to show you what your purpose is here on earth so that you can make the most of it. Since life is short, ask yourself the question, *What can I do here that will have a lasting impact?*

Anything that you do for Christ and His kingdom will last into eternity. The impact that you have on other people will also last. So invest in those around you, recognizing that you will spend eternity with your fellow believers. And also, don't sweat the small stuff. Don't get so caught up in the details and stress of life that you lose sight of the big picture. After all, life on this earth is just a speck of dust compared to the eternity you get to spend in heaven.

Lord, help me understand how fleeting my life is.

GOD LOVES YOU

This is love: not that we loved God, but that he loved us and sent his Son as an atoning sacrifice for our sins.

1 JOHN 4:10 NIV

God loves you. Do you know that? Do you believe that? Do you *really* believe that? The Almighty God who created and sustains the entire universe loves you and knows you by name. That is amazing! His love for you is not just a casual love. He doesn't love you because He has to or because He wants you to do something for Him. He loves you enough that He sent His Son to die in your place. Your sins would have condemned you to death. But instead of letting you die for your sins, God decided to send His Son to die for you. That is remarkable love. It is impossible to understand how deeply He loves you.

Maybe you have been hurt in the past because someone didn't love you the way that they should have. Maybe they didn't care for you or left you feeling abandoned. Or maybe right now you're struggling because you are feeling unloved or unlovable. But no matter what the circumstance, you can be confident that God has, does, and always will love you. And, unlike the love that you may receive on this earth, His love is perfect and unfailing. So go to Him when you feel lonely, scared, or abandoned. He will always be there to care for and protect you.

. . . .

Lord, You loved me enough to send Your Son to die for me. I can't possibly understand how much You love me, and I can't possibly be grateful enough for Your gift.

BY GRACE

For it is by grace you have been saved, through
faith—and this is not from yourselves, it is the gift
of God—not by works, so that no one can boast.

EPHESIANS 2:8–9 NIV

You have been saved by grace. This means that you did nothing to earn your salvation. It means that God chose you to be one of His children simply because He decided to have mercy on you. You have no right to feel arrogant about your salvation. It is a gift that was bought with the precious blood of Christ. This is a debt that you could never possibly pay back. So be humbled by it and forever grateful for the grace that God chose to give you.

Since you cannot earn your salvation, this also means that you have no need to feel guilty. You do not have to live up to some standard to keep your salvation. It was given as a gift that you can't lose. So if you make mistakes or feel like you have failed God, don't let guilt have any power over you. Your mistakes and failures do not affect your standing before God. Live in the forgiveness and grace that Christ purchased for you with His life. Let your thankfulness for the gift of salvation spur you on to love God more and follow Him more closely.

Lord, thank You for bestowing Your overwhelming grace on me. I'm so grateful that I cannot earn or lose my salvation.

DAY 31

YOUR NAME

But now, this is what the LORD says—he who created you,
Jacob, he who formed you, Israel: "Do not fear, for I have
redeemed you; I have summoned you by name; you are mine."

ISAIAH 43:1 NIV

What does it mean when someone knows your name? It means that they know who you are. They have interacted with you enough to be able to remember your name. Someone who doesn't know or care about you would not know your name.

God knows your name. Really think about that—it's pretty amazing. There are billions of people on this earth. In the whole scheme of history, you are just a small speck of dust among a lot of other specks of dust. And yet God knows your name. You are infinitely more important to Him than a speck of dust. He knows your thoughts, what you like and don't like, your greatest fears, and your greatest desires. In fact, He knows you better than anyone else. Isn't it incredible that you are known that well *by God*?

In Isaiah 43:1, God tells you not to fear. Think about it—what is there to fear when you know that the all-powerful God knows you by name and loves you? You belong to Him and are safe under His protection.

Lord, You know me so well—better even than I
know myself. Thank You for singling me out of all
the billions of other people on the earth and taking
time to know me personally and love me deeply.

DAY 32

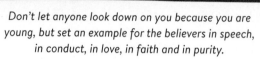

PURITY

Don't let anyone look down on you because you are young, but set an example for the believers in speech, in conduct, in love, in faith and in purity.

1 TIMOTHY 4:12 NIV

Remember the last time you had that sick feeling in the pit of your stomach? You know the one—when you regret what you said, what you did, or how you reacted. You wish you could take it all back. You wish it could be undone. You dread the coming punishment. Maybe you lost your temper or temptation got the best of you. Maybe it was a lie.

Think about it a moment. Our God wants you to never experience that defeat again.

Reread today's scripture. Let's be honest. The synonyms of *purity* can sound pretty boring: moral, wholesome, decent, and spotless.

Truthfully, a life of purity is anything but simple or boring. It requires strength, self-control, and discipline. Do you wonder how it's even possible? You make *what God says* more important than what you feel or think. You make the decision to stay close to the Lord and be obedient to His commands minute by minute and day by day.

The perks? You can live without that sick regret. You can respect yourself. You will develop a close friendship with Jesus. He loves you, you know.

Father, teach me Your Word and Your will for
me. I commit to obedience. I want to live my
life as an example to other people. Amen.

BE CAREFUL WHAT YOU SEE

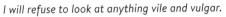

I will refuse to look at anything vile and vulgar.
PSALM 101:3 NLT

How many times have you heard it: "I know there are a few wordy-dirties and a bad scene or two, but it was really a great movie!" The reply is usually something like, "Oh, that won't affect me."

Seeing or hearing what we consider a "little" sin *does* have consequences. It will weaken your conscience and can alter your feelings and thoughts. You don't think so? Advertising agencies all over the world will contradict you! Why else would companies spend huge amounts of money, knowing that a television ad will run only thirty seconds during an hour-long program? Why would a company pay thousands of dollars for a billboard that is seen for only a split second by a traveler driving on a busy highway? *We are affected by what we see.*

In Genesis 3:6 (NIV), Satan tempted Eve to think about the fruit God had forbidden: "When the woman saw that the fruit of the tree was good for food and pleasing to the eye, and also desirable for gaining wisdom, she took some and ate it."

A look became a temptation, which resulted in a wrong decision—sin. Guard your heart by guarding your eyes. No "small peeks." Keep your eyes fixed on Jesus.

Dear Father, help me understand purity from
Your perspective—with no compromise. Amen.

DAY 34

KNOWING HIM

"Be still, and know that I am God."

PSALM 46:10 NIV

What can you tell me about George Washington? What about Abraham Lincoln? I will wait while you think a moment. Now, I understand that you know *about* them, but how well do you *know them*? (Yes. Trick question.)

For years my closest friend was my grandmother. As she aged, she felt bad about not being able to participate in things she had always loved. She felt it made her less interesting and even less lovable. Actually, we grew closer because we spent so much unhurried time together.

Do you see the difference? You can know *about* someone, but you don't *know them* without quality time together.

Now that you understand the difference, consider this: You know *about* the Father, but do you *know Him*? Do you talk with Him as problems come to mind? Do you ask His opinion on friends or issues? Do you thank Him? Are you His friend? He tells us in John 15:14–15 (NIV): "You are my friends if you do what I command. I no longer call you servants. . . . Instead, I have called you friends."

Jesus wants to be your best friend. Slow down and spend time with Him. Read the Bible, talk to Him (pray), and then quietly listen.

Dear Father, I want to be Your friend. I want to listen.
Teach me how to hear and understand Your Word. Amen.

MASTERPIECE

*For we are God's masterpiece, He has created
us anew in Christ Jesus, so we can do the
good things he planned for us long ago.*
EPHESIANS 2:10 NLT

The baby was born prematurely, requiring shots of adrenaline into her chest to prompt the tiny heart to find its rhythm. The minutes of oxygen deprivation caused the baby's body to grow unevenly. Slightly different-sized hands, feet, and legs went unnoticed by most people. Pain, however, began to restrict the little girl's activities.

As she grew, she felt like her body was a mistake. Clothes would not fit correctly, and shoe shopping was almost impossible. Even one of her brothers had teased, "When God created everything, He said it was good. . .except for you. After creating you, He said, 'Oh, that will do.' "

To escape pain, the girl with the tomboy tendencies began to avoid sports and lean toward the guitar. Amazingly, she discovered that her hands and arms were "made" for guitar. Her left hand, because of its increased size and span, could handle chords not easily achieved by others. Music and leading worship became her passion.

What she had seen as defects, God had planned for purpose. What she had deemed restrictions, God had used to direct her to that purpose.

Dear Father, help me see myself from Your perspective.
Show me that "flaws" have function and my pain has purpose.
Help me understand how much You love me. Amen.

DAY 36

OFF THE LEASH

"You must love the LORD your God and always obey his requirements, decrees, regulations, and commands."

DEUTERONOMY 11:1 NLT

The dog managed to slip his neck out of his collar and run. Carrie called him back, but he pretended not to hear. The dog ran in and out of the woods and through multiple neighbors' yards. He absolutely refused to go to the house. Carrie was suddenly ashamed as she watched the dog, realizing she was watching the embodiment of her own stubbornness.

The dog knew what his master wanted but refused to be obedient. He never strayed too far—stayed close to his home—but knew that when he surrendered, he would be on a leash.

Carrie knew she too wanted the security of her Master—Jesus—without the restraints of obedience. She knew she stayed close enough to appease her conscience but enjoyed feeling like she could make her own decisions and maintain some level of independence. She had secretly begun to resent what she believed to be unnecessary limitations. She wanted to choose her friends, her clothes, and her curfew!

The dog ran for hours, but Carrie loved him too much to close the door until he was inside. She realized neither her parents nor the Lord had closed the door on her either. She also realized that her partial obedience wasn't obedience at all.

Dear Father, I know You say I cannot be lukewarm.
I cannot be mediocre. Forgive me. I want to be
100 percent devoted to You and Your will. Amen.

NOT FAIR!

*"From everyone who has been given much, much
will be demanded; and from the one who has been
entrusted with much, much more will be asked."*

LUKE 12:48 NIV

Our Father wants us to become like Christ. He wants us to learn to love, to serve, and to forgive. He teaches us through experiences that play out like school grades—the more we grow, the harder the next lesson; anything failed has to be repeated. Then, the more we learn, the more responsibility He requires. Lesson. Test. Repeat. . .

We must work to "grow up" and take responsibility. We must try to be diligent in our improvements. Yet we often feel surrounded by people whose lives seem easier. We are even required to show mercy and patience to people who do not seem to be working or progressing at the same pace that we are. Sometimes life doesn't seem fair!

We must remember that it is our job to love and God's job to judge. We are simply responsible for our own work and attitude. The more we know, the more we are required to do, and the more we have, the more we are required to give. Got it?

Dear Father, help me remember that I can never repay
You for what You have done for me and I can never give
back to You as much as You have already given to me.
Forgive me for judging others. I want to show as much
mercy to other people as You have shown to me. Amen.

DAY 38

ROCK SOLID, PART 1

"For who is God besides the Lord?
And who is the Rock except our God?"
2 SAMUEL 22:32 NIV

How about a lesson on rocks? I know it sounds pretty boring, but stick with me a minute.

I don't mean a pebble—nothing small or cutesy—I mean a rock large enough for a cave to be carved in the side. Torrential rains, high winds, or a bone-chilling blizzard would not change it. It would not move. It would be secure and steady. It could not burn. It could not leak or blow away. It would be immovable and dependable.

The point? Several times in scripture, our God compares Himself to a rock. He does not change. His promises are true. He is always dependable. He can be trusted. He is all-powerful. He is never panicked. He wants to be your Father. Consider the words of Romans 8:38–39 (NIV): "For I am convinced that neither death nor life, neither angels nor demons, neither the present nor the future, nor any powers, neither height nor depth, nor anything else in all creation will be able to separate us from the love of God that is in Christ Jesus our Lord."

Remember. He loves you. That will not change. It's etched in stone.

Dear Father, help me understand the height, depth,
and width of Your love for me. Help me open my
heart to Your love and never doubt it. Amen.

ROCK SOLID, PART 2

"You must be holy because I am holy."
1 PETER 1:16 NLT

When we accept Jesus as our Savior, we take on the name "Christian." In the same way that we resemble our human mother and father, we should grow to look more like our heavenly Father. People should look at us and see the resemblance.

Think about it this way. We are prone to adjust our personality according to our surroundings. We might act differently at church than we would with people we want to impress at school. We might treat teachers differently than we would treat our parents.

But God does not change. His personality and promises remain the same. Therefore, we should not change either. We should be firm in our beliefs. We should be immovable in our morals. We should not waver, wobble, or waffle. He is not evil—we should have nothing in us that appears to be evil. He loves—we should love. He is good—we should be good. He does not compromise—we should not compromise.

Our standards, morals, and principles should not change. They should not shift. They should not be variable. They must be rock solid—set in stone.

Dear Father, forgive me for my tendency to compromise in an effort to fit in with others. Please give me the courage to stand firm. I want people to look at me and see You. Amen.

DAY 40

AS I HAVE LOVED YOU

*"A new command I give you: Love one another.
As I have loved you, so you must love one another."*

JOHN 13:34 NIV

What do we know about God's love and the characteristics it produces?

- His "love never fails" (1 CORINTHIANS 13:8 NIV),
- He has "loved you with an everlasting love" (JEREMIAH 31:3 NIV),
- His compassions "are new every morning" (LAMENTATIONS 3:23 NIV),
- "He is patient" (2 PETER 3:9 NIV),
- "He does not treat us as our sins deserve" (PSALM 103:10 NIV),
- . . .and the list goes on and on.

Do you feel secure knowing that He loves you completely and that forgiveness is always available? Think about it for a moment. Feel it.

Time to be honest: Do you depend on mercy for your own actions yet want justice for someone who has hurt you? Do you find your own bad attitudes justifiable but believe others deserve punishment? Ask yourself: *Am I willing to forgive and love others in the same way that God loves me?*

Dear Father, I don't always feel loving toward the people who hurt me. Help me see others as Your children. Help me think with Your mind and love with Your heart. Would You love them through me? Amen.

DAY 41

FIRST THINGS FIRST

*"'Love the Lord your God with all your heart and with
all your soul and with all your strength and with all
your mind;' and, 'Love your neighbor as yourself.'"*

LUKE 10:27 NIV

Sunday school teachers say you should love the Lord. Grandmothers tell you to love others. But do you skip the end of Luke 10:27? Go back and read closely. . ."*Love your neighbor as yourself*".

Do you love yourself? How well do you love yourself? Are you as kind to the girl who looks back at you from the mirror as you are to your best friend? Are you as patient with yourself as you are with a little old lady at church? Are you as gentle with yourself as you are with a small child who is lost at the mall?

Why not? You are God's child. He loves you. He treasures you. You are created in His image. From the moment you accept Christ as your Savior, His Spirit lives in you! Say this aloud: "God loves me. He treasures me. He adores me. He wants me to feel His love—to accept His love. Then I can pass it on to people around me."

Does that seem like a strange concept? Well, you know that snobby girl who makes you feel self-conscious? Or the loud boy who tries to be the center of attention? They are all insecure in the deepest part of their hearts—desperate to be accepted. Yes. We are all the same—desperate to be loved.

Father, please fill me with Your love. Fill me up to overflowing.
Let it spill out on the thirsty people around me. Amen.

DAY 42

PROVE IT!

*Don't suppress the Spirit, and don't stifle those who
have a word from the Master. On the other hand,
don't be gullible. Check out everything, and keep only
what's good. Throw out anything tainted with evil.*

1 THESSALONIANS 5:19–22 MSG

Small children learn very basic truths through Bible stories—that
God loves, forgives, and protects people in difficult situations. They
learn about Jesus.

Fast forward a few years and children learn a new skill. . .reading.
Once we learn to read, our responsibility for learning God's Word
totally changes! Anytime you hear a preacher or a teacher discuss
a topic that is different from how you have understood it, go to the
Bible. Google it. Read everything you can about the subject. Do *not*
accept anything into your beliefs, your faith, your *theology*, unless
it is proven in scripture.

People are teaching some weird stuff! A lot of it is altered from
the Bible. On the other hand, our God has said and done some
really strange things! Awesome things! Wild things! We have the
responsibility and the privilege to study His Word and to know Him
as our God, our King, our Creator, our Abba. Are you wondering
what *Abba* means? It's in the Bible. It means Papa. He loves us and
calls us His children. The Bible also says He sings over us. Can you
imagine the Creator of the universe calling your name and singing
to you? You have so much to learn! He loves you!

Dear Father, as I read the Bible, help me get to know You! Amen.

WEDDING PLANS

The LORD God said, "It is not good for the man to be alone. I will make a helper suitable for him."

GENESIS 2:18 NIV

Have you begun wedding planning? Do you dream about candlelight flickering in a church as you whisper promises that will take a lifetime to fulfill? Hold on a second. I am not talking about daydreams but real preparation.

Starting today, pray for your future husband. He is probably close to your age and going through a lot of the same insecurities that you're experiencing. Pray for his salvation—that he will be hungry to study the Bible and learn God's truths. Pray that he has Christian friends who will help him live a strong, moral life. Pray that he will stay pure and not fall into any sort of immorality or addiction. Pray that he will apply himself in school so he can provide for your family. Pray that he will have a good work ethic but will also take time to laugh and play. Pray that he has mentors to teach him strength in kindness. Pray for his parents to protect him and love him. Pray for him to be protected from evil.

Pray for him every day, beginning today, for the rest of your life.

Father, I pray protection and blessing on my future husband. Please give him a hunger for wisdom and purity, and a hunger to follow You. Amen.

THE GIFT IS YOU

*Run from anything that stimulates youthful lusts. Instead,
pursue righteous living, faithfulness, love, and peace.*
2 TIMOTHY 2:22 NLT

One day you will probably stand face-to-face with the man you love. You will take vows of "For better or worse, in sickness and in health. . ." You will have opened a multitude of wedding gifts, and people will ask you, "What is your favorite gift?" hoping it will be the one they gave you.

I have not met your future husband. I have no clue about his height, weight, skin tone, musical preference, or facial hair. But I do know one thing about that man. I know what *his* favorite gift will be; it's a no-brainer. His favorite gift will be you! You heard right. You. Don't you think he deserves the very best YOU, you can offer him?

Pretend for a minute. . .that you begin a journal for your future husband. That every time you hold someone's hand, give or accept a hug or a kiss—any time you give anything of yourself away—you write a note about it. That you plan on giving him the journal the day you marry him. . . *What would you want written in it?* Wouldn't you want to hand him a book with completely clean pages? Wouldn't you want to tell him that he had always been worth the wait?

Father, please help me remain completely pure. I need your
gift of self-control to strengthen me at all times. I want to
stand before my husband as a spotless and pure bride. Amen.

GOD HEARTS YOU!

*You have searched me, Lᴏʀᴅ, and you know me. You know
when I sit and when I rise; you perceive my thoughts
from afar. You discern my going out and my lying down;
you are familiar with all my ways. Before a word is on
my tongue you, Lᴏʀᴅ, know it completely. You hem me
in behind and before, and you lay your hand upon me.*

PSALM 139:1–5 NIV

Do you know that God loves you? I don't mean just a little. He adores you. He treasures you. Don't believe for one minute that you are an afterthought. He knows where you are, what you are thinking, and what you are about to say before you say it.

He created you with care—every detail before and after your birth: "You knit me together in my mother's womb. I praise you because I am fearfully and wonderfully made; your works are wonderful.... Your eyes saw my unformed body; all the days ordained for me were written in your book before one of them came to be. How precious to me are your thoughts, God! How vast is the sum of them! Were I to count them, they would outnumber the grains of sand" (Psalm 139:13–14, 16–18 NIV).

He created you. He knows you. He loves you. Do you wonder how much? Once you accept Him as your Savior, He calls you His bride!

Father, I want to live a pure life. I want to follow
Your commandments and honor You with
my life. I want to be Your bride. Amen.

DAY 46

KNOWING IT BY HEART

*I have hidden your word in my heart
that I might not sin against you.*
PSALM 119:11 NIV

The soldiers were introduced as they stepped off the military plane. They were prisoners of war who were being returned to their country and their families.

One was asked how he survived the years of solitary confinement. He said they would wait for the silence of night when a new prisoner was brought into camp. Using Morse code they would ask if he knew any Bible verses. He said they had collected a handful of verses they repeated constantly. He quoted a few quickly.

Think about it. We have Bibles lying around everywhere; Bibles on our computers and smartphones. But do we *know it*? If all Bibles suddenly disappeared, how much of God's Word do you have in your head and heart? Don't say you can't memorize it! You can probably sing dozens of songs and quote more than a dozen commercials right now!

If someone wrote you a love note, *you would read it until you could repeat it!* The Bible is a 66-book love letter from the Father to *you*. Write verses on index cards or sticky notes. Stick one on your bathroom mirror and have one on your nightstand. If you memorize only one or two weekly, think about how much of God's truth you will have internalized within a few years! Begin making it a priority today.

Dear Father, thank You for Your Word—for Your promises and Your instruction. Plant it deeply in my heart. Amen.

DAY 47

STICKS AND STONES

The tongue has the power of life and death. . .
PROVERBS 18:21 NIV

. . .but words can never harm me.

What a lie! What a terrible, pathetic lie! Words *do* hurt! They shame. They demean. They criticize. They wound. They humiliate. They expose secrets. They crush confidence. They minimize worth. They shatter security. They destroy relationships.

Words can also love. They can build up. They can comfort. They can console. They sympathize. They teach. They encourage. They inspire. They motivate. They nurture. They can heal.

Please, please be very careful with your words! Your words can attract people to you or repel people from you. They also reveal your heart. Have you seen someone mash their finger and been surprised at the words that came flying out of their mouth? Scripture says, "For the mouth speaks what the heart is full of" (Luke 6:45 NIV).

Stated a different way, you are like a tube of toothpaste—whatever is inside of you squirts out when pressure is applied!

Guard your heart. Do not allow someone's words to distort your view of yourself. Ask God to protect your heart from false criticism. Likewise, guard your mouth. Be careful of how your words affect others. Ask God to remind you of Ephesians 4:29 (MSG): "Watch the way you talk. Let nothing foul or dirty come out of your mouth. Say only what helps, each word a gift."

Father, I want my words to be gifts to others. Amen.

BIG FAITH

Without faith it is impossible to please God.
HEBREWS 11:6 NIV

Does it seem like faith came easily to people in the Bible? Because you know how their stories end, do you have a hard time understanding their struggles? Shouldn't the hair stand up on the back of your neck as you imagine the hungry lions when Daniel was forced into the den? Can you imagine the nausea from the rolling, swaying ark. . . multiplied by the smells of the animals? Have you felt Joseph's fear from the bottom of the well as he wondered if he would ever walk on solid ground again?

Somehow we miss the depth of trust—the solid faith—in Almighty God these people had. Why? Do we just not understand how great our God truly is?

Think about it. "Who has scooped up the ocean in his two hands, or measured the sky between his thumb and little finger?" (Isaiah 40:12 MSG). Our God is the Creator of the universe.

He has power over everything: "Then Jesus came to them and said, 'All authority in heaven and on earth has been given to me' " (Matthew 28:18 NIV).

He is in control of the biggest, yet He cares for the smallest: "Are not two sparrows sold for a penny? Yet not one of them will fall to the ground outside your Father's care" (Matthew 10:29 NIV).

He cares about *you*. Trust Him.

Father, I want my faith to increase because
You are the one true God. Amen.

WHEN IT'S BORING

*"Obedience is better than sacrifice, and submission
is better than offering the fat of rams."*
1 SAMUEL 15:22 NLT

I never quite understood today's verse. I would read it and react like my Boston terrier—head tilted to the side with a confused look on my face. So I decided to dissect it.

I realized the two sentences were parallel. The first part of each sentence refers to God's commands. We are commanded to be obedient. We are commanded to submit. The second part of each sentence ("sacrifice" and "fat of rams") refers to payment for sin. Suddenly I understood. The Lord desires what is better: obedience rather than begging forgiveness for sin.

The Lord is merciful. He always loves. He certainly forgives. But He wants us to bypass sin and its consequences. He wants the best for us through obedience to His commands. He wants us to have a foundation of moral purity. Does it sound boring? Maybe sometimes. But it's always right. Always.

What happens when we choose to ignore God's commands? Just remember that our religious razzle-dazzle does not negate our sin. He sees. He knows. He's willing to forgive. But life would be much better if we would simply choose to obey. . .first.

Father, forgive me for my willful disobedience.
I confess it. I want to live a life of purity. Amen.

DAY 50

COMMUNITY

As iron sharpens iron, so one person sharpens another.
PROVERBS 27:17 NIV

Sometimes we pretend to be excited that God made us unique and original, but believing we are different actually gives us a sick feeling in the pit of our stomach. How can we applaud originality when we are desperate for friendship? How do we find the courage to explore unique talents when we are afraid they will exclude us from people around us?

The Bible has a lot to say about friends:

- "A friend loves at all times" (Proverbs 17:17 NIV),

- "The pleasantness of a friend springs from their heartfelt advice" (Proverbs 27:9 NIV),

- "You and I may be mutually encouraged by each other's faith" (Romans 1:12 NIV).

Choose your friends wisely. . .deliberately. No one really has 500 friends like their Facebook profile claims. True friendship is with one or two who hear your heart, offer their shoulder, and carry your concerns to Jesus. And you will do the same for them.

Father, teach me to be a friend—to be willing to listen and willing to take a stand. Thank You for Your example. Amen.

DAY 51

HIS NAME!

The name of the LORD is a fortified tower;
the righteous run to it and are safe.
PROVERBS 18:10 NIV

Remember in kindergarten when the mean boys would call the other students names? Fatso, Beanpole, Dumbo, and Pinocchio were among the favorites. The names were descriptive and, even now, give a mental image of the child they were directed at.

In scripture, God was into name-calling, but in a different way. When He wanted to further explain Himself—introduce Himself—to His people, He would use one of His names to explain His character.

When people were sick, He introduced Himself as Jehovah Rapha, the God who Heals. When they were in need, He introduced Himself as Jehovah Jireh, the God who Provides.

Are you facing a huge problem? El Elyon, the Most High God, is in control! Do you feel like no one understands you? El Roi is the God who Sees. He sees every detail, understands and cares. Feeling alone in the middle of a conflict? Jehovah Nissi is your Banner. He goes ahead of you!

He is our Creator, our Righteousness, our Shepherd, our Savior, and Friend! He is everything we need! We are never alone. We can always run to Him and be safe.

Father, thank You for always being with me.
Teach me to depend on You more fully. Amen.

EVERYONE IS LISTENING

Set a guard over my mouth, LORD; keep watch over the door of my lips. Do not let my heart be drawn to what is evil so that I take part in wicked deeds along with those who are evildoers.

PSALM 141:3–4 NIV

Just a few short years ago, a person could make a few rude or crude comments and they would have been forgotten within a short amount of time. No more. Screenshots of Facebook posts or comments on Twitter archive every rant or tantrum permanently!

Words can easily be twisted and misunderstood. Have you ever written something hoping that the reader would recognize that you had used your "teasing font" or your "sarcastic font"? The written word carries heavy responsibility. Some good rules:

- NEVER say anything on social media you would not want read in front of your parents.

- NEVER say anything *about* a person you would not say *to* the person.

- NEVER "like," "share," or "comment" on anything you would not have written.

The ultimate test: Would you want to read and explain your words to Jesus Christ? Remember, it is called *social* media for a reason! Nothing about it is private. Guard your words. They are powerful.

Father, let the words of my mouth
be acceptable in Your sight. Amen.

SPEAK THE TRUTH

*The LORD detests lying lips, but he
delights in those who tell the truth.*
PROVERBS 12:22 NLT

The school secretary called the young mother and asked her to pick her son up from school. He had been suspended from riding the school bus. The mom went straight to the principal's office. After hearing the accusations, she motioned for her son to come outside with her. The principal asked her to have a seat and discuss the circumstances. She declined until she had a moment with the child.

The young boy's account was different than the adult's. The mother went into the school office and defended her son. In spite of the principal's attitude, she did not waver. After a few phone calls, the principal admitted the boy's account had been accurate. The suspension was lifted immediately.

How could a mom believe an eight-year-old instead of school officials? Well, *I did it because I knew my son. He had a reputation for being honest with me. I knew I could trust him.*

Be *that* person. Be honest. Stand for truth. Be credible. Do not stretch, bend, fold, or mutilate the truth. Be honest even when you know you were wrong, *especially* when you know you were wrong. Offer apologies when necessary, but always tell the truth.

Father, I want to be known for being a person of
my word. Teach me to guard my words. Amen.

SMALL IS NOT INSIGNIFICANT

For we are God's handiwork, created in Christ Jesus to do good works, which God prepared in advance for us to do.
EPHESIANS 2:10 NIV

Consider this: Just as there was only one Moses, one Joseph, and one Peter, there is only one Billy Graham and one *you*. Don't roll your eyes! Huge numbers of people were influenced by each of these men. . .3,000 people accepted Jesus as their Savior after one of Peter's sermons! But the numbers aren't what was really special about these men; it was their obedience to do the "good works, which God prepared in advance."

You may not expect to teach in front of thousands—but what about the fifteen who may listen on a Sunday morning? Or the person at the lunch table who needs encouragement because of problems at home? God is in the small. He cares about the day-to-day. He is interested in the one sheep that is separated from the ninety-nine (Luke 15:4, Matthew 18:12).

Do you feel that your life lacks importance because you are not chosen for "greatness"? Check out Galilee, Bethlehem, and Nazareth. They were small towns. Consider Jesus' humble beginnings. Would you dare call His life insignificant?

You are important too. You have been entrusted with your very own special mission and purpose because God loves you.

Father, show me what You have planned for me. I want to accomplish exactly what You have prepared for me. Amen.

LIMPING AND LEANING

Now to him who is able to do immeasurably more than all we ask or imagine, according to his power that is at work within us.
EPHESIANS 3:20 NIV

Life is sometimes hard and confusing. When we roll the problems or fears over and over in our minds, we can become overwhelmed. We feel incompetent to face people and situations.

Instead of focusing on our weakness, we need to focus on God's strength—His power! Think about it: What has His power accomplished? He spoke the world into being. He breathed life into man and woman. He directed Noah to build an ark on dry land. He parted the Red Sea. He instructed Peter to walk on water. He protected Daniel in the lions' den. He fed 5,000 with five loaves and two fish. He raised people from the dead!

The truth is, we spend way too much energy trying to limp around and handle things on our own rather than leaning on the Father, who is able to do "immeasurably more than all we ask or imagine." Instead of worrying about issues, we should pray about them. We should ask God for specific direction, wisdom, and strength. Then we should thank Him for providing the answers.

Father, forgive me for trying to be independent.
You said we should come to You as children.
Teach me how to lean on You. Amen.

DAY 56

EVIL FOR EVIL

Do not repay anyone evil for evil.
ROMANS 12:17 NIV

Maybe she tried to steal your homework. Maybe she tried to steal your reputation. Either way, you have two choices: revenge or forgiveness. You know how you feel, but you want to do what scripture says. First Corinthians 13:4–7 (NIV) spells it out:

You know revenge would be easy and maybe a little gratifying.

"Love is patient, love is kind."

You are so glad you are not like her! It would feel good to put her in her place.

"It does not boast, it is not proud."

You think it is time she was treated the same way.

"It does not dishonor others, it is not self-seeking."

This same thing has happened over and over and someone needs to stand up to her!

"It is not easily angered, it keeps no record of wrongs."

Two can play her game!

"Love does not delight in evil but rejoices with the truth."

You are really tired of trying to be nice to her.

"It always protects, always trusts, always hopes, always perseveres."

Be honest. Are you glad that God continues to love you? Are you thankful that He willingly forgives you? Are you willing to be used by Him to offer forgiveness to someone else?

Father, please love and forgive others through me. Amen.

CHRIST ALONE

*Follow God's example, therefore, as dearly loved children
and walk in the way of love, just as Christ loved us and gave
himself up for us as a fragrant offering and sacrifice to God.*

EPHESIANS 5:1-2 NIV

Life can be confusing! One minute you are treated like a child; the next minute you are expected to act like an adult. One minute you are told to think for yourself; the next minute you are told you are not old enough to make your own decisions.

What should you do? First: Obey your parents.

Second: Don't base your actions or decisions on other people's opinions. Do not work to pattern your life after others. Do not try to resemble the clique. Realize that people will sometimes offer poor advice. People make bad decisions. People hurt one another.

Instead, make it your goal to imitate God. Imitate His love, kindness, and goodness. Imitate Jesus. Try to live with complete honesty, purity, and selflessness. Try to act and react in all situations just as you would if Christ was with you—*He is*, you know.

He sees everything you do. He listens to everything you say. He feels everything you feel. He knows everything you need. He knows your heart. *He loves you.*

. . . .

Father, I want to act and react obediently to You. I want to live my life for You. Please love other people through me. Amen.

DAY 58

CHANGE

Jesus Christ is the same yesterday and today and forever.
HEBREWS 13:8 NIV

The kids laughed at their parents' high school yearbooks. The clothing was ridiculous! Hairstyles were hideous. Makeup was clownish. Everything had changed since they were young, right? Wrong. The outsides looked different, but everything else was the same—exactly the same.

Kids were worried about not fitting in and having friends. Girls were deciding what they were willing to do to attract a boyfriend. Boys were deciding how to attract girls. People were sneaking around to smoke, drink, or whatever else. . .ignoring the legal, moral, and physical consequences. Kids were scarring themselves through physical relationships meant only for marriage and wounding themselves emotionally with pornography. The year was different, but the loneliness, guilt, and gnawing hunger to be loved were the same. The pain of compromise was the same. The need to be wanted was the same.

Take a deep breath and listen. Jesus loves you. He is not an imaginary friend. He is not "there" if you believe but nonexistent if you ignore Him. He knows you. He sees what you go through. He has always loved you more fully and deeply than you can even love yourself. If you have never accepted His forgiveness, He is offering it. If you mess up over and over, He doesn't love you any less. You are not alone. Not ever.

Father, I know my fear of being alone or unloved does not match up with the truth that You are with me and love me. You never change. Forgive my doubt. Amen.

DAY 59

CONTAGIOUS EMOTION

The tongue can bring death or life.
PROVERBS 18:21 NLT

Imagine. Your mom's remark about your outfit as you leave the house makes you feel a little self-conscious. You run into your best friend and she pretty much ignores you. A little while later, one of your teachers reprimands you in front of the class. Just like that, you are suddenly overwhelmed by an accumulation of embarrassment, loneliness, and feelings of failure.

The rest of the story? Your mom was upset because she forgot the car payment was due last week. Your friend was preoccupied because she had not studied for a quiz she was about to take. The teacher had been arguing with her husband before coming to school. *None of them meant you any harm.* Their careless words, however, negatively affected your feelings about yourself and, therefore, the way you would approach others around you.

When people are critical of you, weigh their words. Are they correct? Are they well meaning? Are they covered in love? Use the same filter when you start to speak. Are your words correct? Are they kind? Will they wound? Are they self-serving?

Father, help me avoid being wounded by careless
words, and please help me avoid wounding anyone
else. Teach me to be an encourager. Amen.

BEASTIES IN THE SKY

Do not be anxious about anything, but in every situation, by prayer and petition, with thanksgiving, present your requests to God. And the peace of God, which transcends all understanding, will guard your hearts and your minds in Christ Jesus.

PHILIPPIANS 4:6–7 NIV

One day after school, Ashton went for a walk. There were clouds in the sky and there were clouds in her heart. She decided to try to find pictures in the clouds to cheer herself up, but when she started the game, everything she saw in the fluffy white shapes looked mean; everything had teeth. It was as if a violent zoo had filled up the heavens. *Great, that's just what I need,* she thought.

On the way home, she decided to tell God how great He is. She thanked Him for her friends; she thanked Him for her family; she thanked Him for bringing good out of bad, for being in control of her life and loving her.

Suddenly, the clouds that were in the sky and those lingering in her heart were changed! The whole sky was filled with animals running and playing.

Do you feel sad today? One way to feel happier and to have more joy is to remind yourself how great God is by talking with Him. Sing Him a song about how much you are thankful for His love and how powerful you know He is. Then the bad weather inside you will change too.

. . . .

Lord Jesus, please help me focus on how amazing and wonderful You are. Then my worry and my sadness will turn into joy. Amen.

IT'S OKAY TO MAKE MISTAKES

*You make your saving help my shield, and your right
hand sustains me; your help has made me great.*

PSALM 18:35 NIV

Have you ever seen very young girls dance? Lots of times they are having so much fun that they don't know if they are messing up. They are just having a fun time twirling, prancing, and skipping.

When you were little, you were just like this. You didn't know that you could make mistakes. You sang, even if you didn't sing perfectly; you danced, even if you missed a step; and you drew pictures, even if they weren't perfect. You didn't worry about messing up.

But when you got a little older, maybe you forgot that it's okay to make mistakes, that being perfect isn't possible, and that before you can learn to do anything really well, you'll sometimes mess up and that's okay. Think about it. Before babies can walk, they fall down. Before they can talk, they jabber. Why should it be different when we get older? We'll still make mistakes, and it's okay.

Remember, if you worry about doing something perfectly the first time, you may never start. Everyone who does anything great starts out learning and making mistakes. Today, why don't you "dance through life" like a young girl who isn't afraid of messing up?

Lord, thank You for allowing me the freedom to make mistakes and for never letting my mistakes define me. Help me remember not to worry about doing things perfectly so that I will have the courage to try new things that You bring into my life. Thank You, God, for loving me so much! Amen.

DAY 62

YOU CAN DO IT!

If God is for us, who can be against us?
ROMANS 8:31 NIV

Avery wants to play the piano. She is excited about taking lessons, but she isn't excited about what one of the girls at school has been saying to her: "Avery, I don't think you'll be good at the piano." Maybe you have had something like this happen to you. Maybe you want to learn to do something new, but someone has made you wonder if you can do it or if you'll be good at it.

Here is something that will encourage you: All throughout life there will be people who think that you can't do something, or they will tell you it's not possible. Maybe they will say: "You can't be a chemist. You're not smart enough;" "You can't be a singer. You're not pretty enough;" "You can't be a teacher. You're not patient enough."

No matter what you want to do, God is the only One who needs to decide if you can do it. He is the One who gives us talents and abilities. He is the One who puts dreams in our hearts.

Sometimes the best way to move toward what you would like to do is to ignore negative and unkind things people may say and go for what you want to accomplish instead. As you do, your courage will grow.

Do you have a dream? If it's a plan for you from God, He is the only One who needs to believe you can do it. Live for Him.

Lord, thank You for the ability to do the things You have created for me to do. If You have placed a dream in my heart, I can accomplish it. No one can stop me from doing what You have made me for. That's such great news! Amen.

HIDE-AND-SEEK AND GOD

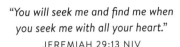

*"You will seek me and find me when
you seek me with all your heart."*
JEREMIAH 29:13 NIV

Have you ever played hide-and-seek? Did you wait in the hall closet while your heart pounded and you thought, *I hope no one finds me!*

What's really great about God is that He isn't interested in remaining hidden. Instead, He wants you to discover Him and learn more about Him by praying and reading the Bible. The Bible is the main way that He speaks to people He loves—including you.

God can be found when you seek Him with your whole heart. You don't have to say your prayers a certain way, go to one special church, or wear your hair a particular way. He is most interested in your heart. And when you look for Him with all your heart, you will find Him, guaranteed.

Then, when you do find Him, it will be like finding one of your friends during hide-and-seek. Because God invites you to seek Him and find Him; He is really happy when you do.

. . . .

Lord, it is so awesome that You want me to find You! You aren't going to keep Yourself from me where I can't discover Your thoughts for me. You have expressed them freely to me through the Bible. Help me seek You with all my heart. Amen.

GOD SEES THE "PARADE" OF YOUR LIFE

*"Therefore I tell you, do not worry about your life, what you
will eat or drink; or about your body, what you will wear. Is
not life more than food, and the body more than clothes?
Look at the birds of the air; they do not sow or reap or
store away in barns, and yet your heavenly Father feeds
them. Are you not much more valuable than they?"*

MATTHEW 6:25–26 NIV

Every year Allison likes to go to a special parade in her town. She likes to sit on the curb and watch each of the floats pass one by one.

Life is like a parade. The events that happen in our lives happen one at a time. We get up. We go to school. We take a test. All those things don't happen all at once, and we can't reflect on them until they've "passed by," just like a float in a parade.

Because this is true, there are times when you might worry because you can't see what's coming. But remember that God is like a helicopter over the "parade" of your life. Because He has created your life, because He doesn't experience time the same way we do, He can see everything that has happened to you and will happen to you. So nothing surprises Him—and He is in control. He will help you with what is coming. He will prepare you for the things ahead. He knows your life from beginning to end and everything in between. You can trust Him because He sees your whole life as if it has already happened, and He loves you.

I am so excited to know that You see my entire
life, Lord. You have it under control, so I don't
need to worry about the future! Amen.

LET GOD GUIDE YOU

Trust in the Lord with all your heart and lean not on your own understanding; in all your ways submit to him, and he will make your paths straight.
PROVERBS 3:5–6 NIV

When friends ride a two-seater bicycle, one person rides in front and the other person rides in back. The one in the front can see everything that happens. The person in the back pedals but can't see what's ahead like the person in front. She just holds on and helps pedal. And she knows that two people can't steer at the same time. If they did, they would crash.

This is how a relationship with God works. It's as if you are on a two-seater bicycle with Him. You are in the back, pedaling, going places with Him, doing what He has asked you to do. He knows what's coming and is always planning where to go next. He is steering. But if you try to take over, you will crash. It's always best to trust God with where you are going.

Some people try to "take over" their life by ignoring God or by telling Him what to do. Sometimes they disobey Him. But this will never get them where they are supposed to go in life. The best thing to do is trust Him, listen to Him, and cooperate with His plan, just like you would cooperate if you were on the back of a two-seater bicycle.

Lord, thank You for being forever trustworthy. You will never take me somewhere that isn't good for me. And even if I don't understand where You are going, You will get me where I am supposed to be. Just help me keep pedaling and obeying You. Amen.

TROUBLE CAN MAKE YOU STRONGER

*"So do not fear, for I am with you; do not be dismayed,
for I am your God. I will strengthen you and help you;
I will uphold you with my righteous right hand."*

ISAIAH 41:10 NIV

Chloe loved riding horses, but she was afraid too. Every day when she went to her horseback riding lesson, she was afraid that she would fall. Then one afternoon it happened. Her horse stumbled and Chloe wasn't holding tight to the reins. She went tumbling through the air and landed on her behind. But instead of crying, she started to laugh. All of a sudden the thing that she was so terrified of wasn't so scary anymore because she knew that she could handle it.

Life can be kind of like Chloe's experience. You may be afraid of failing, afraid of losing a friend, or afraid of saying something stupid in a group. Sometimes God may allow these things to happen to us so that we are no longer held captive by fear. Once you realize that your fear is unnecessary, you become stronger and more courageous, just like Chloe.

Lord, I know that You only allow those things into my life so that I learn how silly my fear can be. God, help me be strong and courageous each day. I am glad You are on my side. Amen.

DAY 67

HOLD YOUR TONGUE—AND YOUR TEXT

Do not be overcome by evil, but overcome evil with good.
ROMANS 12:21 NIV

Because of social media, email, and all the other quick ways people can communicate, no one has to wait to say anything to anyone. They can just say it right now and their friend will hear it in seconds.

This is a really awesome convenience, but it can also be a curse if we don't know how to control our emotions while using social media or texting. Let's imagine someone hurts your feelings and makes you angry because of something rude they said about you on Facebook. It's unwise to respond right away and say the first thing that comes to mind. It could turn into a big fight, and that won't help anyone. It's better to wait until your emotions calm down. Then ask God if you should respond at all, and if you should respond, what you should say. Our words can create a lot of trouble for us if we don't know how to control them. Ask God to teach you how to be wise and use your words for His glory.

Lord, when my feelings get hurt, I may want to respond in an unkind way—in a way that does not honor You. Help me remember that my words can make a bad situation worse. Teach me to go to You with my feelings when I want to lash out. Amen.

DAY 68

SHAME VS. CONVICTION

*If we confess our sins, he is faithful and just and will forgive
us our sins and purify us from all unrighteousness.*

1 JOHN 1:9 NIV

Elsa cheated on her test. She didn't get caught, but she knew it was wrong. After she made this bad decision, there was a little thought that came into her mind: *You are a bad person.*

When people sin, make mistakes, or make poor choices, sometimes they will think, *You did a bad thing.* This can be God telling you that what you did wasn't right. It's called conviction. Other times we may experience shame like Elsa did. Shame will always make you think that you are bad, not that what you did was bad.

When you do something wrong, remember that you may have sinned and you may be guilty, but you are never bad. You are loved by God, and God wants to help you make good choices.

Lord Jesus, thank You that when I confess my sins, You promise
to wash me and make me clean. I never have to carry guilt as
a punishment and think that I am a bad person. Please help
me make the choices You want me to make, but also help
me remember that when I do sin, You still love me. Amen.

DAY 69

COMPASSION MEANS STOP

When he saw the crowds, he had compassion on them.
MATTHEW 9:36 NIV

In sixth grade, Tamara's English teacher asked her to draw a picture to show what the word *compassion* meant. When she looked the word up in the dictionary, she discovered that when someone feels compassion toward another person, they want to help them.

Tamara wasn't sure how to illustrate this, but then she figured it out. She drew a STOP sign, because a STOP sign shows that when you feel compassion toward someone, you want to help them by keeping them from doing anything that would hurt them.

That's the way God is with us. He is compassionate toward those He has made—including you! So sometimes He will say, *"Stop."* Just like a mom who hollers at her son not to run out into the street because she doesn't want him to get run over. Sometimes the most compassionate thing anyone can do for us is to tell us to stop.

Keep this in mind when God says no to something that you want or He uses the adults in your life to tell you to stop doing something. It's because they love you, have compassion on you, and want to protect you.

Jesus, sometimes (okay, maybe all the time) I want things my way. In my head, I know that Your ways, Your plans, are better than mine, but it's hard for me when You tell me "stop" or "no" or "wait." Give me patience and understanding to see my life through Your compassionate eyes.

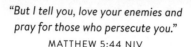

WHEN BULLIES IGNORE BOUNDARIES

*"But I tell you, love your enemies and
pray for those who persecute you."*
MATTHEW 5:44 NIV

Every night Mr. White locks the doors to his home. He doesn't want any intruders to break in. If he wants someone to come inside, he opens the door to them or gives them a key. The lock on the door creates a barrier against bad guys.

Bullies are like bad intruders. They bust into your life and space uninvited. They will be pushy with their words and actions. If you tell them to stop, they just keep going—like an intruder would push right through a locked door.

If you ask someone to stop bothering you, if you tell them you aren't comfortable with what they are doing to you, and they ignore what you say, they aren't respecting your boundaries. They are pushing their way into your life when you didn't open the door to them.

If this happens to you or someone you know, tell an adult until it is resolved. If one adult isn't helping, tell another one. Also, remember that you are loved. No bully can take away that truth. And finally, forgive the person who hurt you and pray for God to help them become more kind.

Lord, please give me courage to stand up for what is right, for myself and for others when I see someone being bullied. Give me the right heart to forgive and to pray for the bully. Amen.

WHEN YOU HAVE A FIGHT WITH A FRIEND

"Therefore, if you are offering your gift at the altar and there remember that your brother or sister has something against you, leave your gift there in front of the altar. First go and be reconciled to them; then come and offer your gift."

MATTHEW 5:23-24 NIV

When Sammie heard that she had hurt her best friend Gina's feelings, she was upset and ashamed. She didn't think they could ever be friends again. But then she went to church and her youth pastor gave her some really good advice.

He reminded her of Jesus' command in Matthew 5 to work out relationship problems if you know someone has something against you. So that's exactly what Sammie did. Plus, she did a few other things that her youth pastor shared with her too.

She said. . .

"I am sorry."

"I was wrong."

"Will you forgive me?"

"Can we be friends again?"

Fortunately, Gina forgave Sammie and they made up. But there are those times when someone else doesn't want to forgive or make up. If that ever happens to you, remember that God still wants you to do what is right, even if the other person won't forgive.

Lord, please help me to always be willing to admit when I am wrong. Help me be someone who always seeks to make peace with others whenever possible. Amen.

HE CARES ABOUT FRIENDSHIP

Cast all your anxiety on him because he cares for you.
1 PETER 5:7 NIV

Sarah was lonely. She had moved with her family to another country, and she really wanted to make a good friend. One night she prayed, *Lord, will You please give me a good friend?* A month or so went by and she didn't meet anyone special.

One Sunday Sarah went to church with her family, and a girl about her age sat down next to her. That's when she felt God quietly impress on her that this was her new friend. Sarah was excited. After church, she turned to the girl, said hi, and asked her name. Her name was Nicola. What was so amazing is that Nicola's family lived right next to Sarah's. They were best friends for months until it was time for Sarah's family to move again. Nicola was sad, so she went to visit Sarah. Sarah had never told Nicola how God had answered her prayer for a friend, but she did that night. They both hugged, and Sarah was reminded that God cares about friendship because He made it.

If you are lonely and you need a friend, pray and ask Jesus to give you one. Then keep your eyes and heart open to people who are around you. You never know when He will answer.

Lord, You tell me to give You all my cares because You care for me. You care if I am lonely. You care if I need a friend. Lord, thank You for bringing the right friends into my life at the right time. Amen.

POPCORN PRAYERS AND LONGER ONES TOO

*"For the eyes of the Lord are on the righteous and
his ears are attentive to their prayer, but the face
of the Lord is against those who do evil."*

1 PETER 3:12 NIV

Some prayers are like popcorn. We pop them up when we are
taking a bath. We pop them up on the bus. We pop them up when
we are standing in line for school lunch. No matter how short or
how long, God hears our prayers—even popcorn prayers. He wants
you to communicate with Him all the time, all throughout the day,
shooting up popcorn prayers.

One thing to keep in mind as you are growing in your relationship
with Jesus is that it's also good to spend time talking with God for
longer periods of time. You can do this by finding a quiet spot to
sit and read the Bible and pray. You can do this at night before you
go to bed. Or you can do it in the morning. But whenever you do
this, it will help you experience more peace and greater joy because
you'll take more time to hear from Him.

Lord, I am so thankful that You hear me all the time,
every day. I am so glad I can always talk to You no
matter where I am. Please teach me also to spend time
learning from Your example in the Bible. Amen.

DAY 74

YOU ARE SOMEONE ELSE'S IDEA

For you created my inmost being; you knit me together in my mother's womb. I praise you because I am fearfully and wonderfully made; your works are wonderful, I know that full well.

PSALM 139:13–14 NIV

Here is a really amazing thought: You didn't dream up yourself. You didn't decide where you would be born, who your parents would be, which country you would be born in, the color of your hair, the color of your eyes, or the way you would laugh. You didn't pick your height or if you are right- or left-handed. You were dreamed up by the Creator of the universe, the same God who made the oceans, mountains, stars, and streams.

When God made you, He made you with the same care that He made the hummingbird, the ostrich, and all the fish in the depths of the sea. And, because He made you with such precision, He gifted you for particular purposes to fulfill in His creation.

It's pretty amazing to think that you were made on purpose, for a purpose, by a magnificent Creator.

Lord, I am fearfully and wonderfully made. How incredible You must be to make so many animals and people—all so unique! Wow! You are so amazing, Lord! Please help me remember that how You have made me is very special. Amen.

GETTING WISDOM IS LIKE STANDING ON YOUR HEAD

If any of you lacks wisdom, you should ask God,
who gives generously to all without finding fault,
and it will be given to you.

JAMES 1:5 NIV

Shannon used to spend hours standing on her head in the living room at home. Have you ever stood on your head like Shannon? If so, you noticed that you see the exact same things as when you are standing up, but your perspective is different when you're upside down.

This is kind of how it is when we receive wisdom from God. Wisdom is what helps us understand life, and God gives it to those who ask Him for it. You could be analyzing a problem, for example, from one perspective, and it may suddenly look totally different when you apply God's wisdom. It's like standing on your head—your world looks different, but in a very good way. Wisdom makes your world look different. It changes your perspective on your problems.

If you aren't sure what to do about something in your life, ask the Lord to give you wisdom, to give you His perspective.

Lord, You are the giver of wisdom. And You promise that You will give wisdom to anyone who asks for it. Lord, please give me wisdom for dealing with the problems in my life. Thank You for helping me. Amen.

LUCK VS. FAITH

"Do not worry about what to say or how to say it."
MATTHEW 10:19 NIV

Have you ever found yourself in a situation where you just didn't know what to say? When you tried to speak, not a single word came to mind. We all find ourselves in the middle of these kinds of moments—just like Cormac Laidir McCarthy.

According to a famous legend, McCarthy was the builder of the Blarney Castle in Ireland in 1446, and he got into trouble when someone was mad at him and wanted to take him to the judge. McCarthy went to a woman named Cliodhna for help. She told him that if he kissed the first stone he found in the morning before he went to court that he would be able to convince the judge through his wonderful use of words to let him go free. McCarthy kissed the first stone he saw, and *voilà!* He received the gift of beautiful speech, and the judge let him go.

That's why people from all over the world visit Blarney Castle every year to kiss the Blarney stone just for fun. They hope that by smooching the rock they will become convincing in their speech.

Of course, we know that kissing a rock doesn't really help anyone speak better or convince anyone of anything. But if you have ever been tongue-tied, there is Someone who can help you with your words: Jesus. If you ever find yourself struggling for the right words, pray and ask Jesus to give them to you at the right time. The Holy Spirit will help you and give you His truth.

Lord, sometimes I don't know what to say, and
sometimes I am afraid to speak. But You will help
me. Thank You that You are always with me. Amen.

COME FIND ME

Look to the Lord and his strength; seek his face always.
1 CHRONICLES 16:11 NIV

Clark's dog, a border collie named Dixie, loves to play hide-and-seek. Clark can hide anywhere in the house and call out, "Come find me," and Dixie will search down the halls, in the rooms, and up the stairs until she finds Clark. When she reaches him, Dixie looks into his eyes as if to say, "Master, why did you want me to come and find you?"

God is always calling to those He loves, *"Come find Me."* He invites them to find Him through prayer. He invites them to find Him through reading the Bible. And He never hides where He can't be found, but He always wants His children to search for Him.

Sometimes people don't answer God when He invites them to come find Him because they think He isn't really listening to them or that He won't really speak to them. But both of these assumptions are untrue. The Bible says that God speaks to those He loves and that He listens to those who call on Him.

Will you say yes when God says, *"Come find Me"*?

Lord, You always want me to come find You, in the same way that Dixie looks for Clark. I am thankful that You hear me and that You are listening when I call. I am truly glad that You care so much for me. Amen.

GOT FRUIT?

*But the fruit of the Spirit is love, joy, peace, forbearance,
kindness, goodness, faithfulness, gentleness and
self-control. Against such things there is no law.*
GALATIANS 5:22–23 NIV

Sam has an apple tree in his backyard. Each year the apple tree blossoms and produces baskets full of juicy fruit that is delicious to eat.

In the same way that an apple tree produces apples, those who belong to Jesus and are living by God's Spirit produce fruit too. Galatians 5:22–23 (ESV) says that "the fruit of the Spirit is love, joy, peace, patience, kindness, goodness, faithfulness, gentleness, [and] self-control."

Imagine that the tree in Sam's backyard started producing fruit that was rotten. None of the fruit could be picked. No one could use it. In the same way, we can produce rotten fruit too if we have a bad attitude. Instead of love, we can produce meanness. Instead of joy, we can be cranky. Instead of patience, we can be impatient. If you don't have some of the fruits of the Spirit, and you know Jesus, ask Him to show you why you are producing rotten fruit. Then ask Him to help you change so you can produce the right fruit for Him again.

Lord, there are days when the fruit I bear isn't very
good. I am cranky or irritable, mean or impatient.
Sometimes I am unkind or selfish. Help me understand
how to change my attitude so that I can produce
good fruit that comes from Your Holy Spirit. Amen.

A GREAT KING

"For God so loved the world that he gave his one and only Son, that whoever believes in him shall not perish but have eternal life."

JOHN 3:16 NIV

When Jesus came riding into Jerusalem on a donkey, all the Jews in the city waved palm branches in celebration because they believed Jesus had come to be king of their nation. They thought he would be an earthly king who would save them from their enemies. But they didn't understand that Jesus was really the King of heaven, the Christ who had come from heaven to save them from their sins so they could spend eternity with the Lord.

They were totally missing the truth of who Jesus was. They saw Him with their eyes, but they didn't understand what God had sent Him to do.

Do you understand what God sent Jesus to do for you? Do you know that God sent Jesus to die on a cross for your sins so that you can be with Jesus forever in heaven and so you can have a relationship with God? Without understanding and believing this truth, you can't go to heaven. It's important for you to know who He is and what He came to do. If you believe Jesus is who He says and that He came to die on the cross for your sins, you may want to pray the prayer below.

Lord, thank You that You came to die on the cross for my sins so that I can go to heaven and have an eternal relationship with You. I believe that You are God, and I accept Your free gift of salvation. Please forgive me for my sins. Amen.

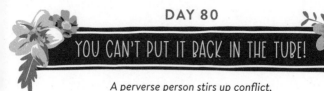

YOU CAN'T PUT IT BACK IN THE TUBE!

A perverse person stirs up conflict,
and a gossip separates close friends.

PROVERBS 16:28 NIV

Rosie *had* a best friend named Abigail—until Rosie said mean things about Abigail to some of the kids at school. Abigail was really hurt by Rosie's gossip, and even though Rosie went to Abigail and asked for her forgiveness, Abigail didn't trust Rosie like she did before.

This can be a very hard lesson. Once gossip leaks out of our lips, we can't get it back. It's kind of like making a mess with toothpaste. If it squirts out of the tube and makes a mess all over, no matter how much we want to put the toothpaste back in the tube, there's no way for it to happen. The mess has already been made, and things won't ever be the same again.

Sure, friends can forgive each other, but, as a rule, it's best to be careful with what we say so that we aren't sorry for the words we have spoken.

. . . .

Lord, please help me be careful with my words so I don't hurt others and so I don't make a mess that is very hard to fix. Help me be kind with my mouth, always building others up.

A LIGHT ON YOUR PATH

Your word is a lamp for my feet, a light on my path.
PSALM 119:105 NIV

Molly went camping every year with her family. At night, sometimes she had to leave the tent and walk a few hundred yards to the campground restroom. Her dad always told her, "Make sure you take the flashlight with you so you can see where you are going." One night as she walked along, she noticed that she could only see a few feet in front of her. The light would only shine on the path where she immediately walked and definitely wouldn't light up more than that.

The Bible says that God's Word is like a light on your path. It won't light up the sky or illuminate too far ahead, just like Molly's flashlight. It will give you just enough light for the step you are on. This is good to remember. When you aren't sure what is going to happen in the future and you begin to worry, remember that God will give you just enough direction and light for the road directly ahead. But He *will* give you light. He will never leave you in the dark.

Lord, thank You for lighting my path. Thank You
for remaining trustworthy as You lead me,
even if I can't see much of the path ahead.

NOT ALL THE SAME ON PURPOSE

Each of you should use whatever gift you have received to serve others, as faithful stewards of God's grace in its various forms.

1 PETER 4:10 NIV

One day Madalyn was eating her sandwich during lunch when her friend, Emilia, sat down by her. "What? You like your peanut butter sandwiches with bananas? Yuck! That's just stupid." Madalyn frowned. Emilia's words made her feel bad. Next, Aaron came to sit by both of the girls. "Madalyn likes her peanut butter sandwiches with bananas. Blech!" Emilia told Aaron. "Yeah, blech!" he said. "I like mine sprinkled with M&Ms." Both the girls laughed.

Some kids think that sameness is necessary in order to be accepted, that being different isn't okay. But God made everyone different, and He gave everyone different tastes and desires for a reason. Can you imagine if everyone in the world liked to drive the same kind of car, wear the same kind of clothes, and laugh the same way? The world would be totally boring. Can you imagine if everyone liked to build things, and no one liked to paint? Nothing would get done if we were all the same.

So the next time someone doesn't appreciate your special differences, remind yourself that God made everyone different for a reason.

. . . .

Lord, thank You so much that I am unique! You made me special! I am so thankful that I am not like everyone else. That means I get to do special things for You in Your kingdom. Amen.

YOUR MOST POWERFUL MUSCLE

Do not let any unwholesome talk come out of your mouths,
but only what is helpful for building others up according
to their needs, that it may benefit those who listen.
EPHESIANS 4:29 NIV

Cade likes to work out at the gym. Five days a week he goes to pump up his muscles because he wants to be a fireman one day. Every day his biceps are getting bigger, and he is able to lift heavier and heavier things. One thing that Cade doesn't know is that his tongue is the most powerful muscle in his whole body. With it, he can encourage someone to overcome an obstacle, pray for them to get well, praise them for their abilities—or he can use his tongue for bad. With it, he can tear people apart, make them feel bad about themselves, or discourage them from trying.

Do you have a friend who is having a tough time? Maybe they are afraid about an upcoming test or they are discouraged about a friendship. Because you have a most powerful muscle called the tongue, just like Cade, you can do amazing things. You can completely change someone's path just by what you say to them. You can make them feel alive in their heart, just like Proverbs 18:21 says.

Be a change maker. Use your strongest muscle to make a difference for someone today.

Lord, please guide me in helping those around me feel life in their hearts and not death by what I say. Help me remember that my tongue is amazing and can be used for good or for evil. It's the most powerful muscle I have. Amen.

DAY 84

GOOD CHANGE IS COMING

But those who hope in the LORD will renew their strength.
They will soar on wings like eagles; they will run and
not grow weary, they will walk and not be faint.

ISAIAH 40:31 NIV

Becca slid out of bed and groaned. "Ugh. It's going to be a bad day just like yesterday. I doubt that things are going to get better."

On Good Friday, the day that Jesus died, the disciples who followed Him didn't think that things would get better either. Jesus was hanging on a cross, and He was their best friend and Lord. They had followed Him for three years while He taught them all about heaven and God's kingdom. Now, He was about ready to die, and they didn't know what they were going to do. They were afraid and sad.

But they didn't know that in three days Jesus would rise from the dead to save His people from their sins. They didn't know God was getting ready to do something more amazing than they had ever seen.

Some days are like this. You wake up like Becca and feel discouraged. But remember that God is always at work, and you never know what wonderful things are coming. It may feel dark in your life now, but if you wait, Jesus will change things for you, just like He did for the disciples. Just keep holding on to hope.

Lord, thank You for always working on my behalf.
Thank You for never leaving me alone, even when
things seem very dark in my life. You are always
moving to bring good change into my life. Amen.

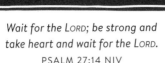

WAIT WITH HOPE

*Wait for the LORD; be strong and
take heart and wait for the LORD.*
PSALM 27:14 NIV

Every day John's dog, Molly, waits by the front door. John walks out the door to go to school, and Molly waits by the door until John comes home. Molly waits because she knows that John is coming back. If she didn't believe he was coming home, she wouldn't wait so patiently.

When is the last time you had to wait for something that you really wanted? Did you wait in confident hope like Molly, or did you wait reluctantly, thinking that only bad things were going to happen?

Sometimes we have to wait on God to do something in our lives or to make a change that we have been asking Him for. If we wait in confident hope like Molly, knowing that our Master will help us, then we will have joy when we wait. If we wait and don't believe that God really cares, then waiting will feel like torture.

If you are waiting for something today, dare to believe that God will come to the rescue. When He comes, He may not give you the exact answer you were looking for, but He will show up to give you the answer you need at exactly the right time.

- -

Lord, please help me wait in confident hope. Keep me from doubting that You will give me an answer. You will never leave me alone without help because You love and care for me. Amen.

DAY 86

GREAT NEWS

For the wages of sin is death, but the gift of
God is eternal life in Christ Jesus our Lord.
ROMANS 6:23 NIV

When you woke up this morning, you probably got yourself ready to face the day, believing it would be like any other. You ate breakfast. You brushed your teeth. In the midst of your normal routine, did you forget that today is a gift? Today is yet another day that God has planned for you and Him to venture through together. We have Jesus to thank for that!

Don't forget Jesus died on the cross. But He didn't stay there for long. God raised Him from the dead three days later! This is what Christianity is all about. This is what life is all about! It's about Jesus' resurrection from the dead. Without His resurrection, there wouldn't be any reason to be a Christian. When Jesus rose after He died on the cross, the power of death was broken. Now everyone who asks Him into their heart and who believes in Him is saved from the power of hell. This is great news!

Today, share the joy of what Christ has done for you with a good friend so that they can partake in the great news too!

Thank You for dying on the cross for my sins, Lord. I
am so grateful that I know the true meaning of life—
to be in an eternal relationship with You. Help me
share this truth with someone else today. Amen.

MORE THAN LOOKS

*Above all else, guard your heart,
for everything you do flows from it.*
PROVERBS 4:23 NIV

Emily looked at herself in the mirror. "Ugh! I hate my hair." She thought about her friend, Sarah. Sarah had long, beautiful hair. It looked like silk. "Mine is so boring. It's not shiny, and it is short and sticks out all over!" She stomped her feet in frustration, grabbed a hat, and slammed the door.

On the way to school, her mom asked Emily why she was so grumpy. "I hate how I look." Emily's mother frowned with compassion and reached for her daughter's arm. "Sweetheart, you are beautiful."

"Mom, you think I am beautiful because I am your daughter." Mom smiled, and Emily continued, "But other people don't think I am beautiful."

Maybe you feel like Emily. Maybe you don't like your hair, your eyes, your height, or your weight. But don't focus so much on what you look like on the outside that you forget to take care of the most important part of you: your heart. Hairstyles change. People get older. They get taller. They get shorter or fatter. But a person's heart can grow more and more beautiful over time if they let Jesus change them.

Sure, make the most of your hair, but don't neglect your heart. People will always notice it and say how beautiful it is if you take care of it.

- -

Lord, thank You for giving me a beautiful
heart. Help me be changed more and more
so that my heart looks like Yours. Amen.

DAY 88

TAKE THE RISK

It has given me great joy to find some of your children walking in the truth, just as the Father commanded us.

2 JOHN 4:18 NIV

A lot of people want to do great things in life, but they don't want to take the chance. *What if I fail? What if I look stupid? What if something happens that ruins my future?* They never get past asking "what if" questions that are bad so they can move on to asking good "what if" questions, like *What if I succeed? What if I do something greater than I have ever done before? What if it turns out really great?*

They focus so much on the negative that they never think about how fantastic things could be.

Is there something in your life that you want to accomplish? Have you been worried that it might turn out horribly? Do you think that it's something that God is leading you to try? Instead of looking at the negative, try looking at the positive. Take out a piece of paper and make a list of all the good things that could happen as a result of taking the risk to do this new, great thing.

And finally, remember that God is with you. Remember that no matter what happens in your life, He will never leave you and He is always at work to make a beautiful story out of all that happens in your life—whether good or bad.

Lord, sometimes I am afraid of making mistakes.
Help me focus on the good that You could bring
to me if I dare take a risk and trust You. Amen.

THE MOST AMAZING LOVE LETTER EVER WRITTEN

Your statutes are my heritage forever;
they are the joy of my heart.
PSALM 119:111 NIV

In his book *When I'm Longing for God,* Dan Stuecher tells a touching story about a great composer named Beethoven. This music man never got married but was in love with a woman that a lot of smart people have spent years trying to identify. They aren't sure who she was, but they call her Beethoven's "Immortal Beloved."

When he was forty-two years old, Beethoven wrote a letter of affection to her. "Oh, why must one be separated from her who is so dear?" he wrote. "However much you love me—my love for you is even greater." After he died, the letter was found in a bureau belonging to Beethoven, without a date or an address.

Some people have wondered if the lady ever knew how important she was to Beethoven because of this secret, undelivered note. Can you imagine being the one who was supposed to receive the letter and never reading it?

God has written you a love letter. It's called the Bible. It's the most beautiful love letter ever written. Remember not to stuff it in a drawer somewhere and never read it. It will give you joy in your heart, direction for your life, and light for your path. Plus, it has some really great stories in it.

Lord, thank You for Your love letter!
Help me spend time with You reading it. Amen.

DAY 90

NOTICE YOUR BLESSINGS NOW

The LORD has done it this very day;
let us rejoice today and be glad.

PSALM 118:24 NIV

"I wish I was older," said Amanda. "I wish I was old enough to drive a car, take myself to the grocery store, and I wish that I didn't have to go to bed when my mom tells me! I can't wait to grow up!"

Have you ever felt like Amanda? Are you in a hurry to grow up, for life to change, for things to be different? Most everyone has wished that their life was different at some time or another. They want things to hurry up and change.

One thing to keep in mind is that when we get in a hurry for things to change, we miss out on the great things that are happening *now*. We miss the friends who make us laugh. We miss the fun of exchanging a joke with a teacher. We miss a lot of things that we are taking for granted because we are looking too far into the future.

If you are in a hurry for life to change, take a minute today and notice as many awesome things as you can that God has given you right now. Many of those things will pass quickly and you won't have them ever again. As you grow, your life will change, and so will the blessings God gives you. So take note of how He is showing His love to you now.

. . . .

Lord, thank You for how You are taking care of me and for all the blessings You have given me right now. I have so much to be grateful for. Help me resist being in such a hurry to grow up that I miss the good things that You are giving me right now. Amen.

HEART FULL OF FLOWERS

I will praise You, O LORD, with my whole heart; I will tell
of all Your marvelous works. I will be glad and rejoice
in You; I will sing praise to Your name, O Most High.

PSALM 9:1–2 NKJV

Look outside the window during class or at home and see the many beautiful things God has placed in our world. The sun seems to hug the earth. The sky puts on its best colors of pink, orange, red, and purple at sunset. . . . All these wonders are God's, and He has placed them on this earth for us, as well as the wonder of His Son, Jesus Christ. When you see a flower, think, *God made that for me. God loves me.*

Sometimes being thankful is extremely hard, especially when your hair wants to look like a bird's nest, your clothes don't fit well, or you're faced with disappointment. We don't know why God withholds certain things from us. But we can be certain that He only gives us what is good for us. It is hard to give thanks when things don't go our way, but when we do give thanks, our hearts are happier. Without giving thanks, our hearts become like a flower that isn't watered. What would happen if there was no rain this spring? All the flowers would wither and wilt; they wouldn't wear their beautiful blooms. When we give thanks, our hearts can grow and bloom.

Lord, help me be more thankful. I feel closer to You when I am thankful. Being thankful is prettier than being fashionable. My heart is Yours, Lord, and I want to thank You for all the reminders of the wonderful gifts that You have blessed me with.

CRAYONS IN A BOX

And David said to his son Solomon, "Be strong and of good courage, and do it; do not fear nor be dismayed, for the LORD God—my God—will be with you. He will not leave you nor forsake you, until you have finished all the work for the service of the house of the LORD."

1 CHRONICLES 28:20 NKJV

Have you ever been in a large crowd? Either at a fair or mall where thousands of people seem to be squished together like crayons in a box and you are the only one traveling against the crowd? Did some people give you funny or mean looks when you squeezed your way past them? It's much easier to walk in their direction rather than making your own way. But there are many times that the Lord calls us to walk against the crowd for Him. The amazing thing is, He walks with us! He is right beside us, moving the crowd, making a path, and picking us up when we fall. How wonderful that He doesn't run away or abandon us when we feel most scared!

God created the whole world, and did you know He created it with you in mind? He makes the flowers pop their heads out of the earth as if to say, "Cheer up, it's spring!" All creation seems to burst forth and sing to the Lord. He has never abandoned the trees, flowers, or birds. Don't you know how much more He loves you than the earth?

. . . .

Lord, help me trust that You are with me. You will never leave me; You will never laugh at me or call me hurtful names. You make me strong and courageous. Help me remember You are always by my side protecting me, even when I'm most scared.

GOD DOESN'T WANT TEXTS

I called on Your name, O LORD, from the lowest pit.
You have heard my voice: "Do not hide Your ear from
my sighing, from my cry for help." You drew near on
the day I called on You, and said, "Do not fear!"
LAMENTATIONS 3:55–57 NKJV

How great is our God that He would hear our cry! In the midst of all the hustle and bustle, He hears us and answers us. God does not see some people as more important or interesting than others. To Him, you are just as important, special, and loved as Selena Gomez or Kate Middleton. Notice in today's verse that we must call on God's name; we cannot just sit around silently hoping for an answer to an unasked question. God delights in hearing your voice and thoughts.

If a friend suddenly stopped talking to you, what would you think? You would be confused, hurt, and sad, and the relationship would not feel like a friendship. See, you cannot have a relationship without communication, and that is exactly why you need to talk to God. The more you talk to Him about good and hard things, the stronger your relationship will be with Him. He does not want a text message relationship with you; He wants to sit down and genuinely hear all that is going on in your heart.

Lord, I am sorry that I have not talked to You as much as I should. Help me listen and speak to You more often. Thank You for hearing me and giving me so many things to celebrate.

AS SURE AS THE DAWN

Let us know, let us pursue the knowledge of the LORD.
His going forth is established as the morning; He will come
to us like the rain, like the latter and former rain to the earth.

HOSEA 6:3 NKJV

What are some things that make you want to stop trying? Is it a hard math question or difficulty getting the ball in the basket or goal? Maybe your best friend has stopped talking to you and you have no clue why. It is easy to give up and "throw in the towel," but what good would quitting do? If you did not work to score the goal, understand the math, or reach out to your friends, you would rightly earn the title of "lazy," "uncaring," or "dud." If you think you have learned everything there is to know about God, you are wrong.

God is greater, mightier, cooler, smarter, funnier, and lovelier than any Hollywood star or person in your life. Knowing Him, reading His Word, and talking to Him through prayer is the greatest adventure you will ever have! God has never stopped loving you; He has never stopped chasing after your heart. God is not "lazy," "uncaring," or a "dud." God reminds us with every sunrise that He is coming back for us, that He has not forgotten us. Don't stop searching for God. Never let Satan or anyone in your life make you think He is boring. Who do you think created laughter? God did! Everything that you enjoy this spring (puddles to splash in, flowers in bloom, rainbows that have no end) were created by God.

God, thank You for all the beauty of springtime. Thank You for the ups and downs in my day, because they fashion me into a young woman who seeks You.

BOASTING IN CHRIST

*God forbid that I should boast except in the cross
of our Lord Jesus Christ, by whom the world has
been crucified to me, and I to the world.*

GALATIANS 6:14 NKJV

You know when someone is proud. They tend to always talk about their skills or talents, possibly even show them off. It is annoying to be around a show-off who wants all the attention. The apostle Paul wrote a letter to the church in Galatia (which was located near modern-day Turkey) that said the only thing he will boast in is Jesus Christ. Now imagine one of your classmates saying one day, "I take pride in the fact that I am a sinner and don't deserve forgiveness, but Jesus Christ saved me! I am proud of Jesus' grace and mercy." Kind of a strange thing to boast about, but what are some things you take pride in? Maybe you have good grades or can sing. Do you have a certain outfit that is super stylish? In comparison to Jesus Christ, these things are worthless. Someday you will not be in school anymore and grades will not matter, and one day your outfit will go out of style, but Jesus never changes. God's love, grace, and power that He showed through Jesus Christ's death and resurrection will never fade away; they are as true today as they were 2,000 years ago! We take pride in the Gospel and Jesus' death and resurrection because we have no hope outside of Jesus Christ.

Lord, forgive me for taking pride in my own abilities; all my gifts are from You. Thank You for the blessings in my life, and help me avoid growing tired or bored of being thankful.

GOD ISN'T SCARED

*"Blessed be the name of God forever and ever,
for wisdom and might are His. And He changes
the times and the seasons; He removes kings and
raises up kings; He gives wisdom to the wise and
knowledge to those who have understanding. He
reveals deep and secret things; He knows what
is in the darkness, and light dwells with Him."*

DANIEL 2:20–22 NKJV

Things like knowledge, wisdom, and authority are all blessings from God. Nothing is outside of God. Everything you interact with on a daily basis (phones, siblings, weather, parents, your crazy hair. . .) all comes from God! Whoa! So does He control everything and know everything? Yes! He knows everything about you, even the places in your heart you do not wish to search.

God knows the scary stuff, the things or secrets we don't want to know, and He is not scared by them. In fact, He is in control of them. The "light" can mean knowledge, healing, or peace, and it lives with God. Light was created by God. Isn't it wonderful to know when you are scared that you have a God who will bring light and peace into the darkest places? In those frightening times, call out to Him, ask Him to calm you, and rely on Him to save you, because He has defeated the darkness.

Lord, I am so glad You control everything! Help me trust You
in the darkest times, knowing that You control the darkness.
Thank You for being a great, strong, and powerful God.

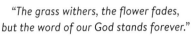

OUT OF STYLE

*"The grass withers, the flower fades,
but the word of our God stands forever."*
ISAIAH 40:8 NKJV

How much change occurs throughout your day? Most likely a whole bunch! You are not the same person each day. You grow a little taller, your opinions about movies or clothes change, and your hair never falls in quite the same way as the day before. The Bible, God's Word, has never changed! The same verses you read in the Old Testament are the same words the Israelites read. God is as constant as the waves on the seashore. His Word does not change, nor does He change His mind. In Isaiah 40:8, we see that God's Word is untouched by time.

Have you ever dealt with a person who can't make up their mind, or have you ever had a hard time deciding on the best outfit for school or a church function? It can be pretty frustrating. Now imagine serving and worshipping a god who changes his mind all the time. Talk about a headache and nightmare! We would always be frustrated. There is such peace and comfort knowing that God's love for you and me, His power and majesty, are untouched by time. God will never go out of style.

Lord, I am so happy that You do not change. Thank You for being a solid rock that I can cling to when frustrating times come.

THE FIRST SHEPHERD

*Behold, the Lord G*OD *shall come with a strong hand, and His
arm shall rule for Him; behold, His reward is with Him, and
His work before Him. He will feed His flock like a shepherd;
He will gather the lambs with His arm, and carry them in
His bosom, and gently lead those who are with young.*

ISAIAH 40:10–11 NKJV

Have you ever held a baby lamb or rabbit? If so, did you feel their heartbeat pulsing faster as they tried to scramble from your arms and then calm down slowly as you stroked their fur? They may have even fallen asleep in the warmth of your arms. This is one picture of how God quiets our worried hearts, but He can't calm your heart unless you give it to Him.

There are many times that we don't believe God will answer or hear our prayers, and His silence makes us nervous. *Should I say yes or no? Do I tell the teacher I saw my classmate cheat on the test? Should I try out for the team or play?* All these questions buzz in our heads like bees to spring flowers, but they never seem to settle. Isaiah gives a beautiful picture of how God handles our buzzing minds and hearts. He draws us near, gathers us into His arms, hugging us as He carries us. We serve an amazing God who brings justice to the wicked and cares tenderly for us. God knows your heart and He delights to hear your prayers, no matter how silly they may sound. Give your heart and questions to God, and know that He will answer you.

Father, please take my worried heart. You are the only
one who can give me true peace. Help me feel Your
hugging presence and know that You are in control.

GOD LITERALLY SAID THIS!

*And the LORD smelled a soothing aroma. Then the LORD said
in His heart, "I will never again curse the ground for man's
sake, although the imagination of man's heart is evil from his
youth; nor will I again destroy every living thing as I have done.
While the earth remains, seedtime and harvest, cold and heat,
winter and summer, and day and night shall not cease."*

GENESIS 8:21–22 NKJV

You've probably heard the story of Noah. Today's verses come right after God brought Noah and all the animals safely out of the ark. Noah built an altar for the Lord out of praise and thanksgiving. God promises that He will never bring about another flood that will cover the whole earth. God also says that as long as the earth remains, He will not disrupt "seedtime and harvest, cold and heat, winter and summer, and day and night." In all of history, have we ever gone a whole year without spring? No, which means God has been faithful to His promise. Each day is a promise kept by God. He has not changed His mind, nor will He deceive us. We can fully trust God, and if you ever doubt that He keeps His promises, just look at the changing seasons, sunrises, and sunsets, because He made them all for you.

Lord God, thank You for the changing seasons and
thank You for the beauty of spring! Thank You that
You do not leave me all to myself. Thank You that
You are constantly watching and caring for me.

PERSEVERE

Let us hold fast the confession of our hope without wavering, for He who promised is faithful. And let us consider one another in order to stir up love and good works, not forsaking the assembling of ourselves together, as is the manner of some, but exhorting one another, and so much the more as you see the Day approaching.

HEBREWS 10:23–25 NKJV

"Holding fast" is the same as holding strong—like grasping a life preserver in rough waves. What do you hold fast to? Is it the knowledge that you might get some time off from school?

Breaks end and you will return to school and studies, but God will never quit on you. The best news is that the One who holds the other end of the lifeline is God, and He is faithful. He will never let go of you.

There are definitely times when God seems distant, but those are times when He is growing your perseverance and trust in Him. If you have ever watched the Olympics or another sporting event, the athletes participating have trained for most of their lives and given all of their time to get in shape and become professionals. God trains you so that in hard and sad times you can trust Him and know that He hears your prayers.

Lord, it is great to know that You train me. Help me recognize the work You are doing in my life and the lives of my friends and family. When things get tough, help me persevere and hope in Your promises.

DAY 101

HE SPINS TIME

I know that whatever God does, it shall be forever.
Nothing can be added to it, and nothing taken from
it. God does it, that men should fear before Him. That
which is has already been, and what is to be has already
been; and God requires an account of what is past.
ECCLESIASTES 3:14–15 NKJV

How many times a day do you look at the clock? We always want time to speed up when we're in school and slow down on the weekends. Did you know that God doesn't rely on time? God doesn't check His watch or look at a clock. Time relies on God because He created it. God's Word and everything He does from creation to the death and resurrection of His Son, Jesus, will last forever! His plan is perfect because He is perfect. In today's verse we read that "nothing can be added to it, and nothing taken from it," so when God says He loves you, He cannot love you more or love you less. He has mapped out your life, and He knows every desire of your heart. God does these wondrous works in your life so that you can know Him more and build a deeper relationship with Him. God is not wishy-washy like TV stars or testy teachers; He is eternal.

Father God, it is crazy to think that nothing about
You or Your plan changes. I change my mind almost
every minute, but I can always rely on You. Thank
You for being an infinite and all-knowing God.

DAY 102

GOD FIGHTS FOR YOU

Strengthen the weak hands, and make firm the feeble knees.
Say to those who are fearful-hearted, "Be strong, do not
fear! Behold, your God will come with vengeance, with
the recompense of God; He will come and save you."

ISAIAH 35:3–4 NKJV

Have you ever talked in front of a large group of people or had to perform on stage? Was there ever a time you were afraid to ride a roller coaster or go to a new school? It seems that every day there is something new to be afraid of. Most of the time we are nervous or scared of embarrassment, and it seems to paralyze us.

Now think of all those scary times and imagine that you had a friend who knew all the answers to the test, spoke perfectly in front of others, always rides in the front seat, and made friends with the whole class on the first day of school. Would you feel more confident with a person like that by your side, who encouraged, loved, and guided you? Of course!

God is that friend. He is strong, mighty, all-knowing, and nothing is outside of His power. He knows all your fears, even the ones you have not faced, and He walks right beside you in the darkest of times. "Be strong, do not fear!" God fights for you and is your Savior. He will rescue you and your heart from the most frightening times.

Father, right now I'm terrified. Calm my heart, Lord.
Help me see Your rescuing hand in this time, and
thank You that You have not left me alone.

DAY 103

ROYALTY

The royal daughter is all glorious within the palace;
her clothing is woven with gold. She shall be
brought to the King in robes of many colors.

PSALM 45:13–14 NKJV

Do you want to know a secret? You are a daughter of the King. When God calls you to be His child, you are adopted into His royal family! How often do you feel like a princess or are treated like royalty? How often do you wish you looked like the girls in magazines or TV shows? There are many times we don't like what we see in the mirror, but do you ever stop to think that God loves you and created you for a great purpose? Go back and read the first verse of today's passage, and pay attention to the words the psalmist uses. Did you catch it? "The royal daughter (that is you) is all glorious within." He is talking about your heart, your compassion, kindness, humor, creativity, imagination, and joy. It is more delightful and fun to hang out with a kind and warmhearted person than it is a rude person, no matter how popular, rich, or pretty they may seem.

God, the King, delights in your heart once you have given it to Him. He loves your company, and He enjoys speaking to you and hearing what is on your mind. He is not an email or text messaging God! He makes us laugh, and He is a God who enjoys joy. How great is our King, and we are His daughters!

Lord, thank You for making me a part of Your family, and thank You that You are the great and mighty King who I can call Father.

DAY 104

WHO HOLDS YOUR ARMS UP?

And so it was, when Moses held up his hand, that Israel prevailed; and when he let down his hand, Amalek prevailed. But Moses' hands became heavy; so they took a stone and put it under him, and he sat on it. And Aaron and Hur supported his hands, one on one side, and the other on the other side; and his hands were steady until the going down of the sun.

EXODUS 17:11–12 NKJV

One of the many ways God does not leave us alone is through friends and family. There have been plenty of times that you were not feeling well. Maybe you were sick or someone had made a mean comment about you and God sent a friend, sibling, or parent to come encourage you. Moses was in a difficult state and physically exhausted when God provided Aaron and Hur to support him for hours and hours.

God uses the people in your life to help you along in the hard times and good times. Sometimes encouragement and discipline seem unfair and harsh, but God uses everything to make you stronger and more secure in Him. God is always looking out for your good. The family and friends in your life are not mistakes. God put you exactly where you need to be even though at times it may not feel like a perfect or fair life.

Lord, thank You for the people in my life. I
have been blessed to have friends, teachers,
coaches, and family who love and support me.

WAITING ROOM

My soul waits for the Lord more than those who watch for the morning—yes, more than those who watch for the morning. O Israel, hope in the Lord; for with the Lord there is mercy, and with Him is abundant redemption.

PSALM 130:6-7 NKJV

What is the longest you have ever waited for someone or something? Was it a vacation to the beach or Disney World? Maybe you were going to see your best friend or grandparents. Whatever you waited for, the time probably seemed to pass so slowly! In today's psalm, David was being pursued by men who wanted to kill him, and David was waiting on the Lord to rescue him. Talk about a nail-biter! You would definitely want the Lord to answer your cries in that situation— and fast! But David anchored his hope in the one person he knew could save him; he anchored his hope in God.

God is loving-kindness, mercy, and the only true peace on this earth. Nothing is outside of God's plan, and nothing that happens ever startles or surprises God. With such power and might, it is no wonder David waited expectantly for God to rescue him. And at the right time, God did rescue David from his enemies. Our only redemption, safety, and love in this world is the Lord.

Father, may I hope in You at all times. Thank You for not leaving me to be captured by my enemies. You hear me and answer my cry because You love me.

YOU, HE CALLED YOU

But now, thus says the LORD, who created you, O Jacob, and He who formed you, O Israel: "Fear not, for I have redeemed you; I have called you by your name; you are Mine. When you pass through the waters, I will be with you; and through the rivers, they shall not overflow you. When you walk through the fire, you shall not be burned, nor shall the flame scorch you. For I am the LORD your God, the Holy One of Israel, your Savior; I gave Egypt for your ransom, Ethiopia and Seba in your place. Since you were precious in My sight, you have been honored, and I have loved you."

ISAIAH 43:1–4 NKJV

When the Lord speaks to Israel, He is speaking to His children. Go back through today's passage, and wherever you see "O Jacob" and "O Israel," insert your name. Now reread the passage with your name in those spots. God is talking to you. You are His child. He "formed" you, "redeemed" you, and "called" you by name; even before your parents knew your name, God saw you and called you. God promises that you are His and He will not sell you for gold; He will not give up on you. When you walk through dark and confusing times, He will be with you. He is your Lord and Protector. He is the ultimate Father who will lead, comfort, discipline, grow, and fight for you!

I love You, Lord. In fire and darkness, in scary, sad, and happy times, You are always by my side, sometimes carrying me when I can't walk. Thank You.

WRAPPED UP LIKE A BLANKET

*But it is good for me to draw near to God; I have put my
trust in the Lord God, that I may declare all Your works.*

PSALM 73:28 NKJV

Have you ever been extremely cold and all you can think of is getting close to a warm fire or snuggling up in a cozy blanket? And once you do, there is instant relief. You feel safe, and the warmth starts to melt your icy fingers and nose. It is a great feeling because our minds and bodies know that it is good to be warm when it is cold outside. Do you know that it is just as good to be near to God and to put your trust in Him? The nearness of God is like having the best soccer player on your soccer team—you can't be beat! God never fails. The nearness of God is knowing that the thunder and lightning may crash and boom but you are safe and snug in your bed. Being near God means having the Ruler of the universe on your side watching over you. Have you ever felt God's comfort and security as though He is sitting right next to you?

We can draw close to God through studying His Word, praise, and prayer. Anything you do for His glory will draw you closer into His wonderful presence. Think of your favorite spot in the world, a spot that makes you feel calm and happy. Those places and joyful moments are given to you by God. He made them just for you!

Father God, thank You for the peace and rest You give me.
Help me draw near to You through scripture and prayer.
Help me worship You in the hard times and happy times.

EVERY LAST PENNY

He called His disciples to Himself and said to them,
"Assuredly, I say to you that this poor widow has put in
more than all those who have given to the treasury; for
they all put in out of their abundance, but she out of her
poverty put in all that she had, her whole livelihood."

MARK 12:43–44 NKJV

Have you ever gotten a gift that you really wanted? Were you thankful and super excited? Of course—you got exactly what you wanted! It is easy to give thanks when you have that thing you desire (money, the newest game, a cool phone). But what if the gift your grandma gave you was the ugliest color in the world? That is when gratitude and a thankful heart are really hard to muster.

In today's passage, Jesus points out that a poor widow gave her last penny. Without money, how could she buy food or pay rent? But she never hesitated to give to the Lord, and she was blessed tenfold because of her sacrifice.

Jesus wants every last penny you have, and He's not speaking about just money. Jesus wants your time, thoughts, actions, worship, conversation, and heart. Sometimes He asks us to give up our pride or be kind to a person who has been mean, but Jesus blesses us abundantly beyond what we can imagine in return. The more you break away from selfish actions, the more free and more blessed you will be.

God, I don't always want to do the things You tell me to do, but help me obey. I want to follow Your will and call. I give You every last penny of myself.

DAY 109

HOPE IN A SHEPHERD

*Now faith is the substance of things hoped
for, the evidence of things not seen.*
HEBREWS 11:1 NKJV

Even though we can't see the wind, we can feel its power and presence when we step outside. How can you believe in something you cannot see? Faith is much more than believing without seeing. You know the sun will rise in the morning, and you know that you will turn a year older each year, but faith is hoping in what God will bring forth during the day and in the future. We tend to place our hope and faith in things that do not always succeed. Have you ever been let down by a friend or parent? It hurts when what we expected didn't come true.

There is only one person who will never fail us. God will always provide; He will always come through in the brightest and darkest of times. God is more constant than the seasons, and He will never be late to pick you up or watch your game. God will always provide what is best for you. Though you may not exactly like His plan, He will never harm you. Jesus is called the Good Shepherd, and a good shepherd does not hurt or handle his sheep roughly. Jesus gently speaks to us in our pain and hurt. He is the Savior and Friend we hope in.

Father, I am so blessed to have You as my God. Thank
You that You will never harm me or yell at me. You
speak so kindly to me. Thank You for loving me.

DAY 110

HURRICANE HEARTACHE

God is in the midst of her, she shall not be moved;
God shall help her, just at the break of dawn.
PSALM 46:5 NKJV

Have you ever seen pictures of towns after a tornado or hurricane has struck them? Everything has been flattened, houses and trees. The result is a mess. There are times when our hearts and lives feel that wrecked and broken, as though an emotional hurricane has swept through. What can we do when a loved one or beloved pet has passed away, or when all the things in our lives seem to be going wrong? We turn to God.

Today's verse gives us a very important truth about living and surviving through rough and tragic times. When God "is in the midst of her, she shall not be moved." In other words, with God as the center and focus of our lives and souls, no emotional pain will conquer us, because Jesus protects our hearts. Did you see the sun rise this morning? Did the birds chirp a springtime song, or did the rain dance a jig on the roof? All these little ordinary moments—the bird's song, the rain's refreshment, and the bright sun—are promises that God protects you. He cannot be your protector, though, unless you choose to make Him the center and focus of your life. But once you do, He will never leave you.

Lord, I can't make things right. I don't have the power or
energy to fix everything, though there is so much that
is broken. With You, nothing is impossible. Please be the
center of my life. Help me focus on You; I love You. I know
You will come as sure as the springtime to save me.

ANNOYING SIBLINGS

*"These things I have spoken to you, that in Me you may
have peace. In the world you will have tribulation;
but be of good cheer, I have overcome the world."*
JOHN 16:33 NKJV

Does it ever feel like nothing will change—as though your brother
or sister will never stop pestering you, your outfits will never be in
style, and the cute boy in second period will never smile at you or
notice you? Did you know that Jesus faced every possible temptation
and struggle that we do today? His younger siblings teased Him,
other kids at school or in the town bullied Him, and He wasn't a rich
child, so His clothes were probably ordinary.

In today's verse, Jesus is talking to His disciples, and His message
is troubling but hopeful. Jesus knows that we will face trials and
"tribulation." That the road we walk will be rocky and hilly, sometimes
dark and sinister, but because of His sacrifice on the cross, because
He was tempted and overcame sin, He is the victor of death and sin.
He overcame the evil and sin in this world so that we can find peace
in Him! He is telling us to cheer up; all the troubles will end, and He
will get us through these hard and frustrating times.

Jesus, thank You for noticing my troubles.
Thank You for conquering the evil in this world
and knowing what I am going through.

WHAT TO DO?

*He has shown you, O man, what is good; and what
does the LORD require of you but to do justly, to
love mercy, and to walk humbly with your God?*

MICAH 6:8 NKJV

Do you ever wonder, *What should I do?* or, *What do I say?* Maybe a friend has asked you for the answer on a test. Or you overheard others talking behind a person's back.

Whatever the circumstance, God has given us the answer. He has told us "to do justly, to love mercy, and to walk humbly with your God." By walking humbly with God, we take on a personal relationship with Him through praying and reading His Word. The Bible is a way to find out more about God's character and power, as well as His love and glory. He is the greatest teacher we'll ever have. Can you learn a lesson if you don't listen or ask Him questions? Of course not!

What would be "justice" and "mercy" in the scenarios above? Justice would be not giving your friend the answer, because that would make you both cheaters, and mercy would be encouraging others not to gossip. There are many times when God calls us to do the right thing, and it is often very difficult to obey. When we do obey, God blesses us beyond our imagination.

Father God, help me stand strong, obey, and act justly
in hard times. Please forgive me for the times that I
have disappointed You, and thank You for loving me.

SING LIKE NO ONE IS AROUND!

Sing, O daughter of Zion! Shout, O Israel! Be glad and rejoice with all your heart, O daughter of Jerusalem! The LORD has taken away your judgments, He has cast out your enemy. The King of Israel, the LORD, is in your midst; you shall see disaster no more.
ZEPHANIAH 3:14-15 NKJV

Shout for joy! Jump up and down! Sing with the birds and buzzing bees! All the colors of spring are yelling the glory of God! Why are they so happy? Because they know their God has redeemed them and that the Lord provides for them. The Lord has taken away all your debt and all your sin so that you may be called His child. The Lord God has taken your enemies down; no one can defeat our God.

We serve a King, and He is the King of kings and Lord of lords. There is no one greater or stronger than Him. Satan cannot defeat Christ because Christ came down and defeated all sin and death. Rejoice and sing loudly as if no one is around you! Did you know you have been purchased at a great cost? Did you know that Christ is the *only* One who could save us from death? There is no plan B outside of Christ. He knows you by name and protects you every time you take a breath.

Sing with creation, and rejoice with all your heart that God reigns. No one can take Him from His throne!

Oh God! How You have loved me and protected me! I don't need to fear a single thing because You are with me. Thank You for Your Son and His defeat of death!

DAY 114

WILDERNESS TRAINING

*"Therefore, behold, I will allure her, will bring her
into the wilderness, and speak comfort to her."*

HOSEA 2:14 NKJV

What makes something scary? When we are scared, there seem to be a million different thoughts racing through our heads. Hosea 2:14 shows that God is in control of the scary places. In fact, He brings us into those difficult times. Why would He take us into a terrifying place? Good question. God is always concerned about your welfare, and He will never give you a difficult teacher, class, or friend that you can't handle with His help. God uses those scary and hard times to make us stronger and trust Him. He brings us into the "wilderness" and speaks "comfort" to us. He never leaves us, even though we may feel abandoned. All the times you've felt as though you've failed or made a huge mistake, God is right next to you speaking comfort. God's comfort comes in many shapes and sizes. He comforts us through song, the birds singing in the trees. He gives us laughter and all the new baby animals being born. He shows us beauty through the budding flowers. God has wrapped us up in a blanket of creation for us to enjoy!

God, thank You for giving me comfort. Thank You
for being in control and making me stronger. Help
me rely on You in scary times and call on Your
name. Thank You for always being with me.

FLOURISH LIKE THE LILIES

"I will be like the dew to Israel; he shall grow like the lily, and lengthen his roots like Lebanon. His branches shall spread; his beauty shall be like an olive tree, and his fragrance like Lebanon. Those who dwell under his shadow shall return; they shall be revived like grain."

HOSEA 14:5–7 NKJV

Have you ever had an exhausting day, and when you finally crawl into your soft bed it seems like your whole body relaxes with relief? When your heart is troubled and someone gives you an encouraging word or you remember one of God's promises, does a sense of peace cover you like a warm blanket?

When we plant our hopes, dreams, and heart in the Lord, He will grow us "like the lily." Lilies are elegant, white, and sweet-smelling flowers that are beautiful to behold. What a glorious picture of how our hearts flourish in the Lord! No plant can grow without water and sunlight; it needs both to survive. Likewise, we cannot grow and blossom unless we sink our roots into the refreshing love of the Lord and seek His light.

God provides comfort in His shadow and shade, just like a big oak tree on a hot summer day. In today's verse, we glimpse God's refreshing character. He is not only beautiful, but He also smells wonderful! All the fragrance of springtime flowers and rain are part of His aroma, and what a wonderful scent it is! Relax in the Lord, go to Him, and know that He will grow and strengthen you.

Lord, thank You for rest and peace. Thank You for being my shade and quiet place. Help me think of Your words and promises. I love You.

SIX KEPT PROMISES

The LORD is near to all who call upon Him, to all who call upon Him in truth. He will fulfill the desire of those who fear Him; He also will hear their cry and save them. The LORD preserves all who love Him, but all the wicked He will destroy. My mouth shall speak the praise of the LORD, and all flesh shall bless His holy name forever and ever.

PSALM 145:18–21 NKJV

Our God is an attentive God, meaning He knows everything that is going on in your heart and mind. You cannot hide anything from God: a lie, a secret crush, or the fact that you cannot stand vegetables. He knows you better than your parents, siblings, or closest friends. His ability to be with you at all times, know your pain, and hear your cry for help is called *omnipresence*. Because God is so great and powerful, He can be everywhere at once. How? We don't know because He has not told us, but it is a promise that He will always be with us.

In today's verse, count how many promises God makes to us. Did you count six? The psalmist declares that the Lord will do the following: He is right next to all who call on Him in truth, He will fulfill the desire of those who love Him, He hears their cries, He saves His children, He protects all who love Him, and He destroys the wicked. How many times have you made six promises and kept them all? Probably not often, but God has kept His promises for thousands of years and will continue to honor them until His return!

Dear Lord, thank You for keeping Your promises and for always being close to me in happy and sad times.

SOMETHING OLD FOR SOMETHING NEW

"Remember the former things of old, for I am God, and there is no other; I am God, and there is none like Me."
ISAIAH 46:9 NKJV

Why do we study history? Why is it important to know how wars began, what people ate, and where the Great Wall was built? Because we can learn from these events and apply them to our lives today. Even in the modern world of iPhones, tablet computers, Google glasses, and electric cars, the lessons we learned from medieval knights and the pilgrims are still very important.

Life will be overwhelming at times: You may have a solo in the school performance or you may have three tests and two quizzes on the same day! Take a deep breath and remember past times when God answered your prayers and calmed your heart. Maybe a certain worship song calmed your anxiety or a friend spoke kind and encouraging words that made you glad.

Look at God's beautiful creation and know that if He feeds all the birds bobbing in the trees, He will definitely take care of your worries. Rely on God; remember His good works. There is no other person like God; He is in His own league. He has protected and bailed us out more times than we realize. Give thanks that He is unchanging and will never stop loving you. Thank Him for His goodness.

Dear God, thank You, thank You for saving me. Thank You for all the past times You have answered my cries and healed my heart! Help me avoid getting worried and anxious when times get crazy. May I always call on Your name, because without You I am weak, but You are strong.

DAY 118

NICKNAMES

*For unto us a Child is born, unto us a Son is given;
and the government will be upon His shoulder. And
His name will be called Wonderful, Counselor, Mighty
God, Everlasting Father, Prince of Peace.*

ISAIAH 9:6 NKJV

How many names do you have? Well, you have a first, middle, and last. Maybe a few nicknames too. Each of your names means something different about you. There are so many names for God throughout the Bible because His character is more infinite than the galaxy!

First, He is Wonderful. What do you consider wonderful? Maybe it is a magenta sunset or a hug from a best friend or loved one. Whatever you think is wonderful is part of Christ's beauty and the wonder of His sacrifice.

Counselor. This means Jesus knows the desires, fears, dreams, and sorrows of your heart, and He wants to hear what you have to say.

Mighty God. This name implies that there is nothing God cannot do; nothing is outside of His power and control.

Everlasting Father. This one indicates that God will never leave you; He will shepherd and guide you forever.

Finally, Prince of Peace. Jesus is royal, and He gives peace to all His children, which is exactly why we ask Him for peace when worries come our way.

Dear Jesus, You have so many wonderful names.
Thank You for being the most wonderful part of my life!

DRIPPING WITH HONEY

*The heart of the wise teaches his mouth, and adds
learning to his lips. Pleasant words are like a honeycomb,
sweetness to the soul and health to the bones.*

PROVERBS 16:23–24 NKJV

Speaking kindly and keeping others' feelings in mind when you talk is a great gift! Think of all the times a compliment about your clothes, talents, schoolwork, or character has made your day. The quickest way to make a friend is to give a compliment, and the easiest way to ruin someone's day is to say something rude or harsh. To give a compliment or encouraging word is better than giving chocolate!

What you believe in your heart will be obvious in how you speak. "The heart of the wise" thinks before speaking or making a comment. There are many times that we say things we wish we could take back. It's embarrassing and humiliating, and sometimes we are punished for the words we say. Learn from those mistakes and ask yourself, *Is this something I'd like to have said about me?* or, *Would this be encouraging or mean?* Give compliments that you truly mean—don't lie—and see how much easier it becomes to speak kindly.

Dear God, forgive me for speaking mean and hurtful
things about others. It only makes me feel worse and never
better. Help me find true compliments to give others,
and please give me the words they need to hear.

DAY 120

HE WINS

Then the women said to Naomi, "Blessed be the
LORD, who has not left you this day without a close
relative; and may his name be famous in Israel!"

RUTH 4:14 NKJV

What are some of the first things that pop into your head every morning? Are they, *Ugh! School! What am I going to wear today?* or *I am so ready for this test.* We think about tons of things during the day: gym class, shopping, what gross food the cafeteria is serving, and how much you love a certain song on the radio. But how much thought do you put into God? Is He in your thoughts at any other time besides when you pray before bed?

God, because He is always with us through the Holy Spirit, pays a lot of attention to our hearts and minds. As Ruth 4:14 proclaims, He has not left us without a redeemer, and His name is to be more remembered than all the Hollywood stars in history! God is the ultimate celebrity because He sent His Son to save us from death and sin. When was the last time One Direction did something like that for you?

Outside of Christ there is only darkness. Don't be fooled into thinking that there are other ways to find true peace. Remember that Jesus is the Prince of Peace. Satan will distract you at all costs from thinking about God and thanking Him. Praise the Lord that He has won the battle! We know one thing about the future, and it's that our Lord and Savior is coming back for us because He wins.

Dear Lord, I am so glad to know that You have won the fight and You are the victor! Thank You for saving me, and help me tell others about Your great love and sacrifice.

JUST. TWO. RULES.

One of [the Pharisees], an expert in religious law, tried to trap him with this question: "Teacher, which is the most important commandment in the law of Moses?" Jesus replied, "'You must love the LORD your God with all your heart, all your soul, and all your mind.' This is the first and greatest commandment. A second is equally important: 'Love your neighbor as yourself.' The entire law and all the demands of the prophets are based on these two commandments."

MATTHEW 22:35–40 NLT

Don't you just love rules? Rules at school, rules in sports, rules at home. Sure, we all have to live by the rules around us so that everything runs smoothly, but it's a lot of rules, and it's easy to feel like we'll never measure up or get them all right. But Jesus showed us how to simplify everything with *just two rules.*

Instead of arguing with those who tried to trick Him, Jesus gave them and us a great answer and blessing. His simple reply is all the guidance and direction we need.

Just two rules. Two things to remember. Two points to consider. Only. Two. Only two rules to guide you to live a life that honors God. That's because when you have to decide something, just answer the questions, *How will this choice love God? How will this choice love someone else?* Like Jesus said, if we let everything we do follow these two rules, all the other rules don't matter so much.

Lord, thank You for Your two rules—the only ones I need. You make my life simple. Amen.

DAY 122

WHERE IT STARTED

We love because God first loved us.
1 JOHN 4:19 NCV

Every moment God says, "*I love you.*" If that's all you ever remembered about Him, that would be enough.

No matter what we're doing or where we are, God's love surrounds us. John wrote many words about God's love, the love that's part of God's unchanging nature. He first *loved* us—not judged us or taught us or trained us—but *loved* us. His "I love you" means "*I cherish you and protect you, guide you and comfort you. I lead you and teach you, hold you and help you. I'm your biggest fan. I'm your Father, full of forgiveness and grace, wisdom and security. I'm everywhere, but my favorite place is your heart.*"

He first looked at you and said to Himself, "*Wow, that young lady is Mine, all Mine, and I love her more than she'll ever know. I'll love her every moment, and in that love, I'll grow her and redeem her and challenge her to be all that I've prepared her to be in this amazing life in front of her!*"

And in God's love we see how we can love those around us too. It's about hope and help and seeing the best that's yet to come. It's an enduring love modeled by God that we can share. It's a peaceful love that comforts others the way God comforts us. It's a growing love that never stops because God's love never stops.

He loves us, we love Him, and away we go!

Father, help me remember—and let
others see—all I mean to You. Amen.

DAY 123

NEVER EVER GIVE UP

*Keep your eyes open, hold tight to your convictions, give it
all you've got, be resolute, and love without stopping.*
1 CORINTHIANS 16:13–14 MSG

Do you ever wonder if you're following Jesus right? Do you run into things you don't understand and situations you can't control? Life is more tangled up than the insides of a broken cell phone, and that's why Jesus simplifies and clarifies things for us. He never says give up. He never says you can't make it. He never stops following you or unfriends you. Paul's pointers to the church members at Corinth guide us too.

Keep your eyes open—look for Jesus in all you do and claim His strength in every situation.

Hold tight to your convictions—don't let anybody make you doubt your faith or God's ability and grace.

Give it all you've got—Jesus needs bold and brave disciples today, just as He did when He walked the earth, and He has special work for you.

Be resolute—finish that work! Keep your focus on the goals Jesus has given you. You'll complete some quickly, some take time, and some are ongoing. Keep at it.

Love without stopping—that's what Jesus does. He loves you through every good moment and every tough moment. Love Him back, and pass that love on to others.

No matter what's happening, these guidelines will work you through it. Jesus' love straightens it all out.

. . . .

Thank You, Lord, for always teaching me and guiding
me. You know how I can get lost sometimes,
and I know Your directions never fail. Amen.

RECEIVING GRACE, REFLECTING GOD

"Therefore, I tell you, her many sins have been forgiven—as her great love has shown. But whoever has been forgiven little loves little."

LUKE 7:47 NIV

The woman in Jesus' story is an example to us today of great love and devotion from her *and* Jesus. The woman led with her heart, despite her mistakes in the past and perhaps her fear of Jesus because she'd done some wrong things. We never have to be afraid of Jesus or His reaction to us—it will always be one of love and forgiveness.

Every day is full of choices and options. We make the wrong decision sometimes. Others do too. But this story shows us that Jesus is waiting for us to come to Him with the mess, to just love Him and leave everything else at His feet and let Him choose how to handle it. Here's a hint—He'll always choose love! He'll use it to teach us and make us stronger so we'll know what it means to feel His great love and then be able to share it.

No matter how much we love Him, He loves us more, and with that example of love and mercy, we can pass it all on to others. We can be generous and kind and forgiving because our love will never be misplaced when it's given as Jesus gives it to us.

We receive God's grace and reflect Him to others. It's a simple and simply wonderful plan.

Lord, thank You for Your love and Your mercy. Please know my gratitude and make me merciful too. Amen.

ONE PRAYER, EVERY DAY

His mother said to the servants, "Do whatever he tells you."
JOHN 2:5 NIV

Sometimes our minds can feel like a computer that's lost its operating system. Sure, we've got plenty of computing that needs doing, but our poor processor has no idea how to process, what to do, where to start.

The confusion comes from everywhere, but the solution comes from one place—one strong, easy-to-find, never-out-of-range place—prayer.

Early in Jesus' ministry, He and His friends attended a wedding in Cana in Galilee. The custom at the time was for the host to share wine with all the guests, but the host ran out. Jesus' mother gave the problem to Him and then told the servants to obey His directions, whatever they were. They did and water from the well became wine for everyone.

Mary's wise words gave them—and us—comfort and direction. All our confusion can be tossed away like an old password when we "do whatever He tells [us]."

So when your computer freezes up—in your mind, your heart, your thoughts—find the Jesus answer key and the instructions you need. Keep your prayers and your follow-through simple.

. . . .

Jesus, please help me remember that You respond
to all my prayers with comfort and direction. Please
help me do whatever You tell me in every moment.
Thank You for Your guidance and care. Amen.

HELP WANTED: ME!

"O Sovereign Lord," I said, "I can't speak for you! I'm too young!"
JEREMIAH 1:6 NLT

Some jobs for God can feel easy—being kind, being grateful, even telling others about Him and Jesus. Other jobs are tougher, and we don't always feel ready. Jeremiah was young and scared when God called him to a big job. He said no. But God isn't in the habit of taking no for an answer, because when He asks us to do something, He's already planned it, and He prepares us to accomplish it.

We don't have God's long-range vision, but we can simply trust Him to know what He's doing. He loves us so much that He would never set us up to fail. People might do that—ask you to do something you know you're too young or inexperienced to do or lead you to the wrong place, but not God. The jobs He gives you fit you perfectly, and you're never too young to say yes.

Maybe you'll start slow, maybe you'll master a few things and grow your confidence in yourself so that you don't feel so afraid. Good. Remember that your courage comes from your faith in God to give you whatever you need. God comforted and reassured Jeremiah so that he could carry out the big job ahead. He'll do the same for you.

Go ahead and answer, *Yes, Lord, I'm young but I'm Yours. Let's go!*

. . . .

Here I am, Lord. Please help me along on the big jobs
You've created for me. Thank You for trusting me,
and help me trust You more every day. Amen.

HE CALLS YOUR NAME

Jesus said to her, "Mary." She turned toward him and cried out in Aramaic, "Rabboni!" (which means "Teacher").

JOHN 20:16 NIV

Learn what Jesus' voice sounds like. It's never mean, never unloving, never wrong.

Mary Magdalene went to be near Jesus in the tomb after He was crucified, but He was gone. She recognized His voice when He called her name.

If a friend turns against you or if someone tells lies about you, those voices are hurtful and mean. If you fail at something, your own voice can be damaging and unkind. If even your family members sometimes don't understand you or you have an argument with one of them, their voices can be cruel and frightening. All those other voices, including your own, are part of the noise of the world, but they're a mumble compared to the voice of Jesus.

Listen for Jesus' voice in every situation. Is He prompting you to make an apology? Is He guiding you through the next step of a difficult process? Is He reminding you of your worth and value to Him?

Know Jesus' voice by knowing *Him.* Spend time learning about His life and ministry and understand how He leads those who love Him. He calls *your name* every moment with love, guidance, and compassion. Listen. His words will be simple, but they will explain everything you need to know.

. . . .

Please help me hear You, understand You, and follow Your loving words, Jesus. Thank You for always calling my name and never forgetting about me. Help me silence all other voices and respond to Yours in love and trust. Amen.

MOTHER'S COURAGE

*When she saw that he was a fine child, she hid him for
three months. But when she could hide him no longer,
she got a papyrus basket for him and coated it with
tar and pitch. Then she placed the child in it and put it
among the reeds along the bank of the Nile. His sister
stood at a distance to see what would happen to him.*

EXODUS 2:2-4 NIV

You might not even remember the name of Moses' mother (Jochebed),
but it doesn't matter. "Mother" is the name that says it all.

The king of Egypt was afraid of the Israelites becoming powerful,
so he wanted every baby boy killed. You can imagine how horrified
the parents were! Moses' mother made a risky and brave decision
to save her baby son, putting her trust in God—and it worked. The
Pharaoh's daughter rescued Moses, and his mom even got to raise
him for a little while.

When Moses was just a toddler, his mom was separated from
him again, but when she held him, sang to him, told him stories, and
spoke words of God's love, she formed something in him that helped
make him the leader of his people and follower of God that he was.

Look at your mom, grandmothers, aunts, teachers—they each have
their "Moses" story of bravery and trust to tell. Learn it. Repeat it.

Father, please help me honor my mom and
all the strong and courageous women in my
life who've shown me how to make good
choices that benefit others. Thank You
for them today and every day. Amen.

THE FAITH TO FOLLOW THROUGH

Ruth said, "If you say so, I'll do it, just as you've told me."

RUTH 3:5 MSG

We read Ruth's Old Testament book and wonder how it can apply to us, but it's a tremendous story of her faith in God and those He provided to help her. And now she's part of everything we do today. Because of her strength and courage, she became the great-grandmother of David, ancestor to Jesus.

Ruth was married to Naomi's son. Times were very different then, and when he died, Naomi and Ruth were unable to care for themselves. So Naomi decided to go home to Moab. Ruth wasn't from there, and going to a new place was a lot harder then, but Ruth's loyalties and faith led her there. She told Naomi, "Where you go I will go, and where you stay I will stay. Your people will be my people and your God my God" (Ruth 1:16 NIV).

Still, it had to be scary, but Ruth knew God, and she put her faith in Naomi's leadership and direction. Even though they were alone when they got to Moab, Ruth followed Naomi's advice and carried herself with dignity and grace.

She kept her faith in her mother-in-law and the God she chose to serve. She married Boaz and they became parents of their son Obed, father of Jesse, father of David. Her simple, deep faith made it so.

Father, help me keep my faith in You and those You provide to help me. Please guide me in new places and lead me on to the great things in my future. Amen.

IT'S YOUR BOAT

When they had rowed about three or four miles, they saw Jesus approaching the boat, walking on the water; and they were frightened. But he said to them, "It is I; don't be afraid." Then they were willing to take him into the boat, and immediately the boat reached the shore where they were heading.

JOHN 6:19–21 NIV

Jesus sees everything. He sees all the good and the bad around you. He'll "walk on water" in whatever form that means to get to you. So the question isn't whether Jesus is holding the doorknob of your life—it's whether you'll unlock it and let Him in.

The disciples had that same choice. They were scared until they knew that it was Jesus "standing at the door," and then they invited Him in. He didn't jump in their boat uninvited, and He won't come crashing into your life. He's not pushy, but He is sticky—once in, He's in for good. He wants you to do the same as the disciples—have faith in Him and *willingly* ask Him near you. That's because *it's your boat.* You decide who's in and if you want Jesus' help in guiding it. His flawless guidance is all the GPS you'll ever need.

Just like it's your choice to accept or reject a phone call or to post or delete a photo, it's your choice to invite Jesus in or leave Him out. It's the simplest choice with the most personal and powerful results *ever.*

Thank You, Jesus, for the power of choice, and I choose You in my life, everywhere, always. Amen.

ONWARD!

Jesus was quick to comfort them. "Courage, it's me. Don't be afraid." Peter, suddenly bold, said, "Master, if it's really you, call me to come to you on the water." He said, "Come ahead." Jumping out of the boat, Peter walked on the water to Jesus. But when he looked down at the waves churning beneath his feet, he lost his nerve and started to sink. He cried, "Master, save me!" Jesus didn't hesitate. He reached down and grabbed his hand. Then he said, "Faint-heart, what got into you?"

MATTHEW 14:27–31 MSG

When you're scared, it's hard to keep your focus where it should be. Peter learned that on high, shifting waves when he lost his footing and his focus on Jesus.

Even when we're doing something good, something we know Jesus approves of and will help us with, we can still be like Peter, upended by the elements around us. Fear is strong, and we have to fight it with everything we have, no matter how it shows up and tries to drown us. Fear that threatens you like a crashing wave can be anything: others who don't believe in what you're doing, others who are too afraid to have faith themselves, and even your own mind feeding itself with doubt instead of Jesus' words.

All that's just loud undertow that means nothing, because Jesus will never let you go under the scary waves. He'll grab your hand and remind you that He's *always* there.

Thank You, Jesus, for walking with me and having faith in me. Help my faith grow as we go onward everywhere together. Let's go! Amen.

WAKE ME WHEN IT'S TIME

Then the time came for Herod to bring him out for the kill.
That night, even though shackled to two soldiers, one on either
side, Peter slept like a baby. And there were guards at the door
keeping their eyes on the place. Herod was taking no chances!

ACTS 12:6 MSG

Faith means believing in our God to do His job while we do ours.
It means carrying on in hard experiences and being an example to
those around us. Do you ever find yourself worrying about a test
you've already prepared for? Do you spend too much time thinking
about what someone else said or did instead of focusing on what
you can do? Do you ever wonder if God's paying attention to what's
bothering you?

When Peter was in jail, waiting to be tried and possibly killed
for teaching about Jesus, do you know what he was doing? He was
sleeping, of all things. He wasn't screaming or plotting or pouting. He
had prayed and turned everything over to God. He had demonstrated
his devotion and faith to those around him. And then, because he'd
done that part of his job and probably needed rest to carry on, he
closed his eyes and simply slept.

Can you do that the next time you're worrying about something
you can't change? Can you pray, do whatever's required of you, and
then rest in faith, "sleeping like a baby"? Yes you can!

Lord, please help me have Peter's faith when I'm
scared, and help me rest in Your promises. Just
wake me when it's time for more work! Amen.

JOY AT THE DOOR

Still shaking his head, amazed, he went to Mary's house, the Mary who was John Mark's mother. The house was packed with praying friends. When he knocked on the door to the courtyard, a young woman named Rhoda came to see who it was. But when she recognized his voice—Peter's voice!—she was so excited and eager to tell everyone Peter was there that she forgot to open the door and left him standing in the street.

ACTS 12:12–14 MSG

Remember Peter, who was in prison, all full of faith and sleep? Once free, he went to his friends. Now let's meet Rhoda, a young girl who spent her time in service to others, including answering the door. She was with those praying for Peter and didn't know of his miracle escape. When she recognized his voice outside, she was so overjoyed that she ran to tell the others, leaving Peter at the door.

Rhoda may have been embarrassed, but that's okay. Her faith in God joined with her joy at Peter's release, and she couldn't contain it. God probably smiled and thought, *What a wonderful daughter of Mine, unafraid to rejoice in My work. I like that.*

When we react out of love and pure joy for God's grace, He says the same thing about us. Look for miracles, have faith in God to accomplish them, and then tell everyone in the house what new miracle is standing at the door of *your* life.

Thank You, Lord, for answering prayers and bringing miracles to my life every day. Help me celebrate You with those I love. Amen.

SAY IT, MAKE IT COUNT

Run away from infantile indulgence. Run after mature righteousness—faith, love, peace—joining those who are in honest and serious prayer before God. Refuse to get involved in inane discussions; they always end up in fights. God's servant must not be argumentative, but a gentle listener and a teacher who keeps cool, working firmly but patiently with those who refuse to obey. You never know how or when God might sober them up with a change of heart and a turning to the truth, enabling them to escape the Devil's trap, where they are caught and held captive, forced to run his errands.

2 TIMOTHY 2:22–26 MSG

Have you ever heard the saying that God gave us two ears and one mouth for a reason? It's a silly little way of saying we should talk less and listen more. Yet we know people (sometimes it's even us) who have to have the last word, who can't stand to be corrected, who spend a ton of time jabbering about stuff that doesn't even matter.

God says there's a better way. When the arguing and complaining start, spit out your own unhelpful ideas like you would the taste of spoiled food guaranteed to make you sick, because that's what bad thoughts and words do.

Listen twice as much as you talk. Use words that tell the wonderful truth about God and why your faith is in Him. Then at least from *you*, everyone will hear love, hope, compassion, and direction.

Lord, please help me be a good leader in every situation, representing You and telling others about You. Amen.

"DIRECTIONS, PLEASE?"

*They pile heavy burdens on people's shoulders and won't
lift a finger to help. Everything they do is just to show
off in front of others. They even make a big show of
wearing Scripture verses on their foreheads and arms,
and they wear big tassels for everyone to see.*

MATTHEW 23:4–5 CEV

Did you know that in Jesus' time some of the Jewish leaders who
wanted to look impressive wore a box on their heads with a Bible
verse or two inside (called *phylacteries*)? Maybe you know the type.

They act like they're friends with others and then spread rumors
behind their backs. They look like good students but cheat on tests.
The truth is that no matter what others appear to be or how they
portray themselves to others, God knows their hearts.

He knows if your faith is real or if it's paraded around for some
selfish reason. The claim to be God's follower only matters when
you live it. He asks for His words to be written not on your head
but on your *heart* where they can never be removed. Jesus called
the Jewish leaders "blind guides" (Matthew 23:24 NIV), but we know
exactly where we're going.

No matter what comes up, with God's love and directions
imprinted from the inside out, there's no need to unstrap a box
from your head and check for instructions. Simply read your heart
and you'll know how to practice what Jesus preaches.

Lord, I know every day is a chance to be
a guide for others. Please make my words
and my actions wise as I follow You. Amen.

DAY 136

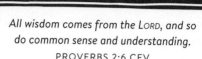

KNOWLEDGE IS POWER

All wisdom comes from the LORD, and so
do common sense and understanding.
PROVERBS 2:6 CEV

You'll hear this statement all your life, and it's true. *Knowledge IS power,* because what you know is something no one can ever take away from you. No one can steal it or hide it. It's yours forever. It's valuable and powerful, so be sure your knowledge comes from the right place.

Some people will tell you what *they* want you to know, maybe try to convince you to do whatever they're doing or make a risky decision. It happens all the time, but your response is simple. To decide if they're leading you the right way or the wrong way, stand their wisdom up alongside God's Word and see if it agrees with it or contradicts it.

And do you know how you'll know? When *you* know God's Word. The knowledge and understanding and wisdom that He gives is the knowledge and understanding and wisdom you need. It's *that* knowledge that's power, and it gives you a plan. When someone comes to you with an idea, take a minute and take a measurement, seeing if it matches what you know from God.

The more you study God's Word, listen to Him, and see Him work in your life, the quicker you'll be able to make those decisions, making your life much simpler. *That's* where you put your trust—in what God tells you and teaches you.

Knowledge is power: God's power.

Please help me learn and follow Your wisdom,
Lord, and claim it for my own. Amen.

HE'S HERE—NOW, ALWAYS, REAL

*"Starting from scratch, he made the entire human race and
made the earth hospitable, with plenty of time and space
for living so we could seek after God, and not just grope
around in the dark but actually find him. He doesn't play
hide-and-seek with us. He's not remote; he's near. We live
and move in him, can't get away from him! One of your poets
said it well: 'We're the God-created.' Well, if we are the God-
created, it doesn't make a lot of sense to think we could hire
a sculptor to chisel a god out of stone for us, does it?"*
ACTS 17:26-29 MSG

Some call it "blind faith" or "misplaced trust" in a God they can't
see or touch. We just say no worries!

Our God needs nothing to survive. He isn't dependent on air,
water, or food the way we are. He spends all His time caring about
us fragile little things who can't even see Him. He wants our trust
yet doesn't demand it. He waits for it.

He's made of love and wisdom and mercy and gives it all to us.
He doesn't post pictures of Himself or create clever hashtags, but
He helps us quicker than the rest between heartbeats. When we
reach for Him, He's already here. If we ask to be part of His work,
He simply shows us the list of stuff we can do, and we succeed when
we trust what we can't see or feel to make everything real.

Thank You, Lord, for being all I need, right beside
me, bigger than anything else—real! Amen.

THE PLACE TO START

In fact, we felt sure that we were going to die.
But this made us stop trusting in ourselves and
start trusting God, who raises the dead to life.
2 CORINTHIANS 1:9 CEV

Paul traveled through some hostile territory to tell the story of Jesus, and he was often in real danger. He told the church in Corinth about being fearful for his life in Asia. He could've kept relying on his own ability, but he found a better source of strength and courage. His fear didn't win. He changed it into faith and trusted God to be with him. God responded, Paul learned, and so can we.

Lesson #1: When you're scared out of your mind, trust God.

Lesson #2: Don't wait until you're scared out of your mind to trust God.

This story doesn't mean we shouldn't be competent and skillful. It's about learning everything you can and doing your best to be a faithful disciple, all while you're trusting God to take care of whatever you can't. When hard, scary things are happening, that's when relying on our trust in God should come *first*. That's when we want to remember God's promises are for us, when we want to remember all the times before that He's helped us and know He's still not scared of anything. He's still the same strong and powerful God who has us in the palm of His hand.

We can't save ourselves, and what's wonderful about that is we don't have to.

Lord, please help me remember You never tune
me out. My trust is the call You wait for. Amen.

YES OR NO?

When Jesus saw him lying there and learned that he had been in this condition for a long time, he asked him, "Do you want to get well?" "Sir," the invalid replied, "I have no one to help me into the pool when the water is stirred. While I am trying to get in, someone else goes down ahead of me." Then Jesus said to him, "Get up! Pick up your mat and walk." At once the man was cured; he picked up his mat and walked.

JOHN 5:6–9 NIV

It's easy to complain and find excuses. The people believed that the pool of Bethesda would heal them if they stepped in the water at the right time, but the man Jesus met couldn't walk. Jesus, in all His love and compassion, didn't pick him up or call for others to do it—He asked the man if he really wanted a better life. *"Do you want to get well?"* might be a question He asks us sometimes, and we can answer like the man in the story.

Do we really want to overcome a fear, break a bad habit, stop following poor role models? *Do we really want to get well?* The man walked because Jesus said he could. He trusted Jesus and began a greater life. What will *you* do when you hear Jesus say you can?

It's a simple question. Let's be ready when He asks, *"Do you want to get well?"*

Jesus, my answer is "Yes!" I want to be well in
You, growing stronger and wiser every day,
doing everything You say I can do. Amen.

BUILDING HIGH, BUILDING WIDE

> *"'Yes, get to work! For I am with you.' The GOD-of-the-Angel-Armies is speaking! 'Put into action the word I covenanted with you when you left Egypt. I'm living and breathing among you right now. Don't be timid. Don't hold back.'"*
>
> HAGGAI 2:5 MSG

The Israelites were trying to rebuild the temple of God after being captives far from home for seventy years. Imagine how afraid and unprepared they felt, and then they met up with a whole town of bullies who didn't want them there. They were tempted to give up, to say the job was just too hard and scary. God had other plans.

He sent them there, and He wasn't going to forget about them or ignore their fear. Haggai the prophet delivered God's message that they needed to keep building. It's a timeless message that comforts and inspires us today. It's so simple, so profound, so God: *"Do not fear, I am with you."*

"Remember who I am," God's saying. *"Do you think these problems and people are bigger than I am? Do you think we should just let them have their way and forget about My plans? That would be a no."*

Following God's lead doesn't mean we become immune to trouble, but it does mean He's there right in the middle of it with us—and He's a whole lot bigger. And just like the Israelites, we'll build temples of our own that He designs, no matter what gets in the way.

Thank You, Lord, for being with me all the time,
just like You promise. Help me not to be afraid
while we build everything You see. Amen.

GUT CHECK TIME

The king wanted [Queen Vashti] to wear her crown and let his people and his officials see how beautiful she was. The king's servants told Queen Vashti what he had said, but she refused to go to him, and this made him terribly angry.

ESTHER 1:11–12 CEV

Have you ever felt pressured in a situation, with little room to refuse whatever was asked of you? It takes courage to stand up for yourself, especially if you have a lot to lose by saying no. The book of Esther tells about two courageous women who did just that. We learn about Esther, but we also learn about Vashti, the queen before Esther, who lost everything but decided that was a risk she was willing to take.

Her husband, King Xerxes, wanted to show her off in front of his guests. She refused, and that's what made the way for Esther to become queen. Who knows what might've happened if Queen Vashti had been less courageous? But she trusted herself enough to make the tough choice. Maybe God was speaking to her somehow, even though we have no indication she even knew God. Still, through her, He made a way for Esther.

The right choice is one of courage and trust in what God has taught us. We can ask ourselves: *Would God want me to do that?* The answer might feel like "trusting your gut" because that's God speaking to you. And when we listen, we'll find the same courage, conviction, and decisiveness Vashti and Esther had.

Thank You, Lord, for leading me the right way.
Help me trust You every time. Amen.

"GOOD MORNING, GOD!"

Listen, GOD! Please, pay attention! Can you make sense of these ramblings, my groans and cries? King-God, I need your help. Every morning you'll hear me at it again. Every morning I lay out the pieces of my life on your altar and watch for fire to descend.

PSALM 5:1–3 MSG

What's the first thing you think of in the morning? Is it school, family, what you're going to wear? Is it a decision you have to make *today*? The best way to attack all of it is with God as your first thought.

David says that he gave everything to God first thing, and it doesn't say he then worried or gave up on getting an answer. Psalm 5:3 in the New International Version says, "I lay my requests before you and wait expectantly." There. Done. He's trusting God to handle it all, and he's expecting God's grace to guide him through the next steps, whatever they are.

God's up all night, waiting for you to wake up and talk to Him. He's ready with the grace you need for the day, like sprinkles on a warm afternoon or a tidal wave you can ride to safety.

Those first thoughts of your morning can guide your entire day. Let them be to God and of God, your expectation and His response. Trust Him to hear you and respond. Trust Him to surround you with His grace, which will allow you to make every day better than the last.

Some days are more of a challenge than others, Lord. I love knowing You're here every moment, no matter what. Amen.

FRIENDS MATTER

Don't fool yourselves. Bad friends will destroy you.
1 CORINTHIANS 15:33 CEV

During the time Paul was preaching and teaching about Jesus, he was talking and writing to people who were influenced by many things, and not all of them were good. Many groups denied Jesus, and they wanted others to turn against Him too. You may have people around you every day who try to influence you the wrong way or convince you to go against what you know to be true. Those are friends you don't need.

God knows that running away from bad friends can be hard, though, and that's why His grace surrounds you and gives you courage and direction, because your choice of friends is so important. For better or worse, we tend to become like those around us. It's part of being human, which can work out for the best, because we can choose to be around godly, kind, and humble people. Just as bad company can take us away from what we know is right and true, good company can help us hold on to it more and become an even better example to those around us.

God helps you find people who'll help you grow, and He also puts people in your life that you can help. Trust Him to continue building your character every day, making you a stronger and wiser friend.

Good influences come from God—be one of them.

Jesus, You said You are my Friend. I believe You.
I trust You. Let me be a good friend to others
and find more good friends to grow with. Amen.

PERFECT FOR YOUR PART

"Here's what I want you to do: Find a quiet, secluded place so you won't be tempted to role-play before God. Just be there as simply and honestly as you can manage. The focus will shift from you to God, and you will begin to sense his grace."

MATTHEW 6:6 MSG

During the school day, you bend to teachers' demands and class rules. During sports time, you put on the team jersey and do your part. During home time, you're the daughter with responsibilities to your parents. If you have brothers or sisters, that's another role, and if you have a job or volunteer, you're hitting your marks there too. You are one committed girl!

And that's all wonderful, just as it should be. But to do your best in all those slices of your life-pie that's getting bigger by the day, you need help. You need God's guiding grace, and you know what? You don't have to be *anything* when you come to Him. You don't have to prepare to talk to Him—He prepares *you* for everything you have to do. You don't have to impress Him—receive from Him. Give Him your love and attention and devotion, and He will give you all the energy and wisdom and ability you need.

Thank Him for His daily grace. Ask for what you need. Receive all that and more. It's never an audition, just dancing high on the stage of God's plans.

. . . .

Father, here I am, and more importantly, here You are.
Thank You for loving me as I am. I love You too. Amen.

RIGHT WORDS, WRONG WORDS

*But you will not really be the one speaking. The Spirit
from your Father will tell you what to say.*
MATTHEW 10:20 CEV

We learn quickly that words matter. What others say to us and about us matters a lot and can have a good or bad impact on how we feel and what we do. Maybe it shouldn't but it does. And sometimes we're wordless as a tree, unable to respond to hurtful things people say or know what to say ourselves when a friend needs comfort. But we can learn what to say every time with God's help, because He *always* has the right words.

Jesus prepared His disciples for the less-than-friendly treatment they might run into as they traveled to preach His teachings and tell others about Him, knowing that others weren't always going to open their doors with hospitality and kindness. *"Don't worry,"* He told His followers. *"Open your heart and then open your mouth—let God speak."* That simple plan of trust still works today for us, no matter what anyone says about us or to us. Our Father's words never fail.

You might meet people who make fun of your faith or condemn you for something or don't see your value to God. Often not responding is the best choice, and hitting DELETE works amazingly well, but when you have to reply, trust God to give you the words. Everyone is listening.

Thank You, Lord, for helping me find the right words and
discouraging me from saying the wrong ones. Remind me
to hear from You before others hear from me. Amen.

MORE THAN ENOUGH

Peter asked [Sapphira], "Tell me, did you sell the property for this amount?" "Yes," she answered, "that's the amount." Then Peter said, "Why did the two of you agree to test the Lord's Spirit? The men who buried Ananias are by the door, and they will carry you out!" At once she fell at Peter's feet and died.

ACTS 5:8–10 CEV

Sapphira and her husband, Ananias, both died because of their greed and mistrust. Who knows what examples they might've been for us if they'd simply been witnesses of God's grace instead of trying to secretly work deals for themselves.

You're learning more and more every day about managing your own money and being responsible for some of your own needs, but that's the point—to be *managers* of what God has given us, not captors. Everything we have is God's. It's our job to use it well and trust Him to continue to provide for us and sustain us every day. God doesn't do anything "barely" or "not quite." He always supplies more than enough when we're following Him in trust and doing our best to carry out His plans.

It's no glory to Him if we go around whining, "Well, God's just not big enough for this project," or, "God didn't make me smart enough to do that," because whatever God's planned for, He's prepared for. And His abundant grace, coupled with our trust and unselfishness, makes it all possible.

Lord, please help me conquer my greed and worry and focus on Your generosity and wisdom. Your supply is overflowing! Amen.

DAY 147

GROWING GIFTS

God's various gifts are handed out everywhere; but they all originate in God's Spirit. God's various ministries are carried out everywhere; but they all originate in God's Spirit. God's various expressions of power are in action everywhere; but God himself is behind it all. Each person is given something to do that shows who God is: Everyone gets in on it, everyone benefits. All kinds of things are handed out by the Spirit, and to all kinds of people!

1 CORINTHIANS 12:4-8 MSG

So what's yours? Do you wonder that sometimes? Do you wish God would just send you a text and tell you what gifts you have and how to use them? Well, He sort of does. More immediate than a text is the evidence of gifts all around you and a special one for you to participate in all the time.

Every day you can practice the gift of encouragement. It doesn't cost a thing, and it helps others focus on God's help and kindness coming through you. Also, when others share their gifts with you, learn from them, thank them, and thank God for putting them in your life.

Keep it simple. See your good qualities and natural abilities as buds, little beginnings to grow. Think about the tiny acorn that grows into the gigantic oak tree and see your God-given gifts as a basket full of acorns. God's grace grows those acorns into your own forest of gifts to share. Start with a little encouragement for yourself.

Thank You, Lord, for all my gifts! Please help me learn from and encourage those around me. We all grow! Amen.

DAY 148

START ANYWHERE, FINISH STRONG

For there is no difference between Jew and Gentile—the same Lord is Lord of all and richly blesses all who call on him.
ROMANS 10:12 NIV

Jesus was born a Jew, but that didn't mean all Jews would follow Him. Many persecuted Him and His disciples. Others who weren't Jewish and were typically the enemies of the Jews trusted and believed Jesus and became His disciples all over the world. We can't change what nationality we are. We can't change when or where we were born or who our parents are or how tall we grow. And none of that matters.

Paul told the Romans and all of us that God doesn't care about any of that stuff—because it's all out of our control. He won't blame us for something we can't create or change. But we can control ourselves and grow and become all He sees for us, and that's what He cares about—not where we start.

So you can't become French if you're born Chinese, but you can become a surgeon because your education is something you can change. You can't grow yourself younger, but you can take care of your body and grow stronger every day. You can't erase mistakes and become sinless like Jesus, but you can correct your wrongs and work every day to make better choices.

The grace Paul was talking about covered the fighting Jews and Gentiles, and the same grace covers you now. God always answers your call.

Lord, help me see the way You do and let nothing stand between me and Your blessings as I grow. Amen.

POWERFUL GRACE

*For we are God's masterpiece. He has created us
anew in Christ Jesus, so we can do the good
things he planned for us long ago.*
EPHESIANS 2:10 NLT

You can't work your way into God's heart. You can't impress Him enough with your good grades or trendiest outfit or newest gadget. He's focused on you—His already-masterpiece—and He cares about how you receive His grace, not because He needs the recognition but because He wants to give you more. The more we use, the more He gives!

When you think you can't learn something or achieve something or overcome something, that's doubt in your heart and mind trying to keep God's grace out—because when grace comes in and you use it, the doubt gets rubbed out like a fading ghost in a cartoon. And then more grace comes in and you use that too. Then more and more. So just tell that doubt that God's already worked out the plan, and He's preparing you and equipping you to achieve it. You're His daughter, the only one who can do the jobs He's prepared for you. Get to work!

That special something that makes you *you* and makes you able to do all you do is God's powerful grace. It's His once-and-forever grace that's saved us from a lifetime lost and abandoned, and it's His every-moment grace that meets us where we need it.

Lord, how much grace do You have to give me?
I know—I'll never use it up! You keep giving it to me
so we can do great things. I like this plan. Amen.

GOD DOESN'T FORGET

*But the king's personal servant completely
forgot about Joseph.*
GENESIS 40:23 CEV

People forget, but God never does.

Joseph knew a few things about sibling rivalry. His brothers even sold him to slave traders thinking they'd be free of him, but Potiphar, an Egyptian captain of the guard for Pharaoh, bought him. Because of Joseph's intelligence and respect, Potiphar put him in charge of running things, but he eventually wound up in prison, accused of something he didn't do.

Even there, Joseph kept trusting God, made friends, and even helped a worker get his job back. Joseph asked the worker to just mention him to Pharaoh when he was released, but like people often do, he forgot. For two more long years, Joseph stayed in prison, forgotten by people, lovingly remembered by God. Once finally released from prison, Joseph went on to save his brothers and many others from starvation because of his wisdom and obedience to God.

For far too long, others have sacrificed so that we are saved today from all kinds of evil, that we're free to worship God in peace. Let us never forget.

Thank You, Lord, for those who live out their wisdom
and obedience to You every day so that we may
live in joy and peace. Let us always remember the
heavy price paid for our freedoms, and help us
honor the memory of those who paid it. Amen.

THAT'S A LOT OF LOVE!

*But now, GOD's Message, the God who made you in the
first place, Jacob, the One who got you started, Israel:
"Don't be afraid, I've redeemed you. I've called your
name. You're mine. When you're in over your head, I'll be
there with you. When you're in rough waters, you will not
go down. When you're between a rock and a hard place,
it won't be a dead end. . . . That's how much you mean
to me! That's how much I love you! I'd sell off the whole
world to get you back, trade the creation just for you."*
ISAIAH 43:1–2, 4 MSG

God doesn't see you and look for the little trash can at the bottom
of the screen. He doesn't lose you and your messages to Him no
matter how many others are filling up His inbox. He knows *you*. He
loves *you*. Just like you are, at this very moment.

He knows your name—no matter who else doesn't, no matter
where you go, no matter what changes about you—because He's
claimed you for His own, forever and ever. He said so. And what
God claims, He blesses, He guides, He protects, He loves.

His love is what caused Him to make you and what keeps Him
near you. It's His precious, everlasting, unfailing, never-let-you-go,
greater-than-you-can-imagine blessing that matters more than
anything, because it's what makes all other things possible.

Keep it simple—believe Him, trust Him, love Him. If we just
loved God back one one-hundredth as much as He loves us, we'd
probably explode. But let's try.

I love You, Lord. You love me. Amen.

FIRST LOVE

"I know your persistence, your courage in my cause, that you never wear out. But you walked away from your first love—why?"
REVELATION 2:3-4 MSG

During this popular season for weddings, you may find yourself witnessing the wonder of a groom in awe of his bride as she makes her way down the aisle. He beams as she approaches in all her radiance. A smile stretches clear across his face, and there's a high probability for tears of joy. This is just a glimpse of the way God loves *you*! In fact, God loves you infinitely more, with overwhelming depth and completeness.

It's impossible not to wonder who you may one day marry and what that day might be like. Yet God Himself is first trying to win you over to an important first love. He longs for you to fall for Him. He encourages us over and over in scripture to focus on His love, the greatest love we'll ever know. He has to remind us because we have a tendency to wander. Our hearts easily stray away, and too often it takes heartbreak for us to see how much we need Him.

Fortunately, no matter how much we get bumped off course, there is always grace from God. He loved us first (1 John 4:19), and He is constantly trying to show us just how much.

God, help me make You my first love. I want to grow into the woman You created me to be. Amen.

DAY 153

AT THE HEART

"Do not consider his appearance or his height, for I have rejected him. The LORD does not look at the things people look at. People look at the outward appearance, but the LORD looks at the heart."

1 SAMUEL 16:7 NIV

The fan pages on social media. Movies on the big screen. They reflect plenty of beauty, that's for sure. Magazines and Snapchats send a lot of pretty pictures your way. If you're not careful, you can get to thinking that you are supposed to look a certain way to be valuable. But that is so far from the truth! God said so.

Looks, finances, family status—none of these matter in God's eyes. He sees you as a standout beauty, no matter what kind of hair day you're having. If your home is a wreck with peeling paint, He doesn't care. If your family vehicle is a ten-year-old minivan, that's quite all right. It's your heart that matters. *You* are what God wants. You matter. And right where you are, God has beautiful plans for you.

Dear God, help me see that the way You made me is beautiful, inside and out. Give me the strength to do the heart work that I need to grow into the strong woman of God You are preparing me to be. Amen.

BALANCING LIFE

Do not conform to the pattern of this world, but be transformed by the renewing of your mind. Then you will be able to test and approve what God's will is—his good, pleasing and perfect will.

ROMANS 12:2 NIV

Olivia spends several hours a day online, and judging by her posts, she seems truly miserable. Claire wants to read all the time. When her friends text her or want to hang out, it seems like she has no time for them. Leah is crazy involved at her church, and it's all she ever talks about. She doesn't take time to really get to know people and hear their hearts.

There are so many activities we can choose to spend our daily life on. Social media, good books, great friends, family time, going to practices, and church activities. In between all the things you get to choose are things you simply should do, like chores and homework.

If you're not careful with your choices, life can get overwhelming and start to feel really out of balance. Making a habit of spending time with God, just reading the Bible and quieting your heart, will help you see and hear what God wants to show you.

Lord, I quiet my heart before You. Help me make
decisions today that give me a balanced life,
shining Your love in me and through me. Amen.

NAVIGATION PLANS

*The LORD directs the steps of the godly. He delights in
every detail of their lives. Though they stumble, they will
never fall, for the LORD holds them by the hand.*

PSALM 37:23-24 NLT

People often ask Zoe what she wants to do when she grows up. She likes it when they leave off the "when you grow up" part. She's in the process of growing up, being more like an adult, and they're noticing. But when she contemplates what job she wants when she's older, she can't help but think about all the adults she knows who still don't know what they want to be! She sees that she has time and that it's a process to decide too.

A mentor is helping Zoe see that God is always working on helping her recognize the gifts He's given her and the many opportunities where she can use them. The best thing, her mentor says, is that when you step out in faith to use your gifts, God helps you grow stronger in them.

Right now Zoe has her hands full navigating her middle school years. She has volleyball games and practices over the summer, 4-H, and youth group too. Each day she is trying to spend time with God. As she reads the Bible and asks God for understanding in applying what He says to her life, she's starting to sort out what is important for her growth and what isn't really a good use of her time.

Dear God, give me eyes to see what is best for my walk
today, that I would grow in strength and wisdom. Amen.

YOU ARE GOOD ENOUGH

There has never been the slightest doubt in my mind that the God who started this great work in you would keep at it and bring it to a flourishing finish on the very day Christ Jesus appears.

PHILIPPIANS 1:6 MSG

Sara feels like nothing she does is ever quite good enough for her parents, for her coach, or for her grades. Life can be so demanding. She tries so hard to do things well, but she feels like she is always coming up short. Or maybe she is putting herself up against the wrong standard.

God says she is good enough, after all. He made her with unique gifts, a great style all her own, and abilities that, little by little, she is getting better at.

God has great plans for the work He began in Sara, and He doesn't quit something He started. He is going to do great things with her life experiences. What she's learning is that those things often don't look like she thought they would! Sometimes she can't see what God's doing at all, and sometimes He shows her much later. She's learning to trust that God is at work, and that means she is always good enough.

God, thank You that You made me good enough
for everything I face. Help me go through my day
with confidence in what You are doing in and around
me, even though I can't see a lot of it. Amen.

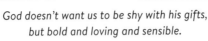

ME? A LEADER?

God doesn't want us to be shy with his gifts,
but bold and loving and sensible.
2 TIMOTHY 1:7 MSG

People often tell Chloe to "be a leader." They intend this to be encouraging, of course, but they don't realize that she has a lot of introvert in her. To her, being a leader doesn't sound like her thing at all. She gets really nervous when she has to say something in front of the class or is chosen to be a group spokesperson in science.

What God has helped her see, though, is that leading isn't always in front of a group and doesn't always involve public speaking. Oftentimes it is just doing the right thing, and if one person sees it and makes a better decision, then she is a leader.

Like at lunch, when Chloe was nice to this one girl other kids were mean to. Soon after she did that, one of her other friends asked a new kid to come sit with them. That was really cool.

She's learning to be brave and grow in the strengths God has put in her. It makes her feel really good about her life!

God, show me today how You want me to lead—
whether it's with words or not. Give me the strength
to choose the right actions today. Amen.

STRUGGLING FRIENDS

*You already know these things, dear friends. So be on
guard; then you will not be carried away by the errors of
these wicked people and lose your own secure footing.*

2 PETER 3:17 NLT

One of Hunter's friends has been making some really bad decisions
lately. It makes Hunter not want to spend too much time with her
so she's not pulled in the wrong direction too. If Hunter's mom
knew the whole story, she wouldn't let Hunter near this friend. Yet
Hunter can't help but think of how Jesus loves every single one of
us no matter what we've done or what we struggle with. Hunter
knows that her friend needs encouragement and grace.

Hunter started praying about this and for her friend. She decided
to talk to her mom and told her how her friend is struggling, how she
needs truth given to her in love, but she also needs grace. Hunter
felt that she was supposed to be a friend who offered those things
to her, that maybe she could be like Jesus in these ways. She asked
her mom to support her in this. Hunter's mom was so surprised by
her maturity and was happy to help. They began praying together
for Hunter's friend and talking through what a healthy balance of
time with her would look like. Her mom had some great ideas for
encouraging healthy decisions for Hunter's friend.

Hunter is so glad she asked God what to do, and thankful for
having a mom who would pray with her and help.

God, guide me today in friendship decisions. Give me
wisdom so that I can grow stronger in my faith. Amen.

THE ROARING

Be alert and of sober mind. Your enemy the devil prowls around like a roaring lion looking for someone to devour.
1 PETER 5:8 NIV

You can feel like you're on the right track. That you're growing just how you should in your faith, your friendships, and your decisions. Then, without you even noticing, you are distracted by something that seemed harmless. Just that fast, you're off track.

The noise of the world around us makes it incredibly difficult to focus on what God wants for us. There are unhealthy messages being thrown out at you all the time. There are people who will lead you astray because they're lost themselves. There are false teachers (2 Peter 2:1), and you never know where they'll turn up. Sometimes certain friends are bad for us, and we have to stop hanging out with them.

The roar of the world around us is a reminder that the enemy is lurking and waiting for a chance to bring us down. Thank God that He is with us always wherever we go. Walking with Him is the only way we can make our way through safely.

God, help me hear Your still, small voice amid the
often deafening noise of the world around me,
that I would walk in strength with You. Amen.

YOUR RADIANT BEAUTY

Your beauty should not come from outward adornment, such as elaborate hairstyles and the wearing of gold jewelry or fine clothes. Rather, it should be that of your inner self, the unfading beauty of a gentle and quiet spirit, which is of great worth in God's sight.

1 PETER 3:3–4 NIV

When Sam was twelve, she wanted Alan to notice her. He seemed nice (and she really liked his hair). He noticed her in the way that he didn't run her over in the hallway. Clearly she wasn't standing out to him though. What she really wanted was for him to think, *Wow! She's really something!* Well, she *was* really something. What she didn't realize then was that she was expecting someone to notice who she really was just by the way she looked.

What Sam learned was that she just needed to concentrate on growing in her knowledge, strengths, and faith. When she relaxed and did that, people noticed the most valuable things about her. These are the people who ended up being her good friends, because strong character and faith mattered to them too. That is beautiful.

God, help me look to You today as I grow. I want to shine for You and attract friends based on who I am rather than how I look. Amen.

REFLECT PURITY

Don't let anyone look down on you because you are young,
but set an example for the believers. . .in purity.
1 TIMOTHY 4:12 NIV

Summer's dad became very upset when he saw the bathing suit she wanted to wear while hanging out with her friends by the pool. "No one should see her like that," she heard him telling her mother. Summer knew he was trying to protect his little girl, but his concern seemed so overboard.

She later came to understand the impact of her clothing choices, how they affect others and potentially her faith walk too.

No one is perfect, not one. Yet we are asked to strive to do our best. For Summer, that meant thinking about how she dresses and acts so that her decisions would set a good example. Whether we're young and just figuring these things out or a little older and wiser, at every age we want to aim to reflect the purity of Christ.

Dear God, help me listen to You and the wisdom of those who know more than I do. I want to grow stronger in You. Amen.

MINDING MY MESSAGES

The weapons we fight with are not the weapons of the world. On the contrary, they have divine power to demolish strongholds. We demolish arguments and every pretension that sets itself up against the knowledge of God, and we take captive every thought to make it obedient to Christ.

2 CORINTHIANS 10:4-5 NIV

Zoe really liked this one popular song. A lot. She added it to her music library, looked up the lyrics, and read about the band too. It was such a cool song, she sang it a lot for a good week or more. Her brother pointed out that some of the words were questionable, and he explained them a little in detail. Now her mom was paying attention to what he was saying, and Zoe was upset. "I just liked the song," Zoe said. How bad could it be?

She didn't want to talk to them about it. She was just mad. She spent some time in her room alone, thinking and eventually praying. She realized that the parts of the song her brother pointed out were not good messages to hold on to. She started writing down in a journal the good messages in songs she liked, the ones that she should hold on to and think about applying in her life. It became a lot clearer that there were many with negative messages, and Zoe decided to be more careful with the things she let herself think about.

God, help me guard the door of my mind so that I am thinking on things that help me grow strong and faithful. Amen.

FACE-TO-FACE FRIENDS

"Therefore, if you are offering your gift at the altar
and there remember that your brother or sister has
something against you, leave your gift there in front
of the altar. First go and be reconciled to them."
MATTHEW 5:23-24 NIV

Emma found herself in a heated texting conversation with one of her best friends, Jade. It was all a misunderstanding, which Emma was trying to explain, but it wasn't getting across apparently. The messages that kept going back and forth were based on faulty information, and it was compounded with each reply. Emma became so upset, she found herself angry with her friend. She started wondering if Jade could still be her BFF, and that made her really sad.

That night at youth group, Emma's mentor noticed how down she was, and Emma was eager to share her situation. Her mentor encouraged her to talk with her friend in person and go back to the original misunderstanding. She shared with her that whether it's our fault or not, or whether it's just a misunderstanding, God asks us to be the initiators of mending broken relationships (Matthew 18:15).

Emma asked her mom that night if she could walk over to Jade's house. Her honest conversation with Jade taught her valuable lessons. She began taking greater responsibility for her words in texting and realized that face-to-face friendship is always the best.

Dear God, help me be the kind of friend that You instruct
me to be in Your Word: genuine and true. Amen.

DAY 164

UNDERSTANDING THE PARENTS

"As the heavens are higher than the earth, so are my ways higher than your ways and my thoughts than your thoughts."
ISAIAH 55:9 NIV

It can seem absolutely impossible sometimes trying to figure out how your parents think and why they make some of the decisions they do.

They aren't God, but understanding their way of thinking can be *likened* to God in the way that they understand many things that are just way beyond you at this point in your life. As crazy as it sounds, they know a lot more than you, if for no other reason than the simple fact that they've lived through things you haven't yet.

Add to this the fact that the human brain is not fully developed until you're in your twenties. Some studies believe peak brain maturity is reached as late as twenty-eight years of age. (What?!)

Even with their fully developed brains, remember that your parents are still just human. They have hurts in their lives and hearts too. They're not perfect, but they love you more than you can imagine.

Even if your parents don't have it together or make some decisions you question, they are usually trying to protect you and do what's best for you (even when it seems ridiculous).

Dear God, help me in my relationship with my parents. You've placed them in my life to care for me and lead me. Give me understanding and patience as I put my trust in You. Amen.

FREEDOM

And the Spirit and the bride say, "Come!" And let him who hears say, "Come!" And let him who thirsts come. Whoever desires, let him take the water of life freely.

REVELATION 22:17 NKJV

A missionary couple spoke at Sara's church. They couldn't tell everyone where they served because it could put their lives in danger, as well as the lives of those they ministered to. It's pretty crazy to think about this when most of us take our religious freedom completely for granted. We can have church services and openly talk about our faith. It's amazing when you compare America to other countries where people are dying every day for their faith in Christ.

The great freedoms of our nation exemplify the freedom God gives us to choose Him. American soldiers have given their lives and their service to provide and protect the many freedoms we enjoy every day. In a far greater way, Christ gave His life to give us a way to choose a life of freedom in Him.

No matter which nation we live in, though, living free in Christ begins with choosing Him. Then it beautifully unfolds into a lifelong living and learning process.

God, help me be mindful of the freedom You give me, in this nation and, most importantly, in You. Amen.

But because of his great love for us, God, who is rich in mercy, made us alive with Christ even when we were dead in transgressions—it is by grace you have been saved.

EPHESIANS 2:4–5 NIV

Claire's new friend, Brie, who started coming to youth group recently, thinks that the things she's done make it impossible for God to love her. She told Claire some of the things she is ashamed of. Some of them were things she couldn't control because people treated her horribly. Other things she chose to do.

Their pastor shared that there isn't anything we can do that God finds unforgivable. He said there's nothing that keeps God from loving us. Claire and Brie talked about this later when everyone was playing Ping-Pong. "It's just so hard to believe," Brie said, "because I feel too bad to ever be loved by someone good." Yet she wanted what was good. She wanted forgiveness.

They had some great conversations over the next few weeks and asked their pastor some questions too. It took time, but Brie finally accepted God's love and forgiveness. She seems so much happier. It makes Claire pretty happy too!

God, thank You for Your love so great that I can't comprehend it. Help me reflect Your love and grace to those around me so they will be drawn to You. Amen.

HURT

"When you pass through the waters, I will be with you; and when you pass through the rivers, they will not sweep over you. When you walk through the fire, you will not be burned; the flames will not set you ablaze. For I am the LORD your God."

ISAIAH 43:2–3 NIV

Lainey's uncle was divorcing her favorite aunt. Her mother cried a lot lately. The whole family was upset about it all. Lainey wondered if she would still get to see her aunt. Would this happen to her parents too? The week before that, the sweet elderly man who lived next door died. Lainey had helped him with his garden. She was already sad about losing him, and now her favorite aunt might be out of her life too. How could things fall apart so fast without warning? As quickly as she could wonder about that, she found out that her youth pastor was moving to another church out of state.

Weeping into her pillow that night, Lainey cried out to God. "What *is* solid and certain in life?"

She really hoped for an audible voice. Instead, what she felt with all her being was God's strong presence with her.

Dear God, thank You for being the constant, certain, solid thing in my life. Help me trust in You during the scary and uncertain times. Amen.

A MENTOR

These older women must train the younger women to love their husbands and their children, to live wisely and be pure.

TITUS 2:4–5 NLT

Sammie's dad was working most of the time, and her mom just wasn't there for her. It wasn't that her mom didn't care, but she seemed to be struggling and distracted by her own issues. It was really hard for Sammie to learn how to work through a lot of things and grow in her faith. Her pastor referred to his mentor many times, so Sammie decided to find a mentor too. If her pastor had one, why shouldn't she? There was a woman at church, Linda, who had spoken before at youth group and often asked Sammie how she was doing. Sammie asked Linda if they could start meeting.

Linda was clearly a busy, working woman balancing motherhood and job responsibilities, but she cheerfully said yes. Sammie's mom was happy that she was seeking the friendship of a trustworthy woman of faith. It was such a great experience for Sammie to talk through the things she was uncertain about. Linda recommended some great books and Bible studies that Sammie loved. Even Sammie's mom started reading some of them, and they began talking more about the things that were on both their hearts.

God, give me wisdom to choose faithful people as role models so I can grow strong and be a mentor someday myself. Amen.

KINDNESS ANYWAY

Be completely humble and gentle; be patient, bearing with one another in love. Make every effort to keep the unity of the Spirit through the bond of peace.

EPHESIANS 4:2–3 NIV

Maddie's younger brother, Henry, frustrates her. Over the weekend she had a birthday sleepover with some friends, and he would not stop running through the house yelling while they were watching a movie. He ate up half the snacks that Mom bought for the night, and it seemed impossible to just enjoy talking to her friends.

Her older brother, Jak, is a little better, but his friends are so awkward and irritating to have around. These boys are ridiculous! Her mom told her that they're just not sure how to act around her and they're just trying to navigate these growing years too. "It's an uncomfortable time in life for everyone," her mom said.

Maddie thought about that and how many uncertain things she faces too. She decided to try following Paul's words she'd read in Ephesians and work on being more patient and kind. The boys are still super silly, but she's noticing improvement, and she knows she's doing what she's supposed to.

God, give me a heart to treat the annoying people in my life with kindness. I need Your help to be more like You. Amen.

GREATEST FATHER LOVE

"Look at the birds of the air; they do not sow or reap or store away in barns, and yet your heavenly Father feeds them. Are you not much more valuable than they?"

MATTHEW 6:26 NIV

Skylar's dad has been gone a little over a year now. It has gotten easier since the shocking day that an aneurysm took him in a moment's time. Fortunately, he left Skylar a great example of fatherly love. His great big heart of love for her has made it easier to see that her heavenly Father loves her. Her dad used to tell her, "He loves you way more than I do. I can't understand that because I love you so much!"

There are a lot of friends in Skylar's life who aren't as blessed as she was. Some of their fathers aren't in their lives at all. Others have been treated badly by their dads. What Skylar realizes is that no matter what our father figures are like, we can always count on our heavenly Father. Looking to Him helps point her friends in that direction too, and His love can't be matched.

God, thank You for the dad You have placed in my life, and thank You for being the perfect Father who loves and protects me exactly as I need. Amen.

FILLED

*"When I discovered your words, I devoured them.
They are my joy and my heart's delight, for I bear
your name, O Lord God of Heaven's Armies."*

JEREMIAH 15:16 NLT

Sometimes there's a hunger to know something and understand. Other times there's a void in you, like an empty spot that you can't seem to fill.

Lara was feeling all this and more when someone she thought was a good friend betrayed her. The girl said awful, untrue things about her that a lot of people thought were true. The damage and hurt were something Lara had not experienced before. Uncertain how to respond, Lara reached out to trusted friends and family. Her mom began praying for and with her. She also pointed her to the psalms in which King David cries out to God about a multitude of struggles and emotions.

Lara gave reading the psalms a try and found herself immersed in sections of David's raw outpouring to God. There was so much encouragement there as she realized that God welcomed her crying out. Not only that, but He could and He would fill the hurting, empty places in her. It was the first time Lara truly understood that the words in the Bible are food for her heart and soul.

Dear God, show me today in Your Word what I need. Fill the gaps in my understanding, or simply help me trust You with those things that are still mysteries to me. Amen.

FINDING GOD'S VOICE

*"Then you will call on me and come and pray to me,
and I will listen to you. You will seek me and find
me when you seek me with all your heart."*

JEREMIAH 29:12–13 NIV

Do you ever wonder how to hear God's voice or if you're already hearing His voice? How can you tell the difference between your own thoughts and temptations and God's actual voice?

Fortunately, God gives us some clear answers to this question in His Word. First of all, we are invited to come boldly before God and inquire of Him (Hebrews 10:19–20). Before Christ's sacrifice on the cross, it was only priests who had this privilege. Even then there were tight limits—they could be struck dead if they didn't do things right! Now we have access to God at any time. This is way more prestigious than you being able to, say, walk right into the president's Oval Office at any time.

God so wants a two-way conversation with us that He never leaves, much like with Adam and Eve in the garden (Genesis 3:8). He is always right here, so you can be sure He wants you to hear Him.

One thing you can count on is that He will never communicate something that doesn't line up with His Word. If we are one of His children (meaning that we have invited Him into our lives), we are given the ability to hear His voice (John 10:27).

So go talk to Him!

Dear God, help me discern Your voice in the midst of
the loudness of this world. I need You today. Amen.

GOOD BOUNDARIES

A person without self-control is like
a city with broken-down walls.
PROVERBS 25:28 NLT

We all know them, the girls who fell into a lapse of lost self-control. They don't know how they got so far off course, but before they knew it, they ended up with a permanently altered plan early in life.

So many things that we know we shouldn't do are enticing, that's for sure. Fortunately, how to avoid a damaging complication in your life is not a mystery. Self-control starts with putting yourself in safe places with healthy boundaries rather than tempting places with broken boundaries. Listen to God's leading, and ask Him to be your strength and wisdom.

You'll be thankful if you can maintain your boundaries of control. Someday it will be a blessing if pregnancy is something you get to experience with full joy when you're married to a great guy. Later in life, these same boundaries can keep you from unhealthy friendships and even affairs that could damage you, your marriage, and your family.

Dear God, help me make strong decisions so that my choices will pave the way to good things in my life. Amen.

THE CHASE

Yet when I surveyed all that my hands had done and what I had toiled to achieve, everything was meaningless, a chasing after the wind; nothing was gained under the sun. . . . I saw that wisdom is better than folly, just as light is better than darkness.

ECCLESIASTES 2:11, 13 NIV

King Solomon was one of the richest men who ever lived, and the Bible tells us that he was also the wisest man who ever lived. He had everything a person could dream of having. He planned his own majestic dream house and had it built exactly as he desired. It sat next to the temple of God Himself, and God granted Solomon wisdom at his disposal.

Yet Solomon, with all his possessions, boundless resources and ability, and beautiful surroundings, came to the conclusion that all his efforts on earth amounted to nothing. Wisdom was his greatest gift.

It seems clear that no one will be given wisdom to match that of Solomon's any time soon, but God does give us the ability to grow wiser. He offers to generously give us wisdom if we will only ask.

Dear God, I need wisdom in the decisions I make each day. Give me what I need so I can make sound choices and grow strong in You. Amen.

CONFUSING EMOTIONS

And now, dear brothers and sisters, one final thing. Fix your
thoughts on what is true, and honorable, and right, and pure,
and lovely, and admirable. Think about things that are excellent
and worthy of praise. Keep putting into practice all you learned
and received from me—everything you heard from me and
saw me doing. Then the God of peace will be with you.

PHILIPPIANS 4:8–9 NLT

Reeling from a terrible day with friends in her neighborhood, Tess couldn't tell if she was more angry or sad about how they were treating one another. When she got home from her friend's house, she had hoped to catch her favorite TV show that was coming on in forty-five minutes. She also wanted to check out a conversation that she heard referenced her on Instagram, but her mom was all over her to get an hour's worth of chores done instead—one of which was taking a dead fish out of the aquarium. Her favorite fish had died!

How many emotions can one person experience at one time? She was sure she would lose it! But, in what seemed a rare moment of maturity, she focused on what was good around her. She had a family who loved her, plenty to eat, and air-conditioning on a pretty warm day. She reminded herself of what was true rather than what was frustrating and sad. It changed her entire outlook, and before she knew it, she felt much more at peace.

God, in the mixture of emotions that come my way, thank You for being the one true God I can rely on to be constant. Amen.

TEMPTATION

The temptations in your life are no different from what others experience. And God is faithful. He will not allow the temptation to be more than you can stand. When you are tempted, he will show you a way out so that you can endure.

1 CORINTHIANS 10:13 NLT

Hannah walked down the block with her friend to the store where they planned to buy a few snacks for the movie they would watch later. A young family walking just ahead of them dropped a twenty-dollar bill and didn't realize it. Hannah hesitated for a moment.

She thought how much more she could buy with that twenty and considered just picking it up and not saying anything. But she felt too bad about it, and besides, she didn't want to involve her friend too. She picked it up and called ahead to the parents of the small children. They were so thankful for her honesty that they let both Hannah and her friend pick out some candy at the store. Even if she hadn't gotten a sweet reward for making the right decision, it felt good to do the right thing.

Dear God, thank You for providing a way out of temptations that come my way. Help me want to choose You. Amen.

POUTING

*Therefore, as God's chosen people, holy and
dearly loved, clothe yourselves with compassion,
kindness, humility, gentleness and patience.*

COLOSSIANS 3:12 NIV

Lizzie's little cousin didn't get her way at the picnic and pouted all
the way to the other side of the pavilion. She leaned her three-
year-old self against a post, looking as sad as she was cute. Lizzie
walked over to her.

"What's wrong, Audree?" asked Lizzie.

"Mommy say no more pop," Audree managed with her bottom
lip sticking out.

"I'm thirteen years old and my mom says that too because she
wants me to be healthy," Lizzie encouraged. "My mom also likes to
make sure I know that I can't always get what I want, which I don't
usually like either!" she said, mocking a stern face.

Audree wasn't buying any of it, so Lizzie scooped her up in her
arms and smiled. "What can we do with what you do have?" she asked
as she picked up the sand toys nearby. "Want to make a castle?"
Audree started to smile. Even though Lizzie was the teacher, she
learned something important that day too.

Dear God, help me do all I can with what You have
given me and be content while I work toward the
things I hope for. I need You, God. Amen.

STUFF

"If you are faithful in little things, you will be faithful in large ones. But if you are dishonest in little things, you won't be honest with greater responsibilities."

LUKE 16:10 NLT

Maggie's dad was always bugging her to put her stuff away. She didn't see the point when she was going to turn around and use it all again. It would be right there ready to go—so much easier in her opinion. The house seemed like it was always a mess, anyway, with their new puppy playing and running all over the place.

Arriving home one afternoon, Maggie dropped her bag on the floor in the living room, her shoes fell off in front of the couch, and she set her phone on the ottoman. She went into the kitchen to get some juice, and by the time she got back, the puppy had chewed a hole clear through her right shoe. She was so mad, and worse, she knew she would have to answer to Dad! Her shoes were only two weeks old. She regretted that this was how she finally recognized the benefits of putting things away.

Dear God, help me with even the little things in life so I can better prepare for the bigger things that come along. Amen.

FITTING IN

"We are here for only a moment, visitors and strangers in the land as our ancestors were before us. Our days on earth are like a passing shadow, gone so soon without a trace."
1 CHRONICLES 29:15 NLT

We're always trying to fit in. We want to look and feel like we belong, which isn't all bad. But when we let the acceptance of others be the measurement of our self-worth, we're on a slippery slope down to places we will not enjoy at all. What if we weren't made to fit in? What if we were meant to follow God's lead instead? And what if that pursuit looked very different from the pursuits of our friends? Would that be okay?

It would.

Sometimes we need to strive to fit in for good reasons—so that we can understand and communicate well with others. But not always. It's important to also embrace and explore the unique qualities and gifts that God gave especially to you. Compared to eternity, this earthly life lasts a very short time, no matter how long we live. So let's not waste any time trying to be something that God never intended for us to be!

Dear God, use my life for Your greater purposes. Help me have the faith I need to walk in Your ways. Amen.

MASTERPIECE ME

Thank you for making me so wonderfully complex! Your workmanship is marvelous—how well I know it. . . . You saw me before I was born. Every day of my life was recorded in your book. Every moment was laid out before a single day had passed. How precious are your thoughts about me, O God.
PSALM 139:14, 16–17 NLT

Who you are is a great discovery of the gifts and opportunities that God has placed in and around you. He granted you specific desires and abilities with a beautiful purpose. Even before you were formed, He had an intricate plan for your life. As you grow, you get to discover the person God made, and is making, as you walk through each day in faith.

Every time you wonder why God allows some frustrating or heartbreaking thing to happen, and each moment that you doubt how you will get through a hard time you are going through, remember this: You are a masterpiece in the making by the Master artisan. It *will* all be beautiful!

Creator God, thank You for how You made me. Guide me as I discover and learn. I need Your hand in my life. Amen.

HE NEVER LEAVES

God is our refuge and strength, an ever-present help in trouble.
Therefore we will not fear, though the earth give way and the
mountains fall into the heart of the sea, though its waters
roar and foam and the mountains quake with their surging.

PSALM 46:1–3 NIV

Sarah excitedly told her teacher how her new shoes would help keep Jesus in her heart. "Every time I look at my sparkly shoes I remember to listen to Jesus, so He never leaves my heart."

"Oh Sarah, Jesus will always be with you, and no matter what you do, He will never stop loving you!" her teacher told her. "It's good to have a reminder like your pretty shoes to encourage you to do what's right, but you couldn't convince God to leave you if you tried. He's with us all the time."

Sarah seemed relieved. Her teacher was surprised to find herself thinking over her own words to her student. She realized how often she needed to remind herself of this truth. God *refuses* to leave us. He may be silent or misunderstood, but He stays.

God, thank You for Your steadfast and unshakable love
for me every day, all the time, anywhere I go. Amen.

MADE FOR CREATIVITY

*So God created mankind in his own image, in the image of
God he created them; male and female he created them.*

GENESIS 1:27 NIV

Humankind was created in God's image. This means that God made us to be like Him. Sin keeps us from being perfect reflections of Him, but despite that, His beauty remains in us.

One important way you bear God's image is through creativity. The Master Creator made us to be "little creators" after Him—we don't speak things into existence, but He gave us the ability to think, make, and speak. Adam first used the creative gift of language to name all the animals in the garden (Genesis 2:19–20). He was also the first poet, speaking beautiful words to mark his wife Eve's arrival (Genesis 2:23).

Whether or not you make fine art (like painting or sculpting), you still shine with God's creativity. The creative impulse radiates out of an awesome cannonball into the pool, in the smile lighting up your face, in a silly joke told at dinner. Our whole lives can be works of art as we practice creativity! And God is delighted through our thankful enjoyment of His gifts.

. . . .

Dear God, thank You for this great gift of creativity.
Help me praise You by using it every day! Amen.

NURTURING THE SOIL

Then he told them many things in parables, saying: "A farmer went out to sow his seed. As he was scattering the seed, some fell along the path, and the birds came and ate it up. Some fell on rocky places, where it did not have much soil. It sprang up quickly, because the soil was shallow. But when the sun came up, the plants were scorched, and they withered because they had no root. Other seed fell among thorns, which grew up and choked the plants. Still other seed fell on good soil, where it produced a crop—a hundred, sixty or thirty times what was sown."

MATTHEW 13:3–8 NIV

When we hear the parable of the sower, we all want to say that we're examples of "good soil"—always growing in God's Word—right? *Right. . .*

Guess what? Your heart is never just one type of soil. At different times, our hearts might be eager to hear the Word (like good soil), but we might abandon it during tough times (rocky soil) or get distracted by more "important" things (thorny soil). Fortunately, God is the Sower *and* the One who nurtures the soil. The Holy Spirit is constantly cultivating our hearts, digging the rocks out, fertilizing, and watering the soil to prepare us to hear God's Word.

If today you're feeling like rocky or weedy soil, ask the Holy Spirit to help you change. The fruit that grows out of His work will be worth all the effort!

Father God, I confess that sometimes I really don't care about Your Word. Please forgive me and keep cultivating my heart! Amen.

MORE THAN A STORY

Finally, my friends, keep your minds on whatever is true, pure, right, holy, friendly, and proper. Don't ever stop thinking about what is truly worthwhile and worthy of praise.

PHILIPPIANS 4:8 CEV

Whether it's a book, a TV show, or a comic strip, we're wired to connect deeply with stories. Paul encouraged his readers to think on what's "truly worthwhile and worthy of praise" because what we spend time thinking about changes us. Stories have amazing power to shift how we think about the world and ourselves.

This summer, take time to think about the stories you're reading and watching. In light of what you know from the Bible, look at the characters and their decisions. Would their actions please God? How? Is there a character that you wish you could be like? Why? You may find that the characters you admire reveal something you need in your own life, or you might decide what actions *not* to take based on their decisions.

Each story you encounter becomes an opportunity to learn more about how stories affect you and for you to grow wiser as you search for truth woven into the fabric of the stories. All truth belongs to God, wherever you find it—it can even be in a story that wasn't written by a Christian! No story is a waste of time when we contemplate it in light of God's Word. Let your reading and watching keep your mind on what is worthwhile and worthy of praise!

Dear Jesus, thank You for books and movies. Please help me stop and look for Your truth in everything. Amen.

INDEPENDENCE

"I will say to the prisoners, 'Come out in freedom,' and to those in darkness, 'Come into the light.' They will be my sheep, grazing in green pastures and on hills that were previously bare."

ISAIAH 49:9 NLT

When you think of freedom, you may automatically think of summer vacation—long, hot days spending time with friends at picnics, the pool, and the movies. But maybe the word *freedom* brings something more serious to mind, especially if your parents or friends of the family serve in the military. You know how much peace can cost in this uncertain world.

As followers of Jesus, freedom runs deeper than the joy of summer or bravely pushing back the danger of war. Jesus saw His people enslaved to sin, and He came to earth to live among us and make us free. He paid the ultimate cost for us so we would no longer be enemies of God; instead, we'd be a part of His family. All we had to do was believe in Him—and He rescued us from the crushing weight of our sin, from the fear of death, from the fear of not being good enough, and brought us into a life of lasting peace with God. Not only are you free from sin, you're also free to thrive—to enjoy the abundant life that the Good Shepherd has for you (John 10:10).

Today, remember the eternal freedom that Jesus has given you!

Jesus, thank You for Your freedom! Thank You for giving Your life so I could be a part of Your family. Amen.

DAY 186

BEAUTIFUL RULES?

The Law of the LORD is perfect; it gives us new life. His teachings last forever, and they give wisdom to ordinary people. The LORD's instruction is right; it makes our hearts glad.

PSALM 19:7-8 CEV

Anywhere we go, we all have to obey rules that don't make sense to us.

"'Keep off the grass'? Why?"

"Ugh! I hate that I'm not tall enough for these roller coasters!"

Have rules ever made us happy? Probably not, but God's rules should. His rules have always been meant for His people's protection, from the Garden of Eden's one rule to the Ten Commandments. God also gave His law to reveal His holy character to us and to help us live in a way that pleases Him. Our unhappy response to His rules is rooted in pride—we think we know better about what's good for us than God does.

Think about it. What sins are fun at first but never turn out well? Fighting with our friends, disobeying our parents, lying. . . Even if there aren't immediate consequences, these things never produce peace in our lives.

Our hearts naturally push against rules, but Jesus can change them. Through His love and His example, He can teach us how to love God's commands. Through His salvation (accomplished by His perfect obedience), we can love God with all our hearts, souls, and minds. . .and by obeying too. Open the Word and ask Jesus to show you the beauty of His commands—He will do it.

Dear Jesus, it's hard for me to see, so please show me how Your commands are perfect. Thank You that You never stop teaching me. Amen.

WHAT LASTS FOREVER?

*I pray that you, being rooted and established in love, may
have power, together with all the Lord's holy people, to grasp
how wide and long and high and deep is the love of Christ,
and to know this love that surpasses knowledge—that you
may be filled to the measure of all the fullness of God.*

EPHESIANS 3:17–19 NIV

If you traveled a million years into the future, what might still be
around from your time? Diamonds, cockroaches, maybe even pieces
of non-biodegradable Styrofoam? There would be one thing for
certain. You can't touch it, but it's more precious than diamonds
and would be there waiting for you as you exited your time machine.

It's the love of Jesus. The Bible says that His love "surpasses
knowledge" with how "wide and long and high and deep" it is. It can
find you whether you go up to the heavens or settle in the depths
of the sea (Psalm 139:8). Even if you had a spaceship, His love could
reach you and hold you close amid the stars in the farthest reaches
of the universe.

His love is unchanging. No matter what you do, you can't stop
Jesus from loving you (2 Timothy 2:13). His forgiveness frees you
from worrying whether you've done enough good things to outweigh
the bad. You're free to grow into a closer relationship with the
almighty Creator without fear. If you trust in Jesus, this love that
lasts forever is yours.

Jesus, I can't begin to understand how precious
Your love is. Thank You for loving me! Thank
You that Your love lasts forever. Amen.

DAY 188

NOT GIVING UP

*And I am certain that God, who began the good work
within you, will continue his work until it is finally
finished on the day when Christ Jesus returns.*

PHILIPPIANS 1:6 NLT

"Why do you have to keep *doing* that?" Have your parents ever said that when they're upset with you? You're trying to obey them better, but it seems like however hard you try, you're stuck struggling with the same things. It feels like you're never going to stop bugging your brother or talking back to your dad. It just happens!

All Christians experience the same thing, and fortunately, God doesn't expect perfection from us. That's why He sent Jesus to live a perfect life, so that His righteousness covers us when we trust in Him for salvation (Romans 3:21–24). God's work in us doesn't stop there. When we trust in Jesus, He gives us the Holy Spirit, and the Spirit works in you every day to teach you to be more like Him— helping you understand scripture (1 Corinthians 2:10–16), helping you pray (Romans 8:26–27), and moving you to grow in the fruit, or character qualities, of the Spirit (Galatians 5:22–23).

If you can't see any change in your life, go back and read Philippians 1:6, and reflect on when you first started following Jesus. Believe it—you *have* been growing, and you'll keep on growing. God doesn't give up on His children.

God, thank You that You're at work in my life even
when it doesn't feel like it. Help me trust You and keep
asking for Your help to grow and change. Amen.

SACRED SPACES

Do you not know that your bodies are temples of the Holy Spirit, who is in you, whom you have received from God?

1 CORINTHIANS 6:19 NIV

Weird question: If you were a building, what would you look like? Do you imagine yourself as Solomon's temple from the Old Testament, covered in gold and beautiful carvings (1 Kings 6)? Or do you picture yourself as a regular house or even a camping tent? You receive so many messages about your body from movies, magazines, and conversations with friends and family. Maybe you feel at home in your body, but there's probably something about it that you wish you could change.

By calling our bodies "temples," the Word declares that our bodies are sacred spaces, inhabited by the third person of the Trinity. When you accepted Jesus, the Holy Spirit didn't look at you and say, "*Well, that's not a temple I want to live in.*" Though you might have trouble liking your body, you were wonderfully made and are deeply loved just the way you are.

Remembering that the Spirit chose to make His home in you, treat your sacred space with kindness. Practice recognizing your God-given beauty, rejoice in all the things you can do, and lovingly care for yourself. This body won't last forever, but you can honor God by caring for His wonderful gift.

Father, thank You for making me a temple for the Holy Spirit. Thank You that You love every part of me, even the parts I have trouble loving. Teach me how to glorify You with how I treat and talk about my body. Amen.

SO ANNOYING!

*If anyone acknowledges that Jesus is the Son of
God, God lives in them and they in God. And so
we know and rely on the love God has for us.*
1 JOHN 4:15–16 NIV

Think of the most annoying person you know. Picture their face. . .
now, remember what Jesus said. "Love the Lord your God with all
your heart and. . . .your neighbor as yourself" (Mark 12:30–31 NIV).
Yep, He even calls you to love *that* person.

Whether it's a sibling or a youth group kid, the Bible has the
solution for how to love the annoying people in our lives. First John
4:20–21 says that if we don't love our brother whom we can see,
how can we claim to love God whom we haven't seen? God's love
reaches all people, no matter what they're like, and He wants us
to love like He does—He lavished love on us before we ever loved
Him back (Romans 5:8).

Fortunately, God doesn't expect us to love in our own strength.
We "rely" on His love for us—when our love runs out, He fills us
with His love and teaches us how to be kind, patient, and to serve
others sincerely. We don't necessarily have to be close friends with
everyone, but we show that we belong to God by how we love others.
Also, chances are you're on someone else's "annoying person" list.
Wouldn't you want them to treat you with God's love too?

God, You know who the annoying people in my life
are. Please help me rely on Your love so that I can
be patient and loving toward them. Amen.

NO MATTER WHAT HAPPENS

*Be cheerful no matter what; pray all the time; thank
God no matter what happens. This is the way God
wants you who belong to Christ Jesus to live.*
1 THESSALONIANS 5:16–18 MSG

Ella turned up her music to drown out the crying. Her mom and dad had already tried everything to calm little James down, but it was no use. *I hate car trips. We've been in the car for two days now!* Her brother seemed to agree, red-faced and wailing. *Yeah, James, we're all miserable; thanks a lot.*

Unexpectedly, the scripture passage from Sunday's lesson came to mind. "'Thank God no matter what happens,' huh?" Ella murmured. *Wouldn't hurt to try.* Looking out at the rolling hills of green cornstalks and the bright blue sky, Ella began to pray silently. *Jesus, thank You for the beautiful day. Thank You that my iPod still has a lot of battery left.* She looked over the seat at her baby brother, who was beating the air with angry fists. *Thank You for James. Can You help him feel better? I think only You can help him at this point. Amen.* James was still crying, but her mood felt lighter.

The corn swayed gently, and the van's tires rumbled along the highway. Later, when Ella was switching to a different album, James drifted off to sleep. Two big sighs of relief came from the front of the van, and Ella smiled. *Thank You, God.*

God, it's hard to always be thankful and cheerful,
but I want to practice. Help me keep on praying
so I can see the blessings You send. Amen.

TREASURE HUNT

*Don't store up treasures on earth! Moths and rust can destroy
them, and thieves can break in and steal them. Instead,
store up your treasures in heaven, where moths and rust
cannot destroy them, and thieves cannot break in and steal
them. Your heart will always be where your treasure is.*
MATTHEW 6:19–21 CEV

In light of today's verses, it might feel silly to mourn one of your
prized possessions that accidentally gets broken or lost, whether it's
a favorite necklace or your favorite book. But the Bible doesn't tell us
to "store up your treasures in heaven" because we're not supposed
to enjoy anything here on earth. God made this beautiful world for
delight—His and ours. Instead, we're given this warning so that we
won't put all our happiness into things that don't last forever—in
this imperfect world, that's setting ourselves up for heartbreak.

There is a treasure that will never break your heart—Jesus, the
most precious One of all. He cares about all your heart's hurts, no
matter how small (1 Peter 5:7). Trusting Him changes how you look
at everything that happens in your life. He gives you strength to
forgive the sibling who ripped your posters, and He's there to listen
when you cry about your mp3 player that went through the wash.
When you treasure your relationship with Him, it gets easier to hold
on gently to earthly treasures because you realize you lack nothing
when you love Jesus (Psalm 23:1). What do you treasure most?

Dear Jesus, help me keep my heart focused
on You, my greatest Treasure. Amen.

FEAR OF THE MAYBES

*"The LORD himself goes before you and will be
with you; he will never leave you nor forsake
you. Do not be afraid; do not be discouraged."*
DEUTERONOMY 31:8 NIV

"Maybe it's going to be too hard and I won't get good grades next year."

"Maybe I won't make the softball team."

"Maybe the older youth group kids will make fun of me."

Have you ever had an attack of the "maybes"? What are you afraid of, deep down? Are you afraid of making the wrong decision and messing everything up?

God has a lot to say about fear in His Word. He frequently reassures His people of His presence (Isaiah 41:10, Matthew 28:20). The possibilities of what could happen are scary, but God is the all-powerful King of the universe—nothing can happen outside of His plan (Isaiah 46:9–10), and His love for you has no end (Lamentations 3:22). Because His perfect love casts out fear (1 John 4:18), you can step out with courage, trusting that He will keep His promise to take care of you no matter what happens.

Sometimes it's hard to feel the reality of His care when the "maybes" close in. For the times when anxiety hits, remind yourself of God's love with a memory verse. Pray in the moment. Seek help from older, wiser Christians. Fear doesn't have to keep you from moving forward—God will go with you every step of the way.

Dear God, whenever I am afraid, I will trust in You.
Thank You that You're always with me! Amen.

IF YOU CAN'T SAY ANYTHING NICE...

*Gossip is no good! It causes hard feelings
and comes between friends.*
PROVERBS 16:28 CEV

The book of Proverbs has several verses about gossiping (11:13, 17:9, 18:8). Why is something that's so fun also so destructive? When we gossip, we share juicy tidbits about what's going wrong in other people's lives. Dragging out those details makes us feel better about the secret messes in our lives—we build ourselves up with the pieces we've torn off others.

Though gossip can make us feel indestructible, it reveals a shaky spot in our hearts—our self-worth. If we think that we have to tear down others in order to be cool or accepted, we have forgotten an important truth. We are enough in Jesus. We no longer have to try to prove ourselves to Him, and we don't have to prove ourselves to anyone else. When we are confident in His profound love, forgiveness, and acceptance of us, we no longer have to camouflage our imperfections in front of others.

Refusing to gossip is one beautiful way to love your neighbor. Praying for those who gossip about you or others is the kindest way you can repay their meanness. Gossip is no good! Make a practice of standing confident in Christ's love and leave gossip far, far behind.

Jesus, help me stop gossiping completely! Let Your truth about
who I am in You fill me with confidence and bravery. Teach
me to share loving words instead of hurtful ones. Amen.

LET THEM FLY AWAY

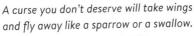

*A curse you don't deserve will take wings
and fly away like a sparrow or a swallow.*

PROVERBS 26:2 CEV

Few things hurt worse than finding out a friend has been gossiping about you behind your back, and the bad things they're saying aren't even true! You want to stop the rumors right away, but they just keep spreading. . . .

If this happens, take heart. As hard as it is to resist defending yourself to everyone, you shouldn't have to if the rumor isn't true. Proverbs 26:2 says that if someone says false, unkind things about you, they won't stick—your character will speak for itself. Luke 6:44 (NIV) says that "each tree is recognized by its own fruit." If your heart is good, you will bring good actions (fruit) out of it, and bad actions if your heart is holding on to evil (Luke 6:45). You, your loyal friends, and God will be able to point to the evidence of good fruit coming from your heart even as others accuse you of bearing bad fruit.

It's tempting to spread gossip in return, but don't repay evil with evil (1 Peter 3:9). Forgive the rumor-starter the best you can (for God has forgiven you) and pile kindness on them, even if that kindness is simply withholding the pounding you want to give them! Trust God to reveal the truth, and let those "sparrows" fly away and nest where they're deserved.

God, it really hurts to be gossiped about. Help me
forgive and lean on Your truth. Help me obey You
by being kind even when I'm really hurting. Amen.

JOY!

You will teach me how to live a holy life. Being with you will fill me with joy; at your right hand I will find pleasure forever.

PSALM 16:11 NCV

Contrary to popular belief, being joyful doesn't mean being happy all the time. When the Bible says to "count it all joy" (James 1:2 KJV), it doesn't mean we have to smile when our friends make fun of us or when we're having a really hard time with our parents. Instead, joy is a constant undercurrent of peace in our hearts—like an underground river that continues to flow even though the land above is dry from lack of rain.

Jesus, the Living Water, is the source of our joy. He has given so many promises—He is always with us to guide us and strengthen us (1 Peter 5:10), He has overcome the hard things we experience (John 16:33), and He will bring peace and beauty out of those situations (Isaiah 61:3). When we are connected to Him and believe His promises through faith, joy runs bubbling through our hearts, watering the places that are cracked and dry—our fears, our anxieties, our embarrassments.

This is what keeps our hearts from staying sunk on bad days. Is your joy a strong stream, or does it feel like a trickle? Spend some time with Jesus. His Word can quench any heart, no matter how parched.

Jesus, I want to trust You more so my joy will grow. Thank You for Your promises! Amen.

ATTITUDE CHECK

*[Jesus] gave himself for us to redeem us from all
wickedness and to purify for himself a people
that are his very own, eager to do what is good.*

TITUS 2:14 NIV

The Bible tells us that when we received Jesus' salvation, God had already prepared good works for us to do (Ephesians 2:10). He's also given each of us gifts we can use to serve others (1 Peter 4:10). Although He also promises to give us the strength we'll need to serve Him, we often don't feel like serving. . .and avoid it. Or we do it but grumble and complain inside.

Unfortunately, our good deeds don't count for much when we have a bad attitude. The Pharisees of Jesus' day did many good works, but they did it so they would be praised by other people, not out of love for God (Matthew 6:2). Jesus called them "whitewashed tombs"—they looked good on the outside but were dead on the inside (Matthew 23:27 NIV). Paul reminds us that without love, good works are like meaningless noise (1 Corinthians 13:1–3).

When you don't feel like serving, pray. Tell God how you are feeling. Like the parable of the two sons working in a vineyard, God would rather you confess an unloving attitude and then do the work He's commanded than the alternative (Matthew 21:28–32). Ask Him to show you opportunities—being kind to your siblings is an everyday way to obey and please God. And that should be the goal of all our service.

God, please forgive me for when I've been selfish
instead of helpful. Help me be eager to serve! Amen.

THE BREAD AND WINE

There is now no condemnation for those who are in Christ Jesus.
ROMANS 8:1 NIV

When your church serves communion, does a knot of dread form in your stomach? During the time of confession, you try to remember all your sins from the week, but the prayer time is never long enough. You nervously take the bread and wine, hoping you aren't eating them in "an unworthy manner" (1 Corinthians 11:27 NIV).

If communion is an anxious time for you, then you might be a little confused about the meal's meaning. Communion isn't about presenting a long list of your sins so that you are allowed to come to Jesus' table. You aren't able to make yourself worthy by your own effort—communion is a celebration of Jesus lifting the judgment for sin from us! The bread and wine remind us of Jesus' sacrifice on the cross and how, by faith, He forgives and cleanses us. While He is glad you want to live right, Jesus doesn't want you to worry that you haven't done well enough to eat at His table. He tells you, *"I know you weren't good enough. That's why I gave Myself. So if you trust in Me for salvation, come and join Me!"*

Next Communion Sunday, remember: Your sins are forgiven now and forever (Psalm 103:12) because you've put your trust in the Savior's love, work, and forgiveness. Come and eat with joy!

Jesus, at communion, help me resist fear and believe the truth that Your salvation has covered all my sins, even the things I forgot to confess. Thank You! Amen.

INTERNET ME

*The LORD's light penetrates the human
spirit, exposing every hidden motive.*
PROVERBS 20:27 NLT

Depending on how internet savvy you are, you probably have an email address, Facebook, Twitter, Instagram—maybe a blog or two. You've been given advice on how to stay safe online and protect your personal info. But have you thought about *who* you are online?

We get to decide who we are every day. We act one way around our parents and another way around our friends—maybe sillier and more relaxed. While these different modes of self-expression are fine, new temptations arise when we realize what we can do online with our identities hidden behind a username. No one would know that it was you who left the mean comment on that video, or that it's your blog that's peppered with gossip about kids in your class. No one would know that you're the one using curse words or visiting websites that you shouldn't.

The internet itself isn't bad. It's a great tool for connection and self-expression. It's awesome to be creative and get to share your excitement for your favorite hobbies or movies with other fans around the world. But resist the temptation to leave behind your conscience when you're online. You may feel anonymous, but God still sees your actions and knows all the motives of your heart. Have you thought about how you can honor Him when you use the internet?

Father God, the internet is such an awesome gift! Please help me remember that You see all that I do online. Help me want to please You with these actions too. Amen.

COURAGE TO ASK

*"So I say to you, ask, and it will be given to you; seek,
and you will find; knock, and it will be opened to you.
For everyone who asks receives, and he who seeks
finds, and to him who knocks it will be opened."*

LUKE 11:9–10 NKJV

Bobbing her knee, Lauren scrolled idly through her phone, trying to be patient as her mom took the call from the hospital.

"Okay. So he's stabilized? Okay. Thank you for letting us know." Her mom ended the call and ran her hand through her rough red hair. "Sounds like Grandpa's doing a little better. The doctor said the fever hasn't come back since last night."

Lauren's eyes widened with recognition. Last night she had woken up and couldn't go back to sleep, her throat tight with worry for Grandpa. She'd tried reading for a while but ended up hiding under the covers, praying hard against her fear. *Please let Grandpa's fever go down. God, I know You can heal him! Please heal him so he can come home.* Finally, she'd been able to fall back asleep.

She gave her mom a hug. "Mom, God answered my prayer! I prayed for the fever to go away!"

Her mom held her close. "He always listens to our prayers, honey. We just need to be bold to believe that He does."

And bold to ask for what we need, thought Lauren. *Thank You, God.*

God, thank You for the privilege to ask You for anything.
Please give me courage to ask for the big things and not
worry. You are strong enough to handle it all! Amen.

THE BLUES

Every good and perfect gift is from above,
coming down from the Father of the heavenly
lights, who does not change like shifting shadows.
JAMES 1:17 NIV

Sometimes the blues hit hard. Maybe it's from looking at your friend's awesome vacation photos on Facebook or just feeling lonely and bored. But even when you're not sure why you're feeling down, your heavenly Father draws near to you, for He comes close to the brokenhearted (Psalm 34:18). He knows your feelings before you tell Him anything, and He is ready and able to comfort you (Matthew 6:8; 11:28).

Some ideas to beat the blues: Take your time. Give yourself permission to feel what you need to feel—pray, write out your thoughts, or make art out of them. Creativity can be a form of prayer. God also comforts us through His many good gifts. When we're feeling down, it's the perfect time to open ourselves to receive them. Spend a day enjoying His creation, something that lifts your spirits. Try visiting the zoo or the aquarium, or picking wildflowers at the park. Maybe it's time for you to finally get that new hair cut or try a new nail polish color. Maybe comfort means playing in the mud or getting friends together for volleyball or having a solo dance party in your room.

Hang in there, and keep talking to God. The Maker of joy will be with you and comfort you on those unexplainably hard days.

God, when I feel really down, help me keep my
eyes and heart open to receive Your gifts. Amen.

MORE THAN MUSCLES

The LORD gives me strength and a song. He has saved me.
Shouts of joy and victory come from the tents of those
who do right: "The LORD has done powerful things."
PSALM 118:14–15 NCV

No doubt you've seen her: the "strong female character." Usually, this character is skilled at physical combat, hiding her emotions, and getting things done with sass. After the movie ends, you might feel a bit inadequate. *I wish I could kick butt like her!*

Despite what movies show us, strength isn't everything. Even if you're a martial arts/computer genius, God's strength is still greater. When you trust in Him, He lets you tap into His power and enables you to do great things, even if you aren't that strong.

Look at the women of the Bible. Though some were warriors— Deborah leading Israel's army and Jael with her tent peg—many of the women in the Bible were ordinary, but they accomplished mighty things through their faith in God. Esther risked her life to rescue her people; Abigail saved her foolish husband by offering hospitality to David; teenaged, unwed Mary carried the Savior in her womb; Anna the prophetess and Hannah, Samuel's mother, prayed earnestly until God answered them; Lydia is celebrated for her business savvy and love for God's people. If you're not that physically strong, don't worry. Strength takes on many forms—showing kindness, praying faithfully, being encouraging, speaking the truth. And you don't do it alone. Listen to God's voice, and trust Him to give you strength for the challenges that await.

God, show me how true strength lies in trusting You. Amen.

TRUST ME

*There are many who say, "You can
trust me!" But can they be trusted?*

PROVERBS 20:6 CEV

How do we prove that we're trustworthy friends? One simple way is by faithfully doing things that show you care for your friends, like remembering birthdays or taking time to listen to them vent when they're having a bad day (instead of changing the subject to be about you) or doing something they like with them even if it's an activity you don't enjoy as much. In all our friendships, we should follow Jesus' command to "love your neighbor as yourself" (Mark 12:31 NIV) and treat our friends how we want to be treated. Don't we want friends who will carry our burdens (Galatians 6:2), speak honestly with us (Ephesians 4:15), and forgive us when we hurt them (1 Peter 4:8)? Someone who will encourage us when we're down (Ecclesiastes 4:9–10) and will tell us when we're doing stupid, sinful things (Proverbs 27:5–6)?

Maybe you don't feel like you have any really trustworthy friends. It's a really tough spot to be in, but as you work on being the most trustworthy friend you can be, maybe God will move a friend to return the favor. Don't feel like you have to share any secrets until you feel like that person has earned your trust. Treat your friends as you would want to be treated, and make your trustworthiness undeniable—you'll be pleasing God in the process!

Jesus, I want to be a trustworthy friend and
have friends I can trust too. Teach me from Your
Word how to be a better friend. Amen.

FEELING OUT OF PLACE

The whole body depends on Christ, and all the parts of the body are joined and held together. Each part does its own work to make the whole body grow and be strong with love.

EPHESIANS 4:16 NCV

You've heard the biblical analogy of the Church (all Christians) being part of the Body of Christ, with each individual part helping out the whole. When you're young, it's easy to feel like you're probably the tonsils or the appendix in the Body—parts that could be taken out and no one would miss.

But God doesn't say that you're only useful to Him when you get older. The Bible says that *each* part helps the Body grow and be strong in love. Paul had to remind Timothy, a new, young pastor, not to let older people look down on him because he was younger but to set an example of faith and purity for all ages (1 Timothy 4:12).

You have God-given talents and skills to offer your fellow Christians and your community. Don't wait! The Body has just as much to learn from you as you can from it. Talk with your parents or someone in your church about ways you can get involved. It doesn't necessarily have to be at church—you can help in your community and do that work joyfully for Jesus too. If you are open and ready to receive it, God has good work for you!

God, I want to feel like I'm part of the Body. Please guide me to opportunities to serve with love in Your Church. Amen.

OH, YEAH. . .

Being confident of this, that he who began a good work in you will carry it on to completion until the day of Christ Jesus.

PHILIPPIANS 1:6 NIV

Maybe you've just realized that you didn't read your Bible at all this past week. It was busy—full of lessons, hanging out with friends, and time with family. Or maybe it was the opposite—a week full of nothing that you spent watching TV, reading, or online.

I'm a terrible Christian, you think. *A real Christian would read the Bible all the time and always pray and not fight with her sisters and listen to Mom and Dad the first time. . .*

Good news: The only thing that makes a Christian "real" is that she trusts in Jesus to save her from her sin. Jesus justified you before God when He died on the cross—there is no more punishment for your sin, and His perfect life covers over your imperfect one. Instead of frantically trying to read the Bible and pray to avoid punishment, we do it because we want to know and love Jesus more. So before you start beating yourself up for forgetting again, talk to Jesus about it. Tell Him you want to love His Word but you're having trouble. His Spirit will work in you, helping you to read and learn from the time you spend in the Word. Don't give up! God has promised that He'll never give up on you.

Jesus, I want to follow You, but reading the Bible
and praying is hard. Remind me that spending time
with You will help me see Your goodness. Amen.

MEANT FOR GOOD

Joseph said to them, "Don't be afraid. Am I in the place of God? You intended to harm me, but God intended it for good to accomplish what is now being done, the saving of many lives."
GENESIS 50:19–20 NIV

Have you ever thought you were stuck in a hopeless situation? When those times come up, reread the story of Joseph in Genesis 37–50. Joseph, Jacob's favorite son, was so hated by his jealous brothers that they sold him into slavery. Joseph served faithfully but then was put in prison after being falsely accused of adultery. He spent years there until God gave him the opportunity to serve Pharaoh by interpreting his dreams about the coming years of plenty and famine, eventually serving as Pharaoh's second-in-command. Later, Joseph was reunited with his brothers. Incredibly, Joseph forgave them. He saw how God turned all the evil they meant him into good—because of Joseph, entire nations were saved from famine!

Whatever hard things we face, God works out everything for the good of those who love Him (Romans 8:28). Nothing we go through is meaningless; often, hard times help us grow closer to God, and we learn how to comfort others better too (2 Corinthians 1:3–4).

Even if it feels like life's taking a wrong turn, God hasn't turned away from you (Joshua 1:5). You can trust Him to guide you and work out the hard things for your good.

God, I can't see how the hard things in my life are going to turn out okay, but I trust You. Help me see the good You'll bring out of them. Amen.

TECH TOYS

Teach us to use wisely all the time we have.
PSALM 90:12 CEV

Isn't technology great? Whether you've got your own phone or you share with a sibling, or you have a laptop, gaming system, or iPad, you already know how to connect with other people online, play games, make art, and so much more.

So how much of your free time would you say you spend on your "tech toys"? They are among God's good gifts to us, but we easily use His gifts in unintentionally hurtful ways. For instance, staring at screens for hours can have long-term effects on your eyesight and upper spine. Also, when you and your family are investing more time in electronics than each other, relationships can suffer too.

Another gift God has given us is free will. We're allowed to choose how we use His gifts—our lives, our talents, our time, our money, our bodies. It makes sense that you might prefer to spend time talking or playing with friends online instead of spending time with family, but challenge yourself: Try taking a Sabbath from your phone or computer. Maybe it'll only be once a month, but leave your screens off for the day and see what you end up doing. Maybe you'll explore a new hobby or drag your family along on an adventure. Enjoy that time—the tech toys will still be there when you get back.

Jesus, thank You for all Your gifts—internet and
computers too. Help me value Your precious
gift of time and use it wisely. Amen.

CRUSHED

*Just as Jerusalem is protected by mountains
on every side, the LORD protects his people by
holding them in his arms now and forever.*

PSALM 125:2 CEV

Crushes are tough. Whether you have a crush or aren't even interested in having a crush right now, you might feel that weird loneliness that comes from wanting someone to notice you—to see you and think you're amazing, fun, beautiful, and the best person to be around. Maybe those feelings seem stupid, but that longing for affection and attention is normal. Just like Adam, you weren't meant to be alone—God made you to be loved, by Him and also by the people surrounding you in your community.

This doesn't mean that He'll make your crush instantly like you back, but God can fill that longing in your heart. You need more than just romantic love to be a well-rounded person—you need the encouraging love from friends your age (and older). Their affection can help lift that strange loneliness, and they can boost your confidence with how they value you and appreciate what makes you who you are.

You also have the loving security of a relationship with your Creator. Know this: Life will be okay whether or not your crush likes you back. God is the Master of your days and the One who loves you best. Whatever you experience, He will hold you in His arms now and forever.

God, please comfort me in the parts of my life
where I feel lonely. Thank You that You care
about everything I go through. Amen.

STARTING THE CONVERSATION

*"Then you will call on me and come and pray to me,
and I will listen to you. You will seek me and find me
when you seek me with all your heart. I will be
found by you," declares the LORD.*

JEREMIAH 29:12–14 NIV

Prayer is kind of weird. Maybe to you it feels more like writing a letter or email than a face-to-face conversation with God. If it feels funny to pray out loud, it definitely helps to write down your prayers; but if you're still not feeling confident in how to start praying, take a look at the Person you're talking to.

We learn about God's character in the Bible. From Jesus, we learn that God is a loving Father who knows what we need before we ask (Matthew 6:8). From Moses, we learn that God listens even when we come to Him with something too big for us to handle (Exodus 32:30–32). From Gideon, we learn that God is gentle with His people when their faith is small (Judges 6:36–40). From the blind man healed by Jesus, we learn that sometimes He lets things into our lives that don't make sense to us, but He will bring glory out of them (John 9).

Starting can be the hardest part of praying. But as you get to know God better, it will get easier to share what's on your mind. And He's promised that if you seek Him, you will find Him.

God, please show Yourself to me in Your Word.
Thank You for always listening when I pray,
and help me pray more often! Amen.

RUSHING AND LAGGING

*The LORD makes firm the steps of the one who
delights in him; though he may stumble, he will
not fall, for the LORD upholds him with his hand.*

PSALM 37:23–24 NIV

When it comes to making decisions, you might be a rusher or a lagger. The rushers are game for anything and jump right in. The laggers wait at the edge, watching the rushers, trying to figure out what's going on before deciding to join (or not—"Are you really going to lick peanut butter off his shoe? Gross!" "C'mon, it'll be awesome!").

Whatever your style, you'll find someone similar to you in the Bible. There are stories about rushers like Peter and Moses, as well as laggers like the disciple Thomas and Jonah. What do they all have in common? Though they all stumbled in one way or another, God worked out their stories for their good because they trusted in Him. Whether His children lag behind or jump ahead, whether they act wisely or make grand mistakes, God will not let them be snatched out of His hand, and He will not let them fall (John 10:28, Psalm 37:24).

The important question is—do you delight in your Creator? Do you make decisions with His beautiful, holy ways in mind? Even when you mess up (and you will), you can trust Him to keep you from falling.

God, I know I'm going to mess up. Thank You that
You keep me from falling when I make mistakes!
Every day is a new day to try again. Amen.

DREAM HARD

*Commit to the LORD whatever you do,
and he will establish your plans.*

PROVERBS 16:3 NIV

What is your wildest dream? What if someone told you that a generous benefactor was willing to fund everything you needed to reach your dream? Not only that, but this person would believe in you 100 percent, even if you made lots of mistakes in the process. How quick would you go for it?

We Christians *have* that generous benefactor, our heavenly Father. He's certainly not a wish-granting genie, but the Bible tells us to bring all our petitions to God (Philippians 4:6). He already knows what you're going to ask, and He gives good gifts to His children who pray in faith (Matthew 6:8; 7:11). Also, God is the One who plants dreams within us—dreams that are according to His plan—when we delight in Him (Psalm 37:4).

Because you have access to the Source of life and deep-down confidence, tell Him your dreams and wishes. Tell it all—worries, needs, anger, doubts—and commit to Him whatever you do. Give those dreams the best you've got, going forth in His strength and trusting Him to show you the way. God might shut some doors on the way, but keep going; He also opens doors to opportunities that we might not have expected. Your generous Father just wants you to ask and follow Him in faith. What's holding you back?

God, help me believe that You care about my dreams.
Help me seek You and commit these dreams to
You and see what You have for me. Amen.

SPEAK TRUTH

The Lord appeared to us in the past, saying:
"I have loved you with an everlasting love;
I have drawn you with unfailing kindness."
JEREMIAH 31:3 NIV

There is a truth you must tell yourself, one you need to hear every day. You get pretty good at lying, telling yourself that you are unlovely and unworthy. You have lots of reasons to explain why you're this way, but those are lies.

The truth? You are loved. Even if you feel anything but loveable. Even if your hair sticks up funny. Even if you've royally messed up.

You are loved. Even if it's hard to believe. Even if the cutie you like hasn't noticed you. Even if you feel the crush of loneliness more often than not.

You are loved. Carve it into the walls of your heart. Run your fingers over the grooves of that truth whether the day is good or sour—find its gleaming light and hang on to it. Know that your name is engraved on God's hands—He will never forget you (Isaiah 49:16).

You are loved. God formed you in secret, with delight (Psalm 139). He calls you His dear one, the apple of His eye (Zechariah 2:8). The Creator of all things bestows His priceless love upon you without stinginess, without waiting for you to love Him first (1 John 4:10).

Do not forget. But when you do, go back to the Word. Read and speak the truth to yourself. *I am loved.*

Father, thank You for loving me so much. Help me to
always remember that You love me completely. Amen.

WHO AM I?

So God created human beings in his own image. In the image
of God he created them; male and female he created them.
GENESIS 1:27 NLT

We've all got questions. Sure, we might not find or have all the answers, but we do know the One who does, and we can seek His wisdom as we find advice from His Word.

Every girl gets to the point where she wants to know who she is and where she came from. We learn from birth who our relatives are, but then we figure out that life is about more than just our families and friends. Ecclesiastes 3:11 tells us that God placed eternity right in each of our hearts from the very beginning. Psalm 139 shows us that God Himself created us inside our mother's womb and that He knows every word we say before we say it.

You are God's beloved creation, and He created you to know Him and know His love for you! No matter what kind of family situation you have grown up in or what you already believe about God, know this: God loves you more than you could ever imagine, and He is a good parent. Even if you have the best parents in the world, God is greater! If you have the worst family situation anyone could imagine, God is bigger than that and will reach down to show you His love if you let Him!

God, I want to know who I really am and who
You are too. Please show me Your love.

IS GOD REAL?

The basic reality of God is plain enough. Open your eyes and there it is! By taking a long and thoughtful look at what God has created, people have always been able to see what their eyes as such can't see.

ROMANS 1:20 MSG

Lee Strobel was an investigative reporter for a large newspaper. After his wife committed her life to Christ, he wanted to prove that God was not real. Through years of research and studying eye-witness accounts of what happened while Jesus was alive, he came to the startling conclusion that it would take *more faith* to believe that Jesus wasn't who He said He was than to keep being an atheist! Did you catch that? He found that it would take more faith on his part to keep believing that there was no God than to accept the facts of history that Jesus was real, that He was God, and that He rose from the dead! Not only is the Bible the inspired Word of God. . .it is also a reliable historical textbook. You can trust what it says about God!

You may have doubts about your faith sometimes, and that's okay. It's what we do with our doubt that matters! God understands our doubts and questions. He wants us to bring them straight to Him so that He can show us how faithful He is! Ask God to show you how real He is. You'll be amazed at the way that He shows up in your life!

God, I want to believe You and trust You with my life. Please help me see You in my world.

WHAT IS GOD LIKE?

*But anyone who does not love does
not know God, for God is love.*
1 JOHN 4:8 NLT

Some of us grow up with a weird view of God. We think He must be really old with a long white beard and sometimes a grumpy face. This is unbiblical and completely incorrect.

Jesus Himself tells us this: "No one has ever seen God, but the one and only Son, who is himself God and is in closest relationship with the Father, has made him known" (John 1:18 NIV). Since Jesus is the only One who has seen God, it's important that we get our ideas about God from Him! So what does Jesus tell us about God?

- "For God so loved the world that he gave his one and only Son, that whoever believes in him shall not perish but have eternal life" (John 3:16 NIV).

- "God is spirit, and those who worship him must worship in spirit and truth" (John 4:24 NCV).

- "The Father and I are one" (John 10:30 NLT).

The one true God of scripture exists as three persons: God the Father; God the Son, Jesus; and God the Holy Spirit. It doesn't have to be confusing, but it is a great mystery! Check out Colossians 1:15 and Isaiah 9:6 for more about who God is!

God, please erase all the wrong ideas I've had about You. Help me know You as the one true loving and living God!

DAY 216

WHAT'S MY PURPOSE?

*Jesus replied, "'You must love the L*ORD *your God with all your heart, all your soul, and all your mind.' This is the first and greatest commandment. A second is equally important: 'Love your neighbor as yourself.'"*

MATTHEW 22:37–39 NLT

What am I supposed to do with my life? Get good grades in school? Go on to college? Have a successful career? Start a family? That's what the majority of people in this world consider their purpose, also known as the American Dream! Those are all great goals. . .but is that really what God wants from us?

Check out what 1 Corinthians 13:1–3 (NLT) tells us:

If I could speak all the languages of earth and of angels, but didn't love others, I would only be a noisy gong or a clanging cymbal. If I had the gift of prophecy, and if I understood all of God's secret plans and possessed all knowledge, and if I had such faith that I could move mountains, but didn't love others, I would be nothing. If I gave everything I have to the poor and even sacrificed my body, I could boast about it; but if I didn't love others, I would have gained nothing.

God's purpose for us might not be easy, but it is simple: Love Him and love others.

. . . .

God, please change my heart to match Your purpose for my life. Help me work hard in all things out of my love for You!

IF GOD LOVES ME, WHY DOES LIFE HURT SOMETIMES?

Be merciful to me, LORD, for I am in distress; my eyes grow weak with sorrow, my soul and body with grief.

PSALM 31:9 NIV

King David was the author of many of the psalms. He experienced times of great blessing, but he also knew his share of deep pain. And still he trusted God no matter what. You can see his great faith in verses like Psalm 37:25 (NIV) where he says, "I was young and now I am old, yet I have never seen the righteous forsaken."

David's pain came about because of the poor choices he made (adultery, murder, lying) and the choices of those close to him (King Saul hunted him, his own son betrayed him). He feared for his life on many occasions, causing him to cry out to God in sorrow and grief. Yet in that same psalm he was able to say, "Praise be to the LORD, for he showed me the wonders of his love" (31:21 NIV).

When life hurts, are you able to look to God and say, "I praise You for Your love for me; I'm hurting but I trust You?"

Psalm 34:18 (NIV) says, "The LORD is close to the brokenhearted and saves those who are crushed in spirit." Jesus meets us in our pain. Sometimes you will never feel closer to God than you will when you are hurting. Reach out for Him. He is always reaching for You.

God, thank You for being with me when I'm sad.
Please take away my hurt and fill me with Your love.

WHO AM I IN CHRIST?

*This means that anyone who belongs to Christ has become
a new person. The old life is gone; a new life has begun!*
2 CORINTHIANS 5:17 NLT

Knowing who you are in Christ will change your life. Once you've accepted Jesus Christ as your personal Lord and Savior, His Spirit comes to live inside of you and changes everything for good. When you do this, God's Word says:

- You are free and clean in the blood of Christ (1 John 1:7, Galatians 5:1),

- you are a precious child of the Father (John 1:12),

- God sings over you (Zephaniah 3:17),

- you are a friend of Christ (John 15:15),

- nothing can separate you from God's love (Romans 8:38–39),

- God sees you as beautiful, and you are wonderfully made (Psalm 139:14, Ecclesiastes 3:11).

Write these down and post them where you'll see them every single day. Are you ready to step into a new life with all that God has in store for you?

. . . .

Dear Jesus, I ask You to come into my heart and be
in charge of my life. Please change me to be like You,
and help me believe all the things You say about me.

WHAT IF I FEEL LONELY?

*Yet I still belong to you; you hold my right hand. You guide
me with your counsel, leading me to a glorious destiny. Whom
have I in heaven but you? I desire you more than anything on
earth. My health may fail, and my spirit may grow weak, but
God remains the strength of my heart; he is mine forever.*
PSALM 73:23–26 NLT

As you get older and change and grow, you'll notice many differences
about you and your friends. Someone you used to be best friends
with might suddenly like new things and new people. You'll find that
you have new likes and dislikes too. It's all part of growing up, but
it can feel really lonely at times.

When we give our lives to Jesus, the Spirit of God miraculously
comes to live inside of us and we are no longer alone! Gods says:
"I will never leave you" (Hebrews 13:5 ESV), and even if you don't
feel like God is with you, He is! That's a promise you can count on.
When you are feeling sad and lonely, tell God about it. He promises
to be close to you when you are feeling down and brokenhearted
(Psalm 34:18).

The next time you're feeling lonely, try writing a prayer to God.
Ask God to fill your heart and help you know that He is near.

God, You promise to be with me always. I'm feeling
alone and sad, and I need Your help. Please fill
my heart with Your presence and love.

WHAT IF I KEEP MESSING UP?

If we claim we have no sin, we are only fooling ourselves and not living in the truth. But if we confess our sins to him, he is faithful and just to forgive us our sins and to cleanse us from all wickedness.

1 JOHN 1:8-9 NLT

When we're growing up, we make a lot of mistakes. We can either learn from our mistakes and make better choices next time. . .or we can keep making the same mistakes and hurting ourselves and others. If we love God, we want to make good decisions and follow His plan for our lives. But sometimes we still mess up. We get selfish. We want our own way. Our friends try to get us to do something we know is wrong, but we do it anyway. Sometimes life is just confusing and hard.

When we make mistakes, God wants us to come to Him and repent. To repent means to ask God to forgive our sins and help us change direction so that we turn away from sin. If you check out Romans 7:14-25, you can see that Paul felt this problem too. He asks God to rescue him from his mistakes and thanks God for His faithfulness to forgive us because of what Jesus did for us on the cross. Paul starts the very next chapter in Romans with this great truth: "There is now no condemnation for those who are in Christ Jesus" (8:1 NIV).

God, I am so thankful and amazed that You took away my sin and mistakes on the cross. Please help me turn away from sin and seek You alone.

HOW DO I FIND HELP FOR MY PROBLEMS?

*If you don't know what you're doing, pray to
the Father. He loves to help. You'll get his help,
and won't be condescended to when you ask for it.
Ask boldly, believingly, without a second thought.*

JAMES 1:5 MSG

Lots of people head straight to the internet whenever they need help. They Google everything looking for answers to all their questions. James 3:17 (NLT) says, "But the wisdom from above is first of all pure. It is also peace loving, gentle at all times, and willing to yield to others. It is full of mercy and the fruit of good deeds. It shows no favoritism and is always sincere." The answers they find online, however, are rarely pure, peace-loving, gentle, and unselfish. You might find the answer you're looking for, but it will be mixed with thousands of differing opinions and you have to sift through a bunch of junk to find some truth.

Pure wisdom is rarely found online unless you're looking up God's Word! When you need wisdom, the Bible tells us that we can ask God for it and He'll give it to us! Just because we asked Him (James 1:5)! You never have to sift through any questionable content to find wisdom from God. Seek the Lord first before you Google and before you ask for advice from others.

God, I definitely need lots of wisdom in this mixed-up
world. Sometimes I get very confused about what is
right and wrong. Please give me the desire to come
to You for the answers to all my questions.

DAY 222

IS GOD WORKING IN MY LIFE?

It was you who split open the sea by your power;
you broke the heads of the monster in the waters.
It was you who crushed the heads of Leviathan and
gave it as food to the creatures of the desert.

PSALM 74:13–14 NIV

Some days we need a good reminder that God is still working in our lives. Maybe God seems far away and you need Him to show up again. In today's psalm, Asaph and his descendants needed help. They felt like God had forgotten them. But instead of giving up on Him, they decided to make a list of what God had already done. They reminded themselves of who God was and how He had already worked on their behalf.

When you are tempted to doubt, speak truth into the moment. Refresh your soul with reminders from God's Word:

- He is always working things out for your good
  (Romans 8:28).

- He is close to the brokenhearted (Psalm 34:18).

- He is not far from any of us (Acts 17:27).

Write down the blessings you have experienced. Take note of hard times you endured and lessons that God taught you. Then when you're tempted to doubt God's presence in your life, go back and remember!

God, thank You for always being with me even when I don't feel You there. I remember how much You love me and care about me. Thank You for working in my life!

HOW CAN I FIND GOOD FRIENDS?

One who has unreliable friends soon comes to ruin,
but there is a friend who sticks closer than a brother.
PROVERBS 18:24 NIV

The Bible talks a lot about being wise in the friends you choose. The late Christian author and speaker Zig Ziglar said, "Life is too short to spend your precious time trying to convince a person who wants to live in gloom and doom otherwise. Give lifting that person your best shot, but don't hang around long enough for his or her bad attitude to pull you down. Instead, surround yourself with optimistic people."

It's so important to surround yourself with friends who love God and lift you up instead of drag you down. You want friends who are trustworthy and kind. A true friend sticks by your side closer than a sibling. This doesn't mean you should hide inside a "Christian bubble," because God wants us to share His love with all people. But do spend a lot of time with people who fill you up with the goodness of God. Then you have the strength and courage to go and fill others up with that same goodness. And you can serve and love unbelievers just like Jesus did!

God, please surround me with people who love You.
Sometimes I have trouble making good friends. Will you
please bring the right people into my life? I trust You to
meet all my needs. . .especially my need for good friends!

HOW CAN I BE A GOOD FRIEND?

*Whoever would foster love covers over an offense, but
whoever repeats the matter separates close friends.*
PROVERBS 17:9 NIV

Imagine this conversation: A friend tells you she heard that another one of your friends hurt your feelings. You may be tempted to share the whole story so that the person listening will feel bad for you in the hopes that it might make you feel a little better. But the Bible says that a good and loving friend will cover over that offense with love and not repeat it by gossiping. Instead, find a way to change the subject and let your friend know it's not something you feel comfortable sharing. Responding in such a way promotes love and protects friendships. You are covering the friend that hurt you with love and grace.

Proverbs 17:17 (NKJV) says, "A friend loves at all times, and a brother is born for adversity." A true friend will promote love at all times. Even when they don't fully understand what their friend is going through. Be that kind of friend. Ask God to help you develop these kinds of friendships. Ask Him to help you respond to friends out of love and to treat friends—and conversations with friends—like you would want to be treated and in the way you would like to be spoken of when you're not around.

God, I really want to be a good friend. Help me
avoid gossip and be loving in my relationships.

DOES GOD LIKE ME?

"The LORD your God is with you, the Mighty Warrior who saves. He will take great delight in you, in his love he will no longer rebuke you, but will rejoice over you with singing."

ZEPHANIAH 3:17 NIV

Hopefully, you have heard a lot about how much God loves you in your lifetime. But "love" and "like" are a little different, right? Do you ever wonder if God likes you? Pastor and author Dr. Charles Stanley says this: "Yes, God likes me. He approves of me. He likes spending time with me. He likes being with me. He likes hearing me when I pray to Him, and He also enjoys talking with me through His Word. I believe He loves me. He knows I make mistakes, but He sees my heart and my desire to know Him better each day." Think about that for a moment. Isn't that so amazing?

When you come to know Jesus as your Savior, God washes all your sins away and He sees you as the perfect girl you are. And you can say with confidence, "God likes me!" He rejoices over you, and the Bible says He even sings about you! You are liked. You are loved. You are His!

Wow, God! This makes my heart smile. Thank You for loving me. . .and for liking me just the way I am. Thank You for Jesus and seeing me as perfect. I love You. I like You a whole lot too.

HOW CAN I KEEP MY EYES ON CHRIST?

Then Peter got down out of the boat, walked on the water and came toward Jesus. But when he saw the wind, he was afraid and, beginning to sink, cried out, "Lord, save me!"

MATTHEW 14:29-30 NIV

When our eyes are focused on Christ, He gives us the ability to rise above the storms of life. But just like Peter, when we get distracted and scared by the waves and problems all around us, we start to sink. Peter cried out to God for help when he realized how crazy and unbelievable it seemed to step out in faith! But the Bible says that "immediately Jesus reached out his hand and caught him" (Matthew 14:31 NIV).

Are you having trouble stepping out in faith and keeping your eyes on Christ? Do you keep looking at your problems instead of looking for God? Ask God to reach out His hand to you just like He did to Peter. Ask Him to forgive you for doubting and give you supernatural power to keep your eyes focused on Him. Trust Him to give you strength and peace in all situations.

God, sometimes I'm scared to step out in faith and do the things You ask me to. I forget to keep my eyes on You, and I look at everyone and everything else instead. Please fill me with Your power to overcome so that I can keep my eyes focused on You!

IS THE BIBLE TRUE?

The instructions of the LORD are perfect, reviving the soul. The decrees of the LORD are trustworthy, making wise the simple. The commandments of the LORD are right, bringing joy to the heart. The commands of the LORD are clear, giving insight for living.

PSALM 19:7–8 NLT

Part of trusting God is trusting in the truth of His Word. As believers, we trust that the Bible is the inspired Word of God. Second Timothy 3:16 (NIV) tells us that all scripture is "God-breathed"! What an amazing truth! God breathed the words of scripture through chosen believers in centuries past, and His words still change lives today.

How can we know the Bible is true? Don't be afraid to search out the truth for yourself. Many an atheist has been converted by trying to prove the Bible wrong! AnswersInGenesis.org says this about the Bible: "It has been confirmed countless times by archaeology and other sciences. It possesses divine insight into the nature of the universe and has made correct predictions about distant future events with perfect accuracy."

God's instructions in the Bible are clear, and they give us wise advice for today. The Word of God can be trusted. If you want to know how to live your life for God. . .if you need wisdom for today and hope for tomorrow. . .if you want to hear God speak to you right now. . .get in God's Word. It will change your life!

God, I want to believe in Your Word. Help me know and understand what You are telling me in scripture. Thank You for the guarantee that Your words are true!

DAY 228

HOW DO I LOVE GOD?

"When you obey my commandments, you remain in my love, just as I obey my Father's commandments and remain in his love."

JOHN 15:10 NLT

In John 15, Jesus tells us how we can show our love for God: by obeying His commands. What are His commands? To love God and love others. Everything else depends on those two things (Matthew 22:36–40).

To love God, you have to know and understand the truth about Him. John 10:27–30 (NIV) says, "My sheep listen to my voice; I know them, and they follow me. I give them eternal life, and they shall never perish; no one can snatch them out of my hand. My Father, who has given them to me, is greater than all; no one can snatch them out of my Father's hand. I and the Father are one."

In Bible times, a gentle shepherd would love and care for his sheep with compassion and kindness. The sheep would listen to the shepherd's voice. Jesus calls us His sheep. In the same way, Jesus wants us to love Him by learning to listen to His voice. Get to know His voice by reading His Word and talking to Him throughout your day. He loves to hear fom you!

God, please help me love You with all my heart and be faithful to obey Your words. I want to please You with my life.

HOW DO I SEE GOD?

O nations of the world, recognize the Lord; recognize that the Lord is glorious and strong. Give to the Lord the glory he deserves! Bring your offering and come into his courts. Worship the Lord in all his holy splendor. Let all the earth tremble before him.

PSALM 96:7-9 NLT

Years ago in a famous newspaper, the religion editor received a letter demanding more evidence for God. The writer wasn't convinced that there was a God. They wanted a sign. They wanted God to show up on the White House lawn and claim that He was real.

Looking outside at the phenomenal creation we live in, or gazing at any human being and recognizing the miracles of the human body, then to demand further proof of the existence of God seems quite silly! God wants us to "see" His hand in everything with eyes of faith. This is part of worship: Recognizing that God is the Creator and Sustainer of our world and everything in it. And also thanking Him for it and taking care of all He has given us. Keep your eyes open and recognize the Lord in all things.

If you're not in the habit of recognizing and "seeing" God in everything, you can start changing that now.

God, please help me see Your hand in all things. Thank You for giving me life and watching over my family and friends. Thank You for my home and my neighborhood. Thank You for creating the stars and knowing me personally in the midst of this great big world. Please open my eyes, Lord!

WHAT IF I FEEL UGLY?

*Charm is deceptive, and beauty does not last; but a
woman who fears the LORD will be greatly praised.*
PROVERBS 31:30 NLT

Do you ever wish you looked just a little bit more like a movie star?
Or maybe you have green eyes and you've always wanted blue.
Or maybe your braces won't come off for one more year and you
absolutely hate to smile.

Cheer up, friend. When God looks at you, He smiles! Braces,
acne, long legs, bony knees. . .it's all part of growing up. God created
you just the way you are with special traits and gifts that only you
can use to serve Him! The Bible says that people look at outward
appearance, but God looks at the heart (1 Samuel 16:7).

A truly beautiful person shines from the inside out. You've seen
the movies! Actresses that are really beautiful but play characters
that have a mean personality aren't loved for very long. And by the
end of the movie, you can hardly stand them! Their bad attitude
makes them look ugly even though they have beautiful features.
So give everyone a great big smile—braces or not! Your beauty
comes from the inside out. A great smile brightens everyone's
day and warms the heart of God. And making God smile is all that
really matters, anyway.

God, when I'm feeling ugly, remind me that I make You smile.
Help me remember that my beauty comes from inside,
and let my smile make someone else happy today too.

HOW DO I KNOW WHICH DIRECTION TO TAKE?

*Now faith is confidence in what we hope for
and assurance about what we do not see.*

HEBREWS 11:1 NIV

Imagine that you are hiking in a forest. As darkness approaches, you realize you better start setting up camp. You hike a bit farther, even as darkness deepens, to find protection from the cold. You keep going down the path, your flashlight guiding you so that you can see just enough to stay on the path. You finally find a safe spot and rest easy for the night. In the morning, you look back and realize the path you were on was extremely dangerous. Any wandering to the left or right would have placed you in great danger. But you trusted your flashlight, and it provided enough light to get you to safety. If you had seen the condition of the path in the light of day, you would have been too scared to move on toward safety. You would have run in the other direction, and that would not have gotten you to where you needed to be.

In the same way, God lights up our path just enough so that we can see how to obey Him—step by step and moment by moment. God's Word is a lamp for our feet, and faith is what drives us down the path. Reading and knowing God's Word provides us with light so our feet know the next steps to take, helping us have enough faith to keep our eyes on God, the One we cannot see.

God, thank You for always having a plan for me. Help me trust in Your Word so I know which direction to take, even when the path looks bleak.

HOW DO I MAKE GOOD DECISIONS?

So letting your sinful nature control your mind leads to death.
But letting the Spirit control your mind leads to life and peace.
ROMANS 8:6 NLT

You have a big choice to make today. Life and death are at stake. You can allow the Spirit to take over. . .or allow your sinful nature to do all the talking. Our sinful nature gets us into all kinds of trouble. When we allow our own nature to control us, we gossip, we do what we want without considering others, we hurt others, we sometimes lie and cheat, and worst of all, we forget about God's Spirit in our hearts.

But when we allow the Spirit of God to take over, we seek the things that God seeks: love, joy, peace, patience, kindness, goodness, faithfulness, gentleness, and self-control (Galatians 5:22–23). Those things lead to life and happiness and wisdom. We make good decisions by choosing to follow God's leading in our lives. We ask ourselves what God would want us to do instead of just doing what everyone else is doing without even thinking about it. Every choice you make matters. Listen as God whispers truth from His Word into your heart each day.

God, today I choose to lay down my own desires and let Your Spirit take control. It's so amazing to me that Your Spirit actually lives inside my heart! Help me to never forget or ignore that! I want to make good decisions that honor You.

HOW DO I LIVE FOR GOD?

Surely the righteous will never be shaken; they will be remembered forever. They will have no fear of bad news; their hearts are steadfast, trusting in the LORD.
PSALM 112:6–7 NIV

The word *steadfast* is defined as "unwavering; firmly established" and "firm in purpose." God's love is unwavering. He has firmly established His love for us by sending His Son, Jesus. His purpose for us is clear and steadfast too: Love God, love others (Luke 10:27).

Take a moment and pray that God will help you trust Him more. While you're at it, pray that God will make you strong, firm, and steadfast in your own faith. Jot down the following verses and pray them for your friends and family members too: "And the God of all grace, who called you to his eternal glory in Christ, after you have suffered a little while, will himself restore you and make you strong, firm and steadfast. To him be the power for ever and ever. Amen" (1 Peter 5:10–11 NIV).

Pastor and author Max Lucado says, "God became a man so we could trust him, became a sacrifice so we could know him, and defeated death so we could follow him." Don't be afraid to follow Him wholeheartedly. His love is steadfast for you. You can trust Him!

God, please make me strong, firm, and steadfast in my purpose and my love for You! Take my hand as I follow after You and lead me closer to You.

WHAT IF I FEEL DISCOURAGED?

"This is my command—be strong and courageous!
Do not be afraid or discouraged. For the LORD
your God is with you wherever you go."
JOSHUA 1:9 NLT

Discouragement is everywhere. Every step in the right direction is often criticized by others. Friends, family, and even well-meaning Christians can lose sight of faith and discourage you from following God's will to the fullest. It's so important to keep your eyes on Christ and concern yourself only with what He wants for you and not what others think. Find encouragement in the One who made you and has perfect plans for your life. Going against the norm takes courage! And God promises to be with you at all times. He is your constant Encourager and Comforter.

Philippians 4:6–7 (NIV) says, "Do not be anxious about anything, but in every situation, by prayer and petition, with thanksgiving, present your requests to God. And the peace of God, which transcends all understanding, will guard your hearts and your minds in Christ Jesus."

If you allow Him to be the center of your life and stop worrying, His peace will guard your heart and mind. Now *that's* encouraging!

Jesus, you are my Friend, my comfort, and my constant Encourager. Help me seek You always and not worry about what others think. Your plan for my life is perfect and full of promise.

WHAT DOES A RELATIONSHIP WITH GOD LOOK LIKE?

*Trust in the Lord and do good. Then you will live safely
in the land and prosper. Take delight in the Lord, and he
will give you your heart's desires. Commit everything
you do to the Lord. Trust him, and he will help you.*

PSALM 37:3–5 NLT

It's easy to look at today's verse and think, *Hey, if I just delight in
the Lord, He'll give me everything I want!* But when we really start to
delight in the Lord, God changes our hearts so completely that all
we ever want is what *He* wants. When you commit everything you
do to the Lord, you will begin to see how your desires line up with
God's desires.

What does this look like in everyday life? Start your morning with
thankfulness. Ask God to bless your day and for opportunities to be
a blessing to those you encounter. Interact with God about each
issue and problem you face. Thank Him for big and little blessings
that come your way. Seek His will and guidance when you make
plans. Pray for loved ones who don't know Christ and friends and
neighbors who need God's help. Remember that He is with you in
each and every moment.

Lord, I commit my whole heart to You—and all my
plans and ideas. I want Your will in my life. Thank
You for Your blessings and Your great love for me.
Show me how to delight in You, Lord. I love You.

WHAT IF I'M AFRAID?

"For I am the LORD your God who takes hold of your right hand and says to you, Do not fear; I will help you."

ISAIAH 41:13 NIV

If there is a scripture you need to have handy in times of trouble, this is it! Post it on your mirror, write it on a sticky note to tack up in your locker or on your laptop, commit it to memory so that the Spirit of God can bring it to mind when you need to hear it most.

Psalm 139 tells us that God created us and knows everything about us. He knows when we sit, when we get up, and He knows every word that's on our tongue before we speak it. Verses 7–10 tell us that no matter where we go, His hand will guide us and hold us. God tells us not to fear literally more than one hundred times in the Bible! Why? Because He is already there making sure that everything is going to work out according to His will (Romans 8:28).

Heading to the emergency room? Repeat Isaiah 41:13 and remember that God is holding your hand. Afraid of the future? Stop worrying and trust the God who loves you and has great plans for you. Facing a problem that you cannot possibly understand? Take hold of God's mighty hand and believe that He will help you.

God, help me resist fear. Take hold of my hand and guide me. I put my faith and trust in You alone.

WHAT IF I'M TEMPTED TO DO THE WRONG THING?

The temptations in your life are no different from what others experience. And God is faithful. He will not allow the temptation to be more than you can stand. When you are tempted, he will show you a way out so that you can endure.

1 CORINTHIANS 10:13 NLT

Is there a temptation in your life that is hard to get rid of? Temptation comes in all shapes and sizes, so what might be tempting to you isn't a problem for someone else. The opposite is also true.

It's so easy to get discouraged when we are tempted and then mess up. Especially when we're tempted by the same thing over and over again. Christopher Columbus said this: "I am a most noteworthy sinner, but I have cried out to the Lord for grace and mercy, and they have covered me completely. I have found the sweetest consolation since I made it my whole purpose to enjoy His marvelous presence."

Here's the encouraging thing: Whenever you face temptation, God promises to provide a way out. In every moment that you are tempted, look for it! Pay attention to the interruptions that occur during moments of temptation and cling to them. They may just be "divine appointments" leading the way out!

Dear God, help me find the way out of every temptation. Let me see Your faithfulness in these situations. Give me Your strength to resist and do the right thing.

DOES GOD UNDERSTAND ME?

For this reason Jesus had to be made like his brothers and sisters in every way so he could be their merciful and faithful high priest in service to God. Then Jesus could die in their place to take away their sins. And now he can help those who are tempted, because he himself suffered and was tempted.

HEBREWS 2:17–18 NCV

God chose to come to earth in human form to be made like us. To understand what it's like to be human. To be able to fully take our place and remove our sins. Because He was fully human while being fully God, He can help. He can comfort. The Bible says that He "comforts us in all our troubles, so that we can comfort those in any trouble with the comfort we ourselves receive from God" (2 Corinthians 1:4 NIV).

It's so encouraging that Jesus was just like us! Our God is not one who wants to remain as a distant high king, out of touch with the commoners. He wants a very personal relationship with each one of us. He lowered Himself to our level so that we could have personal and continual access to Him. His glory knows no bounds, yet He desires to be our friend. Take great comfort in that. He gets you!

God, thank You for the great gift of Your friendship and understanding. Allow me the opportunity to be a friend and comfort to those around me who are in need.

HOW CAN I BE LIKE JESUS ONLINE?

And now, dear brothers and sisters, one final thing.
Fix your thoughts on what is true, and honorable,
and right, and pure, and lovely, and admirable. Think
about things that are excellent and worthy of praise.

PHILIPPIANS 4:8 NLT

Negative and impure thoughts may cross our minds on a daily basis. Social media and TV don't help us out much in that area. Even Christian friends get sucked in and post thoughts and ideas online that make us cringe and hope our parents don't see!

Instead of getting caught up in online gossip and looking at stuff you shouldn't, make it your goal to be a light in what can be a very dark, negative place. Encourage good and right thinking. Comment, post, and share God's love with your friends as much as possible.

For the next month, why not plan to post, text, or write at least one encouraging comment every day? Post encouraging scripture, text a friend a note to make her smile, tweet your favorite quote, or post a happy photo on Instagram.

Before you participate in something online that you know you shouldn't, stop and fix your thoughts on what is true, right, and pure.

Father, help me regard social media as a mission field. Help me be an encouragement to everyone I communicate with online. Keep my eyes away from bad things and help me be like You.

WHAT IF I'M WORRIED?

"Come to me, all you who are weary and burdened, and I will give you rest. Take my yoke upon me and learn from me, for I am gentle and humble in heart, and you will find rest for your souls. For my yoke is easy and my burden is light."

MATTHEW 11:28–30 NIV

Jesus says, "Come to me." Just as He invited the little children to come to Him, Jesus calls us to bring all our burdens and lay them at His feet. He wants to help. He wants to take away the heavy load we're carrying in our hearts.

A yoke is a harness placed over an animal or team of animals for the purpose of dragging something behind or carrying heavy equipment. Jesus liked to use visual imagery to get His meaning across. Can't you just picture all the burdens you are carrying right now strapped to your back like an ox plowing a field? Now imagine yourself unloading each one onto Jesus' shoulders instead. Take a deep breath.

Jesus tells us many times throughout the Gospels not to worry. Worrying about something will never help you. Worry makes things worse and burdens seem larger. Worry clutters up your soul. Jesus wants us to find rest in Him. Hear His gentle words rush over you— "Come to me"—and you'll find rest for your soul.

Jesus, thank You for taking my burdens. I give them fully to You. Help me resist the urge to take them back! I want the rest and peace that You are offering.

WHAT IF I'M A CONTROL FREAK?

*"The LORD himself goes before you and will be
with you; he will never leave you nor forsake you.
Do not be afraid; do not be discouraged."*

DEUTERONOMY 31:8 NIV

How comforting and freeing when we allow God to go before us!
Stop and think about that for a moment: You can relinquish control of
your life and circumstances to the Lord Himself. Relax! His shoulders
are big enough to carry all your burdens. The Lord Himself goes
before you. The problem that has your stomach in knots right now?
Ask the Lord to go before you. The crisis that makes you wish you
could hide under the covers and sleep until it's all over? Trust that
God will never leave you and that He is working everything out.

Joshua 1:9 (NIV) tells us to "be strong and courageous. Do not
be afraid; do not be discouraged, for the LORD your God will be with
you wherever you go." Be encouraged! Even when it feels like it,
you are truly never alone.

If you've trusted Christ as your Savior, the Spirit of God Himself is
alive and well and working inside you at all times. What an astounding
miracle! The Creator of the universe dwells within you and is available
to help you make right choices on a moment-by-moment basis.

Thank You, Lord, for the incredible gift of Your presence
in each and every situation I face. Allow me to remember
this and to call upon Your name as I go about each day.
Forgive me for the times when I try to take control.

DAY 242

HOW CAN I GROW IN MY FAITH?

*Two people are better than one, because they get more
done by working together. If one falls down, the other
can help him up. But it is bad for the person who is alone
and falls, because no one is there to help. . . . A rope
that is woven of three strings is hard to break.*

ECCLESIASTES 4:9-10, 12 NCV

One way you can grow in your faith is to find a mentor. God uses
His people to encourage and strengthen one another. "As iron
sharpens iron, so a friend sharpens a friend" (Proverbs 27:17 NLT).
We get more accomplished in life when we are open to the help
and encouragement of others.

Ask the Lord to guide you in finding a "Three-String" mentor.
Look for a Christian woman with a strong faith in the Lord who is
willing to pray with you, encourage you in your faith, and be honest
with you about your strengths and weaknesses. Make it a priority to
meet together several times a month, and allow your mentor to ask
you some hard questions: Were you faithful to the Lord this week?
Did you gossip? Is there anything you're struggling with right now?
How can I pray for you?

With God, you, and a trusted Christian friend working together,
all three become a rope that is hard to break!

Father, thank You for using Your people to encourage
and sharpen me. Guide me as I seek a mentor who
will help me grow in my relationship with You.

DOES GOD REALLY CARE ABOUT ME?

*I look behind me and you're there, then up ahead and you're
there, too—your reassuring presence, coming and going.
This is too much, too wonderful—I can't take it all in!*

PSALM 139:5-6 MSG

How is it possible for God to care about my thoughts and feelings? Is
that how you feel sometimes? With billions of people to watch over,
how can He possibly know you?

The truth is, He *does* know you. He *does* care. He is the God of
the impossible (Luke 1:37), and He loves you beyond what your mind
can fully understand. He just does. It's a faith thing. Ephesians 3:20
(NKJV) tells us that God is able to do "exceedingly abundantly" more
than what we could ever ask or even think!

Caring about us personally is one of those things.

Think about the heavens, the stars, the universe, the brilliant
colors of the seasons, the miraculous way the human body works.
God is behind *all* of that. And yet the Bible tells us that He even
knows when a bird falls (Matthew 10:29)! And He cares more about
us than anything else in all creation. How is that even possible? What
is impossible to us, is possible with God (Luke 18:27)!

God, please open up my heart to You. I want to know You more
everyday. Give me eyes to see You and ears to hear You. Please
make my faith strong and help me believe that You really do
care about me more than anything else in all of creation.

AN ETERNAL PERSPECTIVE

Then He said to them all, "If anyone desires to come after Me,
let him deny himself, and take up his cross daily, and follow Me."
LUKE 9:23 NKJV

Evie walked slowly up from the school bus stop at the end of her
long driveway. She adjusted her heavy load of homework tucked into
her backpack that pulled hard on her left shoulder. As she entered
the house, she pushed the front door closed with her foot. "Mom,
I'm home," she announced.

"I'm in the kitchen," her mom, Yvette, called as she pulled the
oven door open to put a roast in. Evie's downcast face appeared
around the corner, and she slumped into the stool across from her
mom. "What is it, honey?"

"Over-the-top drama today, and it's so hard not to get sucked into
it. Some people will do anything to be popular. I'm not cool because
I was nice to a new kid today. Most of the girls aren't talking to me,
including Christy, who I thought was my best friend."

"Evie. . ." her mom began, but Evie interrupted her.

"Don't worry, Mom, I'm okay. It's hurtful, but you have taught
me to treat everyone with kindness and respect. I know it's more
important to please Christ over doing what my so-called friends want."

Her mother smiled as Evie continued. "Sure, I want to fit in and
be liked. Who doesn't? But when it comes down to it, the choices I
make today aren't just about today, they're eternal."

Heavenly Father, help me make choices that please You each
day. Remind me that my decisions can last an eternity. Amen.

FRIENDSHIPS BUILT TO LAST

A perverse person stirs up conflict,
and a gossip separates close friends.
PROVERBS 16:28 NIV

A good and trustworthy friend is one of the greatest treasures you'll ever find. When you have someone in your life—whether you've known them forever or it just feels like they have been there that long—it's easy to be yourself. True friends share a give-and-take relationship, offering unconditional love and support. You know they won't misjudge or hurt you. You can laugh, cry, and safely share the deepest secrets of your heart with one another.

Building a friendship that lasts isn't easy. The rough times you journey through together keep your relationship strong. It's important to connect with the people God desires you to have in your life—those who will help you grow stronger in your relationship with Him. Have you given God the opportunity to give you the friends He wants you to have?

God is your Friend too. He wants to mentor you and build a lasting friendship with you and those He puts in your life. Rely on His wisdom, and let Him help your friendships become everything you need them to be for a successful, balanced life.

God, help me evaluate the friendships I have. Show me which relationships are positive and good—the ones You want me to have. Lead me and guide me to be the best friend I can be to others, and help me choose my friends wisely. Amen.

DANCING FOR HIM

This is what the Lord says: "Don't let the wise boast in their wisdom, or the powerful boast in their power, or the rich boast in their riches. But those who wish to boast should boast in this alone: that they truly know me and understand that I am the Lord who demonstrates unfailing love and who brings justice and righteousness to the earth, and that I delight in these things."

JEREMIAH 9:23–24 NLT

"Dance competition is fierce," Tina commented to her friend Allyson as they walked back to the dressing rooms to prepare for their next round of competition.

"I know," Allyson replied, "sometimes I want to quit!"

Tina spun around to face her friend, stopping her abruptly in the hall. "Why would you say that?" she asked.

"Well," she began, "I get tired of the drama from other girls and their moms. They're always bragging on themselves and clucking around like puffed-up chickens. I don't dance so people will look at me."

Tina looked down, feeling a little convicted. "I can get caught up in that, and I know I shouldn't."

"When I dance, I try to remember my ability doesn't come from anything I've done. The Lord gave me that gift. Instead of being one of those 'Hey! Look at me!' kind of girls, I want others to see the Lord's blessing in me."

Lord, You have created me with many gifts, some
I haven't even opened yet. When I'm tempted to
become prideful in my own ability, help me remember
that I am here to point others to You. Amen.

EXPECT IT TO HAPPEN

Keep on being brave! It will bring you great rewards.
Learn to be patient, so that you will please God
and be given what he has promised.
HEBREWS 10:35–36 CEV

Grace was quiet. "Whatcha thinking about?" her dad asked as he turned the car away from their neighborhood and toward her school.

Grace took a deep breath and then let it out with a huff. "I asked God to help me with something, and it's taking a long time."

"Is it something I can help with?" her dad prodded, knowing she liked to work things out on her own.

"Nope! It's a thing at school. People stuff, ya know!"

"Well then, hold on to your faith and believe. Don't give up on what you've asked God for just because it doesn't happen as fast as you want it to happen. Sometimes what we ask for takes time to move the situation around, much like moving a physical mountain into the sea. And when it concerns the hearts of people, He often has to do a lot of work in their hearts first."

"I know, Dad. I'm just a little disappointed. You know it's hard for me to be patient." Grace finally smiled. "I'm not giving up though. I'll just keep believing."

. . . .

God, it's hard to wait for You to work out the details after I pray. Help me keep believing. I know You're working behind the scenes. The Bible says that You will give me the desires of my heart when I pray according to Your purposes and plan. Amen.

SET YOURSELF FREE

*"In a word, what I'm saying is, Grow up. You're kingdom
subjects. Now live like it. Live out your God-created
identity. Live generously and graciously toward
others, the way God lives toward you."*

MATTHEW 5:48 MSG

"Hey Carrie," her brother, Pete, said as she walked through the den.
No answer. "When are you going to give that up? I told you I didn't
break your phone on purpose!"

"Still giving your brother the silent treatment?" her mother asked.

"Yes," she replied angrily. "I'm cut off from the rest of the world
now. Who knows when I'll be able to get another phone."

"You know, your brother isn't the only one you're hurting by
refusing to forgive him. Refusing to forgive can eventually consume
you and destroy your relationships with everyone you care about.
I don't want you to wake up from this and find all you have left is
anger, hurt, and tears."

"I'm going to get a shower," she replied to avoid the response
she knew her mother wanted to hear. As the water poured over
her, she thought about her relationship with her brother, and with
God. She knew she needed to let it go. *"It's just a phone,"* she felt
the Lord whisper. "I know," she said aloud. She got out, put on a
bathrobe, wrapped her hair in a towel, and went to find her brother.

Heavenly Father, it's easy to hold on to anger and
hurt. I want to think I'm punishing the one I don't
want to forgive, but it really hurts me more. Give
me Your grace to let it go. Help me forgive. Amen.

THANKFULNESS FOR PROVISION AND OPPORTUNITY

Indolence wants it all and gets nothing; the energetic
have something to show for their lives.

PROVERBS 13:4 MSG

"Dad," Annie spoke up from the backseat of the car, "I don't get Labor Day. What's the point?" Her little brother, Jason, piped up, "We get out of school for it."

Dad glanced into the rearview mirror and caught Annie's gaze. "It's always the first Monday in September and was made into a holiday following the labor movement years ago. It was a time set aside for everyone to celebrate the social and economic achievements of American workers, especially the contributions workers made to the strength, success, and welfare of our country."

"So we're celebrating hard work and success as a country?" Annie asked.

"Yes," Dad continued, "and as Christ followers, we can also be thankful for the foundation God's Word provides to teach us the importance of hard work in the natural world and in the spiritual world. We thank God for providing everything we need, including the opportunity to earn a living and point others to God with honor and integrity."

God, thank You for giving me opportunities to live a
life for You. Teach me the importance of giving my all
in everything I do. Help me grow and learn a good and
godly work ethic in the natural and spiritual aspects
of my life. May all my efforts honor You. Amen.

YOUR HEART'S MIRROR

*Therefore, whether you eat or drink, or whatever
you do, do all to the glory of God.*
1 CORINTHIANS 10:31 NKJV

Elaine caught a glimpse of herself in the bathroom mirror. *Why do I
have to be so ugly?* she thought. She leaned into the mirror, examining
her freshly washed face. *Alyssa got the beautiful skin, the perfectly
shaped lips, and I got this—freckles and dry skin.*

She jumped suddenly when her older sister, Alyssa, popped her
head into the bathroom. "Sorry, didn't mean to scare you. Are you
going to be much longer," Alyssa inquired softly. "I'd like to get in
here and get a shower."

"I jumped because I thought I might have said what I was thinking
about you out loud."

"Oh yeah? And what were you thinking?" Alyssa said teasingly.

"Just the same ol' thing. You're beautiful and I'm not. I just feel
awkward."

"I know you don't want to hear this," Alyssa began, "but you
are beautiful inside and out. The heart of a person is really what
matters. When people see you—the ones who really want to take
a good look—they see the character and nature of God in you. His
light shines in all you do. That is more important than anything else."

Heavenly Father, I want to be a reflection of Your heart
in all that I do. When I become discouraged and am
tempted to see myself as the world sees me, remind
me of what You see. You created me and made me
who I am. I am beautiful in your sight. Amen.

GO FOR IT ALL

But you are a chosen people, a royal priesthood, a holy nation,
God's special possession, that you may declare the praises of him
who called you out of darkness into his wonderful light. Once
you were not a people, but now you are the people of God; once
you had not received mercy, but now you have received mercy.

1 PETER 2:9–10 NIV

Heidi closed her algebra book and tucked her completed assignment inside her folder before sticking both into her backpack. Her dad walked through the kitchen. "Honey, it's late. Why are you still up?"

"I just had to double-check my pre-algebra assignment. This has been a really hard unit, and I need all the homework points I can get before the final."

Her dad tousled her hair. "I admire your persistence to pursue your goals. I believe God will honor you for all your hard work and help you remember all the things you've learned."

"Can you believe I started with a tutor?" Heidi smiled sleepily. "I have good study habits so I can succeed now and into high school. Without the help of the Lord and encouragement from you and the rest of the family, I would not have gotten to this point. Now, I actually understand what I'm doing—I'm doing math!"

. . . .

Lord, You have given me everything I need to succeed.
I have the mind of Christ and Your ability on my flesh to
accomplish great things. Thank You for wisdom and tenacity
to set goals and achieve them with Your help. Amen.

PROTECT YOUR REPUTATION

*Those who are dominated by the sinful nature think
about sinful things, but those who are controlled by the
Holy Spirit think about things that please the Spirit. . . .
Therefore, dear brothers and sisters, you have no obligation
to do what your sinful nature urges you to do.*

ROMANS 8:5, 12 NLT

Perhaps you have heard the expression "His name is 'Mudd.'"
Surprisingly, it doesn't have anything to do with someone's name
or reputation being dragged through dirt as you might suppose.
Instead, the phrase comes from the circumstances surrounding
a man involved in the life of John Wilkes Booth, the assassin of
President Abraham Lincoln in 1865.

Dr. Samuel A. Mudd went to prison for not reporting his patient's
location after he set Booth's broken leg. The authorities felt Dr.
Mudd misled them by not reporting Booth's location after treating
his injuries. Although President Andrew Johnson pardoned Dr. Mudd
in 1869, his reputation was lost to many.

Honesty, integrity, and trust are characteristics of a person
with honor and a good reputation. Each decision you make is an
opportunity to demonstrate the person God created you to be. Your
choices reflect a picture of your true relationship with God. Within
the quiet moments you share with God, you grow in your faith and
discover His strength to do what is right when character is tested.

God, instill in me a hunger to know You more. Help me grow
in my faith. Let my decisions and choices I make each day
speak loudly of who You desire me to become. Amen.

COMPETITION ISN'T FRIENDLY

*Then I realized that we work and do wonderful things
just because we are jealous of others. . . . For example,
some people don't have friends or family. But they are
never satisfied with what they own, and they never stop
working to get more. They should ask themselves, "Why
am I always working to have more? Who will get what I
leave behind?" What a senseless and miserable life!*

ECCLESIASTES 4:4, 8 CEV

Jenny shut her locker door and turned to see her friend Meagan waving at her with something in her hand. "Jenny! Look what I got," she called as she half ran, half walked down the crowded hallway. *Oh great,* Jenny thought, *another gadget she doesn't need,* as she tried to offer a smile for her excited friend.

As Meagan chatted excitedly, Jenny's mind wandered. *Meagan is always trying to impress people with the things money can buy.* Jenny didn't resent Meagan for having things, but Meagan always had to one-up everyone else. It drove Meagan nuts when someone had something better.

Jenny remembered a conversation she had with her grandmother about King Solomon. "When someone is always trying to outdo someone else, it eventually leads to unfriendly competition," her grandma had told her.

"I'm so happy for you, Meagan," Jenny said—and she really meant it. She slid her arm through her friend's, and they walked together to class.

Lord, help me avoid jealousy when others have
something I want. Help me be truly happy for them
and remember that it's not a competition. Amen.

LOVE—THE GREATEST LAW OF ALL

Love never hurts a neighbor, so loving is obeying all the law.
ROMANS 13:10 NCV

Gretchen's six-year-old little bother, Tyler, was full of questions about the Bible since his Sunday school class began a study on the Ten Commandments. "So why does God have so many rules, Gretchen," he asked. "And how am I s'pose to remember them all?"

"You don't have to think about it like that," Gretchen said softly. "God promises to love us whether we do good or bad. What you do or don't do doesn't make Him love you any more or less."

"Then why all the rules?" Tyler asked.

"God wants us to know what makes Him really happy—like those things listed in the Ten Commandments. The most important thing to remember is, God loves you no matter what—and He wants you to love others—no matter what."

"Even mean people?"

"Yes, even them. When you choose to love others, God will help you have love for them. God doesn't say to let them hurt you or put yourself in danger. Mom and Dad don't want that either. But maybe when you're nice to the mean people, it will help their hearts soften and maybe want to know God."

"What if I can't love them?" Tyler asked.

"Then you can pray and ask God to help you love them, and He will."

. . . .

Thank You, God, for loving me no matter what. Thank You for pouring Your love into my heart and helping me love others—even those who aren't so nice to me. Amen.

TAKE GOD AT HIS WORD

God means what he says. What he says goes. His powerful
Word is sharp as a surgeon's scalpel, cutting through
everything, whether doubt or defense, laying us open
to listen and obey. Nothing and no one can resist God's
Word. We can't get away from it—no matter what.
HEBREWS 4:12-13 MSG

Deedra sat on the front steps of her house with her chin resting in her hands. *I won't cry this time,* she thought to herself, but as the minutes passed without her father in sight, she felt the lump in her throat rise higher. The tears came slowly and without sound.

Her friend Kylie sat down. "Waiting on your dad again?" she asked softly. Deedra nodded. "I'm sorry he didn't show," Kylie continued.

"You'd think I'd be used to it. It's the third time he promised he'd visit, and again, nothing!"

"You know what?" Kyle asked with a big smile on her face. "Now that you're God's child, you have a heavenly Father who always keeps His promises. In His book, the Bible, you can read all about His promises to love you and never leave you. He'll be with you and me both, always!"

"Yes, you are right," Deedra said. "I am learning about God and His promises for my life. He tells it like it is. He's always here for me."

God, when others disappoint me for whatever reason,
help me lean on You. Give me strength to forgive those
who hurt me—whether on purpose or unintentionally.
Thank You for always keeping all Your promises. Amen.

GOD'S DEFINITION OF BEAUTY

Do not let your adornment be merely outward—arranging the hair, wearing gold, or putting on fine apparel—rather let it be the hidden person of the heart, with the incorruptible beauty of a gentle and quiet spirit, which is very precious in the sight of God.

1 PETER 3:3-4 NKJV

The pages of the Bible tell the stories of beautiful people—those perceived as internally beautiful by God and those considered externally beautiful by others. The prophet Samuel wanted to name Jesse's strongest, best-looking son as king, but he was not God's choice. Instead, the scrawny son that slept with the sheep was God's choice because he had a heart after God.

The apostle Peter, in today's verse, is not saying it is wrong to dress up, fix your hair, and wear nice things, but that is not where God looks for beauty. He sees you from the inside out. He knows what you're made of and the attitudes of your heart.

Inner beauty is about the actions someone takes to develop the qualities that God admires. Those with this inner beauty demonstrate acts of unconditional love for God and others: mercy, kindness, gentleness, and patience. They are peacemakers, quick to forgive and keep their hearts pure.

God, You created me and made me lovely. I pray my heart is filled with love, compassion, goodness, and all the other things You admire. Let me become the person who has a heart like Yours. May I live my life from the inside out. Amen.

FOLLOW THE LEADER

*"The one who sent me is with me; he has not left
me alone, for I always do what pleases him."*

JOHN 8:29 NIV

"Do you always do what your parents want you to do?" Tara asked. "Just ask them to drop you at the mall, and then my sister will pick us up and take us to the party. They never have to know."

Lydia held her phone to her ear, listening and trying to decide what to do. Sensing her friend's hesitance, Tara pressed. "Everyone is going to be there. You have to go."

"It's time for dinner," Lydia's mother called from the dining room. "You kids wash up."

"I've got to eat dinner with my family," Lydia reported to Tara as she ended the call.

Lydia sat through dinner with a knot in her stomach. Even if her parents didn't find out, she would know the truth. She made a commitment years ago to follow Jesus. The knot in her stomach would only go away if she followed Him.

After dinner, she texted Tara. I CAN'T LIE TO MY PARENTS. I WON'T BREAK THE TRUST THEY HAVE IN ME. After a few texts in reply from a disappointed Tara, she went into the kitchen to help her mom with the dishes.

Jesus, thank You for setting the right example for me to follow. Help me always choose truth, even when it means rejection from others. I value my relationship with You above anything else. Amen.

LETTING GO OF RESENTMENT

*"But when you are praying, first forgive anyone
you are holding a grudge against, so that your
Father in heaven will forgive your sins, too."*

MARK 11:25 NLT

Hannah slid into the backseat of her mother's car. Normally a chatterbox recounting the events of the day, she was quiet.

"Tough day at school?" her mom asked as she made eye contact with her in the rearview mirror. She could see tears forming in her daughter's eyes. "Oh honey, I'm sorry," she said as she pulled out of the school parking lot.

"It was awful," Hannah choked out. "I don't want to talk about it."

"That's understandable," her mother said. "You're hurt and probably resent the person or persons who caused you pain. The important thing is to pray about it, give it to God, and let it go. Holding on to the hurt or carrying a grudge doesn't hurt them, but it poisons you. Eventually you're going to have to talk to the Lord about it."

"I know," Hannah said softly. "I have to let go of the anger and the desire to get back at them first. It's going to take some work on my part to let go. The Lord will help me when I'm ready."

Lord, it's only natural to want others to pay for the pain
they have caused. That's not Your way. Help me let go of
the anger and hurt. I choose to give it to You now. Give
me the mercy I need to let it go so that I can be free
from the poisonous residue of resentment. Amen.

WHEN YOU DON'T FEEL FAVORED

If you treat one person as being more important than another,
you are sinning. You are guilty of breaking God's law.
JAMES 2:9 NCV

Shelby saw the package on the front porch as they pulled into the driveway. "My gift from Aunt Sue!" she shouted. She pulled her backpack from the car and rushed to pick up the big box. She knew what was inside—her painting—the gift Aunt Sue made for each great-niece or -nephew on their thirteenth birthday.

Aunt Sue, an exceptional artist, had created a beautiful piece of art for Shelby's older sister, Pamela, three years ago on her thirteenth birthday and for their cousin Max on his as well. It was a tradition she'd started with the two oldest that she said she would continue with the rest.

Shelby lifted the box that held the precious canvas, carried it into the house, and placed it on the kitchen table. She very carefully opened the box after cutting away the thick tape. Her eyes fell on the canvas and her heart sank. Max's and Pamela's paintings were tailored to their personalities and favorite colors, but Shelby's gift was generic and could in no way be compared to the gifts her sister and cousin received.

Mom put her arm around Shelby, "I'm sorry you're disappointed. It is a beautiful gift—just less than what you expected."

- -

God, thank You for loving me unconditionally and
favoring me. Help me to love others unconditionally
and to forgive when others show favoritism. Amen.

STANDING TALL

*Be brave and strong! Don't be afraid of the nations on the
other side of the Jordan. The LORD your God will always
be at your side, and he will never abandon you.*

DEUTERONOMY 31:6 CEV

Janna noticed Veronica picking on Cassandra. It wasn't obvious to
anyone else, but Janna had been the recipient of Veronica's bullying
last year. A group began to form around Cassandra's locker, blocking
her way of escape. Janna could hear Veronica's taunts. By the time
Janna stepped into the semicircle, Veronica had pushed Cassandra,
and her books fell to the floor.

Janna took a deep breath and said in a voice as loud as she could,
"I think that's enough, Veronica!" She slipped in between the two
girls and tried to appear taller than she was.

Veronica frowned, "Are you sure you want to get involved? This
has nothing to do with you."

"Consider me involved," Janna said. "I'm not afraid of you anymore,
and I won't let you treat other people like you treated me before."

The bell rang. Veronica made a face and stormed off as the rest
of the crowd disappeared. "Thank you," Cassandra whispered as she
and Janna picked up her books together.

Janna smiled. "It makes standing up to a bully easier when you
don't have to go it alone."

God, thank You for being on my side. No matter what
I face in life, You are with me. Give me courage to
stand tall in the face of adversity and respond with
Your wisdom in each situation I face. Amen.

ASKING FOR HELP

"If you ask for anything in my name, I will do it for you so that the Father's glory will be shown through the Son. If you ask me for anything in my name, I will do it."

JOHN 14:13–14 NCV

It was getting late and dinner was not even close to ready. Shara wanted to cook a meal on her own. She had browned the roast in the skillet like she'd watched her mother do many times, and then put it into the slow cooker, but she'd gotten a late start on the vegetables. She had the carrots cut up, but the potatoes were taking too long to peel.

Shara's mom stuck her head into the kitchen. "Are you doing okay?" she asked.

Shara stopped for a minute. She wanted to tell her mom that she had everything under control, but that would have been a lie. "I wanted so badly to do this on my own, but I didn't realize how long the vegetables would take. So yes, I do need some help!"

"People like to help—they're just waiting to be asked." Her mother smiled and winked.

. . . .

Lord, I don't like to ask for help. I want to be independent, but I need to learn to rely on others—and on You too. There are things I just can't do by myself. Show me who I should ask for help. Also, help me appreciate their assistance and not take it for granted. Amen.

DAY 262

PRAYER—THE OPEN DOOR

Make this your common practice: Confess your sins to each other and pray for each other so that you can live together whole and healed. The prayer of a person living right with God is something powerful to be reckoned with.

JAMES 5:16 MSG

She'd hit Snooze too many times. Madalyn rushed to get ready for school. Suddenly her grandmother's words flooded her mind: *"God wants you to share your life with Him. Time in prayer is the open door to a relationship with Him. Don't forget to invite Him in!"*

Oh, I miss Grandma so much, she thought as she pulled on her clothes and tied her shoes. Many mornings she'd woken up to find her grandmother kneeling at the side of her freshly made bed, speaking to God about the things she was thankful for and the things that concerned her. Grandma taught her how to really talk to God simply by her own example.

Madalyn found that her own conversations with God contained the power to transform her heart, once filled with anger and resentment, and to make lasting changes in her life. As she invited the Holy Spirit to make God's Word real to her, she began to know Him in a tangible way.

She grabbed a breakfast bar and a banana and headed out to the bus stop a little early. She wanted to make sure she had several minutes alone with God since she'd started the day late.

Heavenly Father, thank You for always having time for me. Today I invite You to share in my life. May I never be too busy for You. Amen.

EXTENDED FAMILY

*Let us consider one another in order to stir up love and good
works, not forsaking the assembling of ourselves together,
as is the manner of some, but exhorting one another, and
so much the more as you see the Day approaching.*
HEBREWS 10:24–25 NKJV

"Sometimes church gives me a charge. It's like plugging my spirit
into a charger and powering up for the week," Rylie commented
to her younger sister, Emma, as she sat down at the kitchen table
to help her do her homework.

Dad rinsed out his coffee cup in the sink and chimed in to the
conversation. "I try to go to church expecting God to respond to
our faith. It's about the family of God living, learning, and growing
together. I also experience strength from a faith shared with others.
As believers come together, they grow in every area of their life."

"They are like our second family—our church family," Emma said.

"Yes," Rylie agreed, "just like we help each other in our natural
family. Our faith family encourages us to learn, live, and grow our
faith."

Lord, thank You for my church family. Help me
develop positive relationships with people who
love You and love me. Give me wisdom in how I
can encourage others as I grow in my faith. Amen.

GUARD YOUR GATES

Don't you know that you yourselves are God's temple and
that God's Spirit dwells in your midst? If anyone destroys
God's temple, God will destroy that person; for God's
temple is sacred, and you together are that temple.

1 CORINTHIANS 3:16–17 NIV

Halfway into their conversation, Hope realized her friend Bailey wasn't listening. "Hey, you're not listening to me. What's up?" she asked.

"I'm sorry," Bailey replied. "I've been distracted since I watched that horror movie the other night. I shouldn't have watched it, but I did it anyway."

"Oh," Hope said, "I did that once. It is awful to have those images stuck in your head."

"I convinced myself it wouldn't bother me, but I was so wrong. So what did you do?" Bailey asked.

"I asked God to forgive me for not guarding my heart. We choose what passes through our eyes, ears, and mouths. These are the 'gates' to our thoughts, which impacts the condition of our heart. Then I asked God to help me remove those thoughts and images. I deliberately replaced them with positive ones through prayer, reading the Bible, and I even saw another movie that built hope instead of fear into my thoughts."

"That's good advice!" Bailey said.

. . . .

Lord, thank You for reminding me that my spirit
and mind respond to what I choose to put into
them. Help me choose wisely what I allow to pass
through the gates that protect my heart. Amen.

ARE YOU LISTENING?

"'For this people's heart has become calloused; they hardly hear with their ears, and they have closed their eyes. Otherwise they might see with their eyes, hear with their ears, understand with their hearts and turn, and I would heal them.' But blessed are your eyes because they see, and your ears because they hear."

MATTHEW 13:15–16 NIV

Leann sat down in the swing on Grandma's front porch. She enjoyed the moments she had alone with her grandmother and the quietness of their ranch home that sat a distance back from the main country road. Grandma sat next to her. She took a sip of her hot tea, closed her eyes, and breathed in the fresh, midmorning air. "Are you listening?" she asked her granddaughter.

Leann tilted her head back and squinted her eyes to catch a glimpse of the sun as it slid behind the clouds. The birds were singing. She heard the chatter of two little squirrels chasing each other up and down the tree next to the house.

"Listening is a discipline," Grandma encouraged. "It requires self-control and a desire to hear instead of to be heard. The art of listening helps you interpret your world, understand others, and have a powerful relationship with God."

"Yes, Grandma, I'm learning. The question you asked me comes back to my mind often: 'How can we expect to hear God, who we can't see, when we can't even hear the people in our lives we can see?' "

God, I want to hear You. I take time today to give You my undivided attention. Teach me to listen to You and to others today. Amen.

WHEN YOU'RE SINKING

Peter replied, "Lord, if it is really you, tell me to come to you on the water." "Come on!" Jesus said. Peter then got out of the boat and started walking on the water toward him. But when Peter saw how strong the wind was, he was afraid and started sinking. "Save me, Lord!" he shouted. Right away, Jesus reached out his hand.

MATTHEW 14:28–31 CEV

Fitting in at a new school really mattered to Melissa. She desperately wanted to make friends. When a few of the "cool" kids invited her to have lunch at their table, she hoped it was a good sign.

Melissa excitedly answered their questions about herself and listened intently to their conversation. A red flag went up in her heart as the conversation shifted to what had happened the previous weekend at Jason's house while his parents were out of town. "It was a sweet party, Melissa," Jason bragged. "Maybe you can come to the next one."

She smiled shyly and nodded, but her heart raced. *This is not the type of cool kids my parents would approve of me spending time with. I don't want to lie to my parents in order to go to parties.*

As she exited the lunchroom and stopped by her locker to grab her notebook before her next class, she felt herself sinking. *Lord, save me,* she prayed.

. . . .

Lord, You are faithful to pull me from the raging storm and bring me back to safety. When I'm tempted to compromise Your truth, reach in and rescue me. I trust You! Amen.

TIME FOR GOODBYE

*Then David tore his clothes to show his
sorrow, and all the men with him did also.*
2 SAMUEL 1:11 NCV

Margo walked slowly across the parking lot toward her brother's car.
She didn't want to go home. She was numb. She didn't want to face
the grief in her own heart or on the faces of her family members.
The words *Grandpa is gone* played over and over in her head, growing
louder and louder with each step.

She felt a hand on her shoulder. "Hey! I've tried to catch up with
you all day. What is going on?" Rachel stopped short when she saw
the tears sliding quietly down Margo's face.

"Grandpa's dead," she said. *There, I said it,* she thought.

"Oh Margo! I'm so sorry. I have no words. I'll just wait with you
for your brother to get out of class."

Margo nodded, and Rachel took it as a yes. Then Margo began
to talk about her grandpa through her choking sobs and tears. "It's
not any easier to accept just because we knew he was really sick.
We knew it was going to happen, but I am not ready. Knowing he's
in heaven and that I'll someday see him again doesn't make the pain
of not having him here go away."

· ·

Lord, help me process my emotions and grief in a healthy way.
Help me let go of the pain and embrace Your comfort and
strength. Remind me that I don't have to grieve alone. Amen.

GOD FIRST

But many believed in Jesus, even many of the leaders. But because of the Pharisees, they did not say they believed in him for fear they would be put out of the synagogue. They loved praise from people more than praise from God.

JOHN 12:42–43 NCV

"Everyone wants to be liked," Natalie quipped as she followed her friend Dave to a spot on the bleachers to watch the volleyball game. "We want to feel loved, valued, and accepted by others. So what if we do things sometimes to get people to like us?"

"But why should we have to 'do' stuff to make them like us? Shouldn't they just like us for who we are?" David argued. "I don't want to trade my relationship with God for friends and popularity."

"So you'd rather just be unpopular?" Natalie smirked.

"I hope I would choose to be unpopular rather than go against what I say I believe. It's like I have to pretend to be someone I'm not in order to fit into the popular crowd. I don't want to compromise. I want to believe that those who are truly my friends will accept me and my desire to do things God's way."

- -

God, I want to have lots of friends. I want to fit in and be a part of the popular group. Help me always choose pleasing You over pleasing others. Help me choose good friends who share my faith and understand my choices for You. Amen.

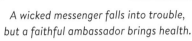

TALKING IT OUT

A wicked messenger falls into trouble,
but a faithful ambassador brings health.
PROVERBS 13:17 NKJV

"It's so complicated," Lydia said in exasperation. "At first I thought living in a blended family would be terrible, but I don't think they are better or worse than any other families—just different."

"How so?" Olivia asked.

"There are just so many people involved. When my mom and stepdad make a decision, they try to consider how it will impact each person. How it will make them feel and if there are things they should talk with anyone about in order to avoid hurt feelings."

"So I imagine it's a real challenge to keep everyone straight. And what about having two houses—your mom's and your dad's?"

"Yes, that can get sticky too. Mom and Dad have different expectations and different rules. I can do some things at Dad's that I can't do at Mom's, and vice versa," Lydia explained. "My mom and dad have worked really hard to hear me and my brother, Michael, out. They listen when we have problems—but that wasn't the way it was at first. We had to learn to talk it out. It took a lot of effort on our part to hear what our parents were saying and for them to really listen to us. In the beginning I did a lot of crying and praying."

Lord, help me understand the dynamics of a blended family. Teach me how to express my feelings in a positive way that will help me and my family grow in You. Amen.

TALK THE TRUTH

"A good man brings good things out of the good stored up in his heart, and an evil man brings evil things out of the evil stored up in his heart. For the mouth speaks what the heart is full of."

LUKE 6:45 NIV

Jessica caught a glimpse of her older brother, Cole, standing in front of the mirror talking to himself. "Are you practicing for a speech?" she asked.

"Nope," Cole smiled. "I'm telling myself the truth. I'm talking to myself about who God says I am."

Jessica shot him a curious look. "How do you do that?"

"I find Bible verses that describe who I am in Christ and then say them to myself."

"Okay. Let's see." Jessica stepped back and watched as her brother began to recite Bible verses.

"In Christ, I am more than a conqueror," Cole began. "I can do all things through Christ who strengthens me." Cole paused between each statement as if he was letting the truth of God's Word sink into his heart and mind.

Jessica glanced at the piece of paper in front of him and saw that each statement on it referenced a Bible verse. Over the weeks that followed, she began to see some little changes in her brother's words and actions. "Hey," she asked him, "could I get a copy of your list of truths too?"

Heavenly Father, thank You for teaching me who I am in Christ. Help me speak only the truth. Remind me to agree with You in who You say I am and who You want me to become. May I grow in Your truth each day. Amen.

A PROMISE IS A PROMISE

Then Moses summoned the leaders of the tribes of Israel and told them, "This is what the LORD has commanded: A man who makes a vow to the LORD or makes a pledge under oath must never break it. He must do exactly what he said he would do."

NUMBERS 30:1–2 NLT

I GOT FREE TICKETS FOR US TO SEE THE MOVIE IN 3-D. Jill texted.

I CAN'T GO. I'M BABYSITTING. Susanna replied.

CAN'T YOU JUST TELL THEM SOMETHING CAME UP? WE HAVE TO USE THE TICKETS TODAY.

NO! I MADE A PROMISE AND I'M KEEPING IT. Susanna texted again. I GAVE MY WORD. IF I START BREAKING PROMISES NOW, NO ONE WILL TRUST ME TO DO WHAT I SAY. I'M SURE SOMEONE ELSE WOULD LOVE TO GO WITH YOU. SORRY I HAVE TO MISS IT.

Jill replied with a sad face emoticon.

Susanna's mother had grown up with lots of promises that were seldom kept. Because of that, Susanna knew what it was like to have parents who kept their promises. She'd seen friends who hoped and expected only to have their dreams dashed by people who didn't keep their promises. She found Christ also kept His promises. She stayed determined to consider her commitments before making them and then, once made, keeping them no matter what.

God, You are the ultimate promise keeper. Thank You for teaching me how important it is for people to be able to trust that I keep my commitments. Give me wisdom in which promises to make and then help me keep them. Amen.

LIFT YOUR VOICE

My dear friends, you always obeyed when I was with you. Now that I am away, you should obey even more. So work with fear and trembling to discover what it really means to be saved. God is working in you to make you willing and able to obey him.

PHILIPPIANS 2:12–13 CEV

"Seems like there is a lot of talk on TV about what you can and can't do at See You at the Pole," Karen commented quietly to a small group in her fifth-period class.

"Not necessarily," Chad commented. "Teachers and employees of the school district have gotten in trouble for sharing their faith, but as students, we have the freedom to plan it. SYATP is specifically designed as a student-led, student-initiated movement of prayer. It's all about us praying together."

"Right," Carlson chimed in. "It can't be left up to youth pastors or teachers. We have to plan it, let our administration know we want to do it, advertise it, and then lead it."

"It's a great opportunity to speak life into our school using the Word of God. We can really have a say in what happens as we take our place as spiritual leaders on our campus. We need to have strong spiritual student leaders who are willing to take a stand."

See You at the Pole is just one example of how you, as a young person, can own your faith. Making a difference starts with you using your gifts and talents right where you are.

Lord, give me courage to take a stand. Give me the words to boldly declare Your will, Your purpose, and Your plans for my school or wherever else You may place me. Amen.

SO VERY TALENTED

*For we are His workmanship, created in Christ
Jesus for good works, which God prepared
beforehand that we should walk in them.*

EPHESIANS 2:10 NKJV

It seemed hard sometimes for Becca to find her place. She wasn't the oldest, nor the youngest—she was the middle child. She wanted to know who she was and how she could set herself apart from everyone else. *"I'm the middle—average. It's so easy to get lost when everything is mediocre. I'll never be better or worse, but just okay,"* she wrote in her journal.

Becca liked to escape into the little gathering of trees at the edge of her family's property. The little sliver of woods had a creek that ran through it. She liked to sit on a rock near the edge and write poetry for hours.

A teacher had taken an interest in Becca's writing and encouraged her to do more. One afternoon, her teacher pulled her aside. "Becca, I hope you don't mind, but I submitted a couple of your poems to a company looking for teen writing talent. I have a letter here requesting permission to print two of them in an upcoming book. Your talent for writing is really developing."

Becca's heart leaped. She had found her passion, and a gift God had given her was starting to take shape.

God, You created me on purpose. You filled me with passion and have given me gifts that will bring You glory. Show me how to open those gifts and use them to please You. Amen.

DAY 274

WHY GOD HAS RULES

Love the LORD your God and keep his requirements,
his decrees, his laws and his commands always.
DEUTERONOMY 11:1 NIV

Sometimes our parents give us rules we don't understand. It may seem like they don't want us to grow up or they're keeping us from having any fun. But the truth is, parents have rules for their children because of love.

When Mom says not to play in the busy street, it's because she doesn't want her daughter to get hurt by a careless driver. When Dad won't allow his daughter to see a certain movie, it's often because he wants to protect her mind from things that might steal her innocence and joy.

God is the same way. He loves His children with His whole heart. He didn't give us a bunch of strict rules to keep us from being happy. His laws do the opposite: They make it possible for us to live a truly joy-filled life. God's rules are set in place to keep us from sin's harmful effects.

If we disobey our parents and play in the busy street, our bodies could be seriously injured. If we disobey God's rules, our spirits can be badly wounded, and sometimes it takes a long time to heal. Because God cares about us so deeply, He wants to keep us safe from harm.

Dear Father, I know Your rules are there to
keep me safe. Help me love You and obey You
always, even when I don't understand. Amen.

AVOIDING SETBACKS

Observe therefore all the commands I am giving you today, so that you may have the strength to go in and take over the land that you are crossing the Jordan to possess, and so that you may live long in the land that the LORD swore to your ancestors to give to them and their descendants, a land flowing with milk and honey.

DEUTERONOMY 11:8–9 NIV

Mistakes set us back. They make us tired and wear us out trying to fix them. For example, if we refuse to study for a test because we'd rather play with our friends, we may fail the test. Then, our grade average is lower, and we have to work a long time to get the grade back to where it should be. Refusal to study was a mistake. It would have been much better to study for the test in the first place.

God wants our lives to be full of joy and peace. He wants us to move forward instead of always having to go back and clean up our messes. He knows if we don't do the right things, we'll mess up and have to work hard to fix our mistakes. But when we obey God's commands, we get things right the first time, and we avoid the hassle of cleaning up the mess we made. Our lives are better, we feel stronger, and we have more joy when we obey God.

Dear Father, I know You are leading me to a beautiful place. Help me follow You and not get sidetracked with things that don't please You. Amen.

GOD HELPS ME

"This is what the LORD says—he who made you, who formed you in the womb, and who will help you: Do not be afraid. . .for I will pour water on the thirsty land, and streams on the dry ground."

ISAIAH 44:2–3 NIV

Every day there are new things to worry about. No matter how old we get or how many things we live through, there will always be something new to bring us stress and anxiety. Whether it's a test in school or mean people or financial troubles at home, life just brings trouble.

But there's good news! God loves us more than we can imagine. He made us, and we belong to Him. He will never let the child He loves, the one He created, go without His help. With every breath He adores us, and He promises to take care of us.

When we ask Him for help, He is there. He doesn't always take away our problems, but He helps us through them. He gives us wisdom and strength to know how to face each hard thing as it comes. When He pours out His wisdom, we can soak it up, like water on dry ground. Then we'll feel nourished and refreshed to face whatever may come.

Dear Father, I'm so glad You always help me when I ask. Please give me wisdom and strength to handle the problems I face right now. I need Your help. Amen.

FEAR AND HOPE

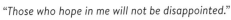

"Those who hope in me will not be disappointed."
ISAIAH 49:23 NIV

Hope and fear are polar opposites. While fear is the belief that something bad will happen, hope is the assurance that something good will happen. God wants us to have hope.

Many people allow fear to control them. They don't try new things because they're afraid of failure. They don't reach out to others or try to make new friends because they're afraid of rejection. But with God, we don't need to be afraid. We don't have to live that way.

God loves us more than we can ever understand, and He wants good things for us. In fact, He's already planned beautiful things for each of us, right now, today. We can enter each situation without fear. We can live each moment with hope, knowing exciting, happy things await us each and every day.

When we believe with our whole hearts that God wants good things for us, we won't be disappointed. He wants us to trust Him, and when we do, He surprises us with joy and peace and blessings we never thought possible. Next time we find ourselves feeling afraid, we can remember that fear is the opposite of hope. With God, there is always the promise of good things to come.

Dear Father, thank You for teaching me the difference between hope and fear. Help me to never be afraid. I want to live in hope, knowing You have good things in store for me. Amen.

HANG IN THERE

"When you pass through the waters, I will be with you; and when you pass through the rivers, they will not sweep over you."

ISAIAH 43:2 NIV

Life is full of ups and downs, highs and lows. There will be times of intense joy. There will be times of great sorrow. And there will be many, many in-between times.

When we go through low times, the times when the pain and tears are more than we can handle, we can hold on to Isaiah 43:2. God will not let those difficult times be the end of the story. As long as we trust Him, He will bring us safely through to a better place.

In that way, life is a little bit like a roller coaster. It dips low only to rise high again. Our lives will have their low points, for certain. But when we pass through those times, we can breathe deeply and cling to our heavenly Father. He will hold us, comfort us, and keep us safe during the most difficult times. And He will eventually bring us out of the valley to a high place of joy and peace again.

Dear Father, when life gets hard, sometimes it feels like it will never get better. During those times, I cry. I get angry. I just want to run away and hide. But I know You won't leave me alone in those times. I know You'll stay with me, and one of these days I'll feel happy again. Thank You for Your love and Your promise of good things to come. Amen.

PLEASANT MEMORIES

*"Forget the former things; do not dwell on the past. . . .
Now it springs up; do you not perceive it? I am making
a way in the wilderness and streams in the wasteland."*

ISAIAH 43:18–19 NIV

It's fun to think about pleasant memories. God gave us our memories as a gift, to remind us how He's shown His love in the past. While it's good to remember the sweet things, sometimes we let our memories control our feelings in a bad way.

If we're not careful, we can feel sad about the past. We forget to be thankful for the good things we have today. Other times, we remember good things from our pasts and we think things will never be that good again. It's wrong to allow our feelings about the past, whether good or bad, to control the way we act and feel today.

The truth is, no matter how pleasant or horrible something may have been, it's gone. We can't change it, and we can't get it back. God wants to do some pretty amazing things in our lives today and every day to come. So while it's okay to smile at sweet memories, we need to spend more time living for God today and thinking about the beautiful future we have in Him.

Dear Father, thank You for my past, for it has helped make me who I am today. Remind me to focus on You, not on things I can't change. Thank You for my beautiful future. Amen.

HIS LOVE NEVER FAILS

"Though the mountains be shaken and the hills be removed, yet my unfailing love for you will not be shaken nor my covenant of peace be removed," says the LORD, who has compassion on you.

ISAIAH 54:10 NIV

In the course of our lives, lots of stuff happens. Wars break out. Disasters occur. People die and people are born. Things are constantly changing. And for most of us, change can be unsettling.

But in the midst of the chaos, in the center of all the change is one thing we can always, always count on: God's love. He is love, and He can never be anything different. He adores us, and that love will never be altered. Though our circumstances may be difficult, He loves us. Though it may feel like He's forgotten us, He hasn't. He sees everything we go through, and He is actively working to make us better people and to take us to a better place.

Remember, nothing lasts forever except God and our relationship with Him. No matter how hard things seem at the moment, our circumstances aren't permanent. We'll survive. We'll get through them. But through it all, God's love will never fail, and it will never change.

Dear Father, thank You for Your unfailing, unchanging love. When things get crazy and it seems like You've forgotten me, remind me. Help me hold on to Your faithfulness when there's nothing else to hold on to. I love You. Amen.

DAY 281

TREES APPLAUD

"You will go out in joy and be led forth in peace; the mountains and hills will burst into song before you, and all the trees of the field will clap their hands."

ISAIAH 55:12 NIV

Today's verse almost sounds like an animated cartoon movie. Birds sing. Forest animals dance. Even the trees wave and clap in delight—all for you, God's child.

But what God wants for His children is even better than a make-believe movie. Every day, in countless ways, He pours out reminders of His love for us. He sends beautiful flowers in spring, gorgeous bright leaves in fall, snow-capped mountains in winter, and crystal-cool waters in the summer. He gives us pets to love and care for, friends to laugh with, and He provides the things we need each day.

Unfortunately, we can get distracted with things that shouldn't matter much, like wondering if we look right or if we're popular or smart enough. God doesn't want us to worry about those things; instead, He says, *"Slow down! Enjoy the good things I've given you that are right in front of you!"*

God wants us to have hearts filled with joy, and He provides constant reminders of His love. Next time you find yourself upset or worried about something, look around. It won't take long to find a tree clapping its hands, just for you.

Dear Father, thank You for the reminders of Your love that You send every day. Help me look for them and feel the joy You want me to feel. I love You. Amen.

NAMING THE STARS

Lift your eyes and look to the heavens: Who created all these? He who brings out the starry host one by one and calls forth each of them by name. Because of his great power and mighty strength, not one of them is missing.

ISAIAH 40:26 NIV

God is a pretty incredible God, isn't He? He created the heavens and the earth, the moon and billions of stars to fill the galaxy. Isaiah 40:26 tells us that He gave each star a name, and He knows that not one of them is missing.

That's a lot of stars.

If God cares that much about stars, how much more must He care about people—who He made in His own image? The stars are His creation, but we are His children. He formed us to be like Him because He longs for a relationship with us. He wants to talk to us, listen to us, laugh and cry with us.

Sometimes, when we feel lonely or discouraged, it can seem like God is distant. Like He's forgotten all about us and He doesn't even know our names anymore. Nothing could be further from the truth.

Just as God knows each of the stars by name, He knows each of us intimately. He never leaves us alone for a moment. He loves us, and that love will never, ever end.

. . . .

Dear Father, thank You for knowing my name. Thank You for loving me and wanting to have a relationship with me. Forgive me for the times I forget about You, for I know You never forget about me. Amen.

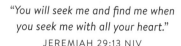

HIDE-AND-SEEK

*"You will seek me and find me when
you seek me with all your heart."*
JEREMIAH 29:13 NIV

Christopher Columbus is credited for discovering America. We can all learn something from him. He was a discoverer. He sought out new things; he knew there were places in the world that hadn't yet been drawn onto the maps, and he wanted to find them.

God wants us to be discoverers too. Only, instead of discovering land, He wants us to discover Him. There are things about God we will never know; He is too great. But that shouldn't stop us from trying to know as much about Him as we can—or from trying to have as close a relationship with Him as we can.

God promises that when we look for Him, we will find Him. He doesn't want to play hide-and-seek with us. But He does want to know we're interested enough to seek Him out. That shows Him we want to have a relationship with Him. When we do, He will greet us with His arms open for a big, welcoming hug.

Dear Father, I want to know You. I long to know everything about You. I want to live in Your presence, and I want You to walk with me in everything I do. I'm looking for You, God. Please help me find You. Amen.

LOVING AND STRONG

One thing God has spoken, two things I have heard: "Power
belongs to you, God, and with you, Lord, is unfailing love";
and "You reward everyone according to what they have done."
PSALM 62:11–12 NIV

Sometimes we focus on only one aspect of God's character. We remember how strong He is, and we may feel afraid. We're scared to mess up because we think God will punish us.

Other times, we remember how loving He is. We may be tempted to take advantage of that love by doing whatever we please. We think, *Oh, God won't punish me for that. He'll just forgive me. It will be all right.*

We must always remember that God is both powerful and loving. He loves us and doesn't want anything bad to happen to us. He also loves other people and wants to protect them. He will take care of us when we trust and obey Him, and He will bless us with good things. But if we disobey or act in a way that would disrespect or hurt someone else, He will protect them too because He loves them as much as He loves each one of us.

We need to always do what is right, because we respect God and His power. But as long as we are doing our best to honor Him and love other people, we can relax. We don't need to fear God, because He loves us in an amazing way.

Dear Father, thank You for Your strength and Your love. I want to love others and protect them the way You do. Amen.

SPIRIT SONG

*Because you are my help, I sing in the shadow of your
wings. I cling to you; your right hand upholds me.*
PSALM 63:7–8 NIV

Sometimes life gets hard and we feel overwhelmed. We cry or get
angry or stressed. No matter how hard we try, we can't seem to
relax. But God says we can feel joy to the point of singing, right in
the middle of the worst trouble, because He is there to help. And
with God helping us, we can always know it's going to be okay.

Next time we're worried about a test, we can study and prepare,
and then our spirits can sing. He will help us do our best. And if we
fail, maybe He'll use that failure to get us even more help.

Next time we're upset about the way a friend is treating us, we
can continue to treat them with love and sing in our hearts. God is
there, and He will help us. He'll either work in that person's heart to
change their attitude or He'll send us another friend, or He'll move
in some other way to protect us.

Even when things are stressful at home, we can trust God and
sing. He is always working to bring about good things in our lives,
as long as we rely on Him.

If everything always went the way we wanted, we wouldn't
need His assistance. Life will have trouble and hardships, but God
is always there to help us.

Dear Father, thank You for guiding me through difficult things.
Help me trust You so much that my spirit sings. Amen.

GOD WILL TAKE CARE OF US

*"Ask and it will be given to you; seek and you will find;
knock and the door will be opened to you. For everyone
who asks receives; the one who seeks finds; and to
the one who knocks, the door will be opened."*

MATTHEW 7:7–8 NIV

God wants us to ask Him for the things we need. When we ask, it shows we trust Him to provide. He often uses others to meet those needs, but He doesn't want us to depend on other things or people more than we depend on Him. He wants us to trust Him completely.

That doesn't mean He'll give us everything we ask for, like a spoiled child. But when we look to Him to provide the things we need, like food, clothing, and even friendship, He will provide. He loves us, and He loves taking care of us.

When we let Him know what we need, we must step back and allow Him to take care of it in His time and in His way. It's tempting to tap our feet and cross our arms impatiently, but we must remember—He is not our servant sent to do what we demand. He is our caring Master, our loving Father. He will take care of us, but we have to trust Him. When we place our confident hope in Him, He will give us the things we need.

Dear Father, thank You for giving me what I need.
Teach me to trust You for everything. Amen.

BRICK HOUSE

"Therefore everyone who hears these words of mine and puts them into practice is like a wise man who built his house on the rock. The rain came down, the streams rose, and the winds blew and beat against that house; yet it did not fall, because it had its foundation on the rock."

MATTHEW 7:24–25 NIV

Have you ever built a sand castle? It's fun to build with sand because it gets wet and squishy and feels nice in our hands. But sand won't hold its shape. As soon as a big wave or a strong wind comes along, *splat!* All our hard work is gone.

When we live our lives based on anything other than God's Word, our lives are kind of like a sand castle. It may feel nice for a minute. For a short time, it may even look beautiful and seem great. But the first time a big wave of stress or a strong wind of trouble comes along, our lives will go *splat*.

But when we base our lives on God's Word and live according to His laws, it's like building a brick house on a cement foundation. It may take more work in the beginning, but when we put in the patience and discipline to pattern our lives after God, we will withstand the storms of trouble and difficulty. A brick house is always sturdier and will protect us better than a sand castle.

Dear Father, thank You for Your wisdom. Help me live for You. I want to build a strong foundation for my life. Amen.

DON'T BE A DRAMA QUEEN

Warn a divisive person once, and then warn him a second time. After that, have nothing to do with them.
TITUS 3:10 NIV

Some people aren't happy unless they're miserable, and they make everyone else miserable with them. While that sounds silly, it's a fact of life. There are drama queens (and drama kings) in this world, and God wants us to stay away from them. And He certainly doesn't want us to be one of them.

God loves everyone, and He wants us to be kind to everyone. But if a person in our lives wants to gossip and bully and stir up trouble, God will deal with them. He wisely instructs us to encourage them to be kind and live at peace with others. If they don't listen the first time, we can encourage them again. But if they still don't listen, God wants us to avoid that person, for they will cause nothing but misery.

Sometimes we can't avoid the person completely, but we can do our best to avoid the drama. We can refuse to take part in gossip. We can try to make peace between everyone involved. We can leave the room, read our Bibles, and pray. If all else fails, we can continue to say kind things to that person or about the person they're slandering. If we try to avoid the drama kings and queens of the world and try to live at peace with everyone, God will honor our commitment to Him.

Dear Father, help me be kind to everyone.
I don't want to be a divisive person. Amen.

DOING MY BEST

*Do your best to present yourself to God as one
approved, a worker who does not need to be ashamed
and who correctly handles the word of truth.*

2 TIMOTHY 2:15 NIV

God is proud of His children. Or at least, He wants to be proud. He wants to look at each of us and say, *"That's My son,"* or *"That's My daughter,"* with a genuine sense of accomplishment. Since He created each of us with a special purpose, He wants us to do our best to live out that purpose.

The key here is finding our purpose and doing our best. If we are lazy and do a sloppy job of things, that doesn't honor God. If we get distracted and jealous because we're not as good as someone else at something, that doesn't honor God either.

Instead of lamenting that we can't sing as well as somebody else or that we're not athletic enough or smart enough or pretty enough, we should do our best in those areas and be satisfied to let someone else shine. And instead of doing a hurry-up job on our homework or cleaning our rooms, we should do our best so we can be proud. Most importantly, we should find the things we're good at, the things God has especially equipped us to do, and become the best we can be at those things so we can point people to Him and live out our purpose in this life.

Dear Father, help me be the best I can be
at the things You want me to do. Amen.

GODLESS CHATTER

*Avoid godless chatter, because those who indulge
in it will become more and more ungodly.*
2 TIMOTHY 2:16 NIV

It's fun to talk about stuff. Conversation is an important way to build relationships. But as we talk to one another, we need to always keep our conversations godly and uplifting.

That means we shouldn't say negative things about other people. When speaking of others, it's best to only say positive, encouraging things about them. That way, we don't hurt others or make them angry at us.

We should also avoid talking about things that wouldn't please God or that would make our parents unhappy. Making plans to disobey or discussing things that are sinful doesn't help us grow into the people God created us to be.

God loves us, and He wants our conversations to reflect His love and His goals for us. So it's fine to discuss a great sports team or a fun new fashion or a yummy recipe, as long as we keep the tone of our words and attitudes positive, uplifting, and encouraging for all who hear.

A good rule of thumb is to talk about things, not people. And we should always let our words reflect God's love, kindness, and compassion.

Dear Father, it's easy to let my conversations get away from me. Sometimes, before I know it, I've said something negative or unkind, or I've focused on something that wouldn't please You. I want to become the person You want me to be. Help me guard my words. Amen.

DECISIONS

Flee the evil desires of youth and pursue righteousness,
faith, love and peace, along with those who
call on the Lord out of a pure heart.

2 TIMOTHY 2:22 NIV

It's normal to want to do things that are wrong. It's called temptation, and even Jesus was tempted. Sometimes the things we're not supposed to do seem more exciting than the things we're allowed to do. We long for the thrill of getting away with something.

But there's a reason God sets boundaries. He loves us so very much, and He doesn't want us to get hurt. He knows that poor decisions made when we're young can affect us for the rest of our lives.

Instead of pursuing the thrill of evil, He wants us to chase after righteousness, faith, love, and peace. When we're faced with a decision, we should ask ourselves, *Is it right? Does it show faith in God? Does it demonstrate love and promote peace?*

God doesn't want us to live for today only; that causes us to make foolish choices. Instead, He wants us to live for eternity, making wise decisions that will lead us to a life filled with love, peace, and joy.

Dear Father, forgive me for wanting to do things
that are wrong. Help me resist temptation and
make choices that will honor You. Amen.

LET IT GO

*Don't have anything to do with foolish and stupid arguments,
because you know they produce quarrels. And the Lord's servant
must be quarrelsome but must be kind to everyone.*

2 TIMOTHY 2:23–24 NIV

There's a popular song titled "Let It Go." It encourages the listener
not to hold back anything. While this is good advice when it comes
to pursuing our goals and dreams, it's not always wise to let our
tongues go when we're offended.

Instead, it's often better to let go of the offense. If someone has
a different opinion about a matter, that's fine. Let them have their
opinion, and you can hold on to yours. We don't always have to argue
about everything. As a matter of fact, unless it's a matter of life and
death, it's usually best to just keep our mouths shut.

If someone does something we don't like, it's often wise to let
that go too without making a big deal of it. The stress and anger
stirred up by a heated argument is usually much worse than the
original offense that caused the argument.

If someone repeatedly offends us, perhaps we can find ways to
avoid that person rather than make an enemy of them by starting
an argument. God loves us, and He doesn't want us losing sleep over
some petty disagreement that could have been avoided if we'd just
chosen to let the offense go.

Dear Father, help me keep my mouth shut when I'm angry. Help
me let offenses go so I can live at peace with others. Amen.

A NOBLE LIFE

In a large house there are articles not only of gold and silver,
but also of wood and clay; some are for special purposes and
some for common use. Those who cleanse themselves from
the latter will be instruments for special purposes, made holy,
useful to the Master and prepared to do any good work.
2 TIMOTHY 2:20–21 NIV

God's children are royalty. Since He is the King of kings, all His children are princes and princesses. He wants us to remain set apart for noble purposes.

But sometimes His children choose to get bogged down with the things of this world. We act and live more like peasants than daughters of the King. We choose to fill our minds with junk instead of things of value.

God wants us to be gold, not garbage. He wants our minds to be filled with silver, not slop. The only way that will happen is if we make a conscious effort to be choosy about how we live and what we put in our minds. When we talk, our conversations should be uplifting. When we watch television or listen to music, the subject matter should be fitting for a child of the King.

Dear Father, I want to be careful about the things I allow into my life. Help me make wise decisions with my words and the things I put in my mind. I want to live a life of nobility. Amen.

ADDITION AND SUBTRACTION

*Do not add to what I command you and do not
subtract from it, but keep the commands of
the LORD your God that I give you.*

DEUTERONOMY 4:2 NIV

Most of us want to obey God when it's easy. But there are times when living by God's standards isn't convenient or fun. In those times, it's tempting to only listen to the parts of God's Word we want to hear and ignore the rest. We'll take one verse we like and ignore another that we don't like. We might even want to add a little bit here and there to make it more comfortable for us to do what we want. We twist His words to justify our actions.

But God says not to ever do that. He wants us to be familiar with His entire Word and obey every part of it. We're not allowed to alter it or change it in any way.

That's hard, because sometimes God's Word may seem to say different things in different places. In one place He encourages compassion, in another place justice. But God never contradicts Himself.

If we're confused about what God's Word says, we can ask a trusted pastor or teacher. But we must always remember that love is the overriding theme in the Bible. If we're not sure what to do, we can ask for wisdom to make certain we're acting in love.

Dear Father, help me obey every part of Your
Word. I don't want to ignore or change any part
of it. Help me to always act in love. Amen.

ALL THE TIME

"I am the Lord, and there is no other; apart from me there is no God. I will strengthen you, though you have not acknowledged me, so that from the rising of the sun to the place of its setting people may know there is none besides me. I am the Lord, and there is no other."

ISAIAH 45:5–6 NIV

When we choose to accept Christ as our Savior, we are marked as His. We belong to God. Throughout His Word, He promises He'll never leave us or turn His back on us. He's there for us all the time, and He wants us to succeed so others will know He's a great God to serve.

But we occasionally get distracted and forget to acknowledge His goodness. He knows that sometimes life gets in the way. We forget to pray or we forget to say "Thank You" to Him.

If we never pray, that's a big problem. But if we make it a habit to seek God, to honor Him in our choices, and to live for Him each day, we don't have to worry that we didn't pray at the exact moment or that we forgot to say thanks for every little thing. He knows our hearts, and when our thoughts are pure, He will strengthen us and take care of us.

God loves us more than we can comprehend, and He wants us to succeed. When His children are strong, we are happy, and that makes others want to know Him more.

Dear Father, thank You for being there for me, even when I forget to acknowledge You. Amen.

LIKE HIM

*"I form the light and create darkness, I bring prosperity and create disaster; I, the L*ORD*, do all these things. You heavens above, rain down righteousness; let the clouds shower it down. Let the earth open wide, let salvation spring up, let righteousness flourish with it; I, the L*ORD*, have created it."*

ISAIAH 45:7–8 NIV

Sometimes it's easy to forget just how big God is. Think about it. He created light and darkness. He calls forth the rain and sprinkles the stars in the heavens and sets the moon in place. That's pretty amazing stuff.

What's even more amazing is that He created you and me in His image. Of all the things He made, He chose each of us to look and act and think like Him. He chose us as His children.

Then He gave us free will. Although He loves us immensely and wants to have a relationship with us, He never forces that relationship. We have a choice to belong to Him, to act and think like Him, or not.

When we choose to have a relationship with God, He causes His righteousness to grow in us. That means as long as we pursue a close relationship with Him, we will continue to become more like Him. And when we become like God, that's pretty amazing stuff.

Dear Father, thank You for creating me to have a relationship with You. Help me make the choice each day to grow in that relationship. I want to be like You. Amen.

SUCH GREAT GOODNESS

How abundant are the good things that you have stored up for those who fear you that you bestow in the sight of all, on those who take refuge in you. In the shelter of your presence you hide them from all human intrigues; you keep them safe in your dwelling from accusing tongues.

PSALM 31:19–20 NIV

Have you ever had a new puppy or kitten? Or better yet, maybe you have a younger brother or sister. When another living thing loves us, obeys us, and runs to us when they're afraid, something happens in our hearts. We become very protective of that person or pet, and we want to take care of them.

If we have enough love in our hearts to care for an animal or another person, think how great God's love for us must be. He created us. He adores us. He wants to give us lovely blessings to make us happy, and He longs to protect us from things that will harm us. God is nothing but good, nothing but love.

He is so full of love for us that He wants to pour out His goodness until we are saturated. When we run to God, we have nothing to fear, for He will always take care of His own.

Dear Father, thank You for Your love and Your goodness. When I feel afraid, remind me to run to You. I love You, and I want to stay close to You and live each day in Your presence. Amen.

WHEN I NEED IT MOST

*Praise be to the LORD, for he showed me the wonders of
his love when I was in a city under siege. In my alarm
I said, "I am cut off from your sight!" Yet you heard
my cry for mercy when I called to you for help.*

PSALM 31:21–22 NIV

Do you ever feel like you're in a bad situation and there's no way
out of it? That's how David felt when King Saul and his army were
chasing him, trying to kill him. At those times, it can feel like God
has forgotten about us, like He doesn't even see us anymore.

But God always sees us. He's always aware of every detail of
our lives, and He cares deeply. Sometimes He rescues us from
bad things before they ever happen and we don't even know to be
thankful. Other times, He leaves us on our own for a while. He wants
to give us the opportunity to stand strong, to be wise, to make good
decisions. He may even let us get a few nicks and bruises along the
way to teach us some valuable lessons.

But He is right there, all the time. He will never leave us, and He
will certainly never let us be defeated. God will always give us help
when we need it most.

Dear Father, thank You for never leaving me alone.
Keep me strong during the hard times and remind
me of Your presence when I need it most. Amen.

HOPE IN THE LORD

Love the LORD, all his faithful people! The LORD preserves
those who are true to him, but the proud he pays back in full.
Be strong and take heart, all you who hope in the LORD.

PSALM 31:23–24 NIV

Hope is a beautiful thing. It is a confident belief that good things are coming your way. Time and again, God tells His children to have hope in Him. We can be strong. We can smile at the future, as long as we are faithful to love Him and follow His commands.

Satan doesn't want us to have any hope. He wants us to be afraid of the future, afraid that bad things will happen. He throws all kinds of frustrations and hurts and heartaches in our direction and tries to convince us that life will always be that way. Or he tries to make us worry about things that will never even happen to us. He's a thief, and he wants to steal our joy.

When we love God and trust Him, we don't have to be afraid. We don't have to believe Satan's lies that bad things will come. Even if they do happen, most things aren't as bad as we thought they'd be. And on the other side of the hurt, God always has a happy ending planned for those who love Him with all their heart.

Dear Father, I love You. Help me recognize fear for
what it is: Satan trying to steal my joy. Remind me to
live with hope—the belief that You have good things
in store for my life each and every day. Amen.

HOW TO BE STRONG

The LORD thunders at the head of his army; his forces are beyond number, and mighty is the army that obeys his command.

JOEL 2:11 NIV

This is a great big world, and each of us is just a tiny part of it. Sometimes we can get overwhelmed and feel insignificant, like we don't matter or we aren't important. But we must never forget that although we're small, our God is mighty and powerful. And when we join with others who also love and serve God, we gain strength.

Obedience to God makes us more powerful, both as individuals and as a group. When we honor Him and live to please Him, He lives in us. And though we may not be able to accomplish much on our own, with God, all things are possible.

With God, we can succeed where we might have failed. With God, we can endure when we might have given up. With God, we can love even the most unlovable people. Obedience to God allows us to be more than we ever thought we could be.

God loves us, and He longs to make us strong in every way. When we live for Him, He lives through us, and everything we do is powered by His presence.

Dear Father, I'm glad to know You're so strong and that I serve in Your army. Help me be an obedient servant. I want the kind of strength that only comes from You. Amen.

GOD'S SECRET FORMULA

Live in harmony with one another. Do not be proud,
but be willing to associate with people of low position.
Do not be conceited. Do not repay anyone evil for evil.
Be careful to do what is right in the eyes of everyone.

ROMANS 12:16–17 NIV

Sometimes we feel that in order for people to like us, we have to associate with the cool crowd. We think if we're friends with the pretty people, the popular people, the ones with the perfectly styled hair and the trendy clothes, others will associate us with those qualities, and they'll like us too.

But there's a flaw in that way of thinking. Most people are thinking more about themselves than they are about anyone else; it's human nature. So even if we're standing next to the most impressive person around, people aren't likely to notice us.

Because God loves us, He taught us a secret formula to make most people like us all the time. If we make them feel good about themselves, they'll like us. If we're nice to everyone and treat everyone with kindness no matter what they look like or how trendy their wardrobe, people will start to notice. They'll realize they have nothing to fear from us because we always treat everyone with respect. They'll know whenever they're around us that they feel safe and wanted. Pretty soon, we'll be popular—not for what we look like or how much money we have but for how we treat others.

Dear Father, help me avoid acting like I'm better than others.
Teach me to be kind to everyone, no matter what. Amen.

ALWAYS THERE

*May the God of hope fill you with all joy and peace
as you trust in him, so that you may overflow
with hope by the power of the Holy Spirit.*

ROMANS 15:13 NIV

Have you ever seen a dad throw his little girl in the air and catch her? Perhaps you remember being that little girl in your own father's arms. It's a delightful thing to watch, for the child usually squeals with delight. Even though she's being thrown in the air and could fall and badly hurt herself, that thought never crosses her mind. She knows her daddy will catch her. In that moment, she's all about the joy, and fear is a thousand miles away.

That's how God wants us to be with Him. When we feel like life is tossing us around, we can smile and laugh and feel total peace and joy in knowing our Father will catch us. He's not going to let us fall. That's called trust.

Somewhere along the way, as we grow up and skin our knees and experience some bangs and bruises, we forget to trust our Father. Instead of squealing with joy, we cry in fear. We forget that He loves us and will always be there to catch us.

Life does carry some hurts, but we don't have to expect them. That expectation steals the joy and peace from our lives. Today and every day, think of that daddy and his little girl and expect joy.

Dear Father, sometimes I forget how good You
are, and I forget to trust You. Remind me to
always expect good things from You. Amen.

HE PRAYS FOR ME

We do not know what we ought to pray for, but the Spirit himself intercedes for us through wordless groans. And he who searches our hearts knows the mind of the Spirit, because the Spirit intercedes for God's people in accordance with the will of God.

ROMANS 8:26–27 NIV

Sometimes we find ourselves in the middle of a confusing situation and we don't even know how to pray. We have no idea what to ask God for because we don't know what the right thing is. That can feel pretty frustrating.

But even in those times, we can trust that God knows what we need. He knows our hearts, and He knows everything about us. He knows what is best, even if we don't. And He is always, always working for our best.

Today's verse tells us that the Holy Spirit prays for us, even when we don't know what to say. He prays for us even when we can't form words to pray ourselves. As long as we're doing our best to stay close to God and please Him, we don't have to worry about the little details of forgetting to pray or not praying right. All we have to do is call out to God in our hearts. He hears and He understands perfectly.

Dear Father, thank You for hearing and understanding the deepest part of me even better than I understand myself. Thank You for always caring and for always seeking my good. Amen.

WISDOM AND INNOCENCE

I want you to be wise about what is good, and innocent about what is evil. The God of peace will soon crush Satan under your feet.

ROMANS 16:19–20 NIV

God likes to see His children have fun, but He wants us to remain innocent about what is evil. He doesn't want us to get drawn in by dark, bloody, frightening tales of murder and the supernatural. He doesn't want us spending our days allowing entertainment to replace Him completely in our thoughts. He doesn't want us to get caught up focusing solely on all the things happening in the world that we cannot control.

Today, if we feel frightened, we can remember that God is overwhelmingly more powerful than evil. And we can remember that in the midst of our fun, our most important task is to share His love and His goodness with everyone we meet.

Dear Father, thank You for giving me wisdom about what is good. Remind me today, and every day, not to be too curious about evil things. Help me stay focused on the pure love, kindness, and compassion that comes from You. Amen.

GROWING UP WITH JESUS

Then he returned to Nazareth with them and was obedient to them. And his mother stored all these things in her heart.

LUKE 2:51 NLT

Can you imagine what it must have been like to grow up in the same neighborhood with Jesus? If you had been alive when He was a boy, would you have wanted to be His friend? The other kids may have thought He was a little different, but most likely, they didn't know about the angels who announced His birth or the shepherds and wise men who came to worship Him.

When He was twelve years old, He went to Jerusalem with His family and their friends for the Jewish celebration of Passover. Afterward, on their way home, Joseph and Mary couldn't find Him. They were frantic and hurried back to search for Him. They finally found Him in the temple, talking to a group of teachers. He acted surprised that they worried. He said, "Didn't you know I'd be doing my Father's business?" (Luke 2:49).

Until then, even though they knew He was special, they probably treated Him just like other children. What He said made it clear that He knew He was from His heavenly Father. But after they got home, He was obedient to His parents.

If the Son of God needed to obey His earthly parents, it sets a wonderful example for children everywhere. Do you suppose kids who knew Him then tried harder to obey their parents when they watched Him?

Dear Jesus, I want to be like You. Help me obey my parents and teachers and any others who have authority over me.

LEARN TO BE HAPPY

*There is a time for everything, and everything
on earth has its special season.*
ECCLESIASTES 3:1 NCV

Don't you sometimes wish you were completely grown up already? People act like you're still a child who can't take care of herself. Everyone tells you what to do and how to do it. You have to remind your parents you don't need a babysitter every time they go out. But when you try to tell them to treat you differently, they say something like, "You're too young to understand. Someday you'll wish you were still a little girl."

What do you think you can do to show them you're growing up? It doesn't help when you get angry because they don't do what you wish they would.

Think about your age as a season. Whether it is summer or winter, there are fun things to do; you can't play in the snow when it's hot outside, but you can swim. Just as the seasons have different opportunities, so does each age.

You will get older. When you are twenty, some of the things you do now won't be appropriate. But there are other activities you'll be able to do then. There is a time for everything. Some days this may feel like a tough age to be, but you can choose to make it better with a happy attitude. Look forward to the years ahead while you have fun now.

Lord Jesus, help me be happy just as I am. I don't
want to get mad at people because they treat me
like a kid. Help me know I'm special right now.

LOOK THROUGH GOD'S EYES

*But the LORD said to Samuel, "Don't judge by his appearance
or height, for I have rejected him. The LORD doesn't see
things the way you see them. People judge by outward
appearance, but the LORD looks at the heart."*

1 SAMUEL 16:7 NLT

How do you suppose other people see you? Do they think you're
pretty? Kind? Funny? Smart?

Today's scripture is about David, when he was a young teen. God
sent Samuel, a prophet, to David's family to anoint the man who
would be the next king of Israel. Of course David's father was thrilled
to think one of his sons would become king. He introduced seven
of his boys, one at a time, starting with the oldest. But the prophet
knew none of them was the one the Lord had chosen.

Finally, Samuel said, "Is this all your sons?"

Their father said, "Well, the youngest is out in the pasture with
the sheep. He's just a boy—surely it's not him."

But God saw David's heart. He knew this young man would
learn to lead the people. David's family just saw a shepherd, but
God saw a king.

What do you think God sees when He looks at you? He sees the
person you will become. He catches a glimpse of your heart and
says, *"She's special!"*

Heavenly Father, I ask You to let me see myself the
way You do. Even when I do something dumb, help
me not to get discouraged. Remind me that You are
working to make me the person You have planned.

LISTEN TO YOUR WORDS

When you talk, you should always be kind and pleasant so you will be able to answer everyone in the way you should.

COLOSSIANS 4:6 NCV

The tone on Emily's phone let her know she had a text. Allison! She was one of the most popular girls in their class.

Emily was excited at what she saw: CAN U COME TO A PARTY FRIDAY NITE? Allison had never acted especially friendly to her before.

Then another text came: DON'T TELL JENNA. SHE'S A PIG!

Emily's excitement evaporated. Jenna was her best friend.

Just then, her mom tapped on the door and came into Emily's room. "Everything okay?"

Emily's mom always seemed to know when something was wrong. "What should I do," Emily said, "when a really popular girl invites me to a party but then says something rude about my friend?" She went on to explain what happened.

"Well, before we talk about the party," her mother said, "you have to decide if you want to get closer to someone like that."

Emily and her mother talked a little longer, and Emily made up her mind. Her friend was more important than a party with someone who said unkind things. She felt more excited about keeping a good friend than about the invitation to Allison's.

. . . .

Dear Lord, help me remember to keep my words kind
and to say things that are positive and encouraging.
I want to please You when I talk to others.

BE A SHINING LIGHT

*Do everything without grumbling or arguing. Then
you will be the pure and innocent children of God. You
live among people who are crooked and evil, but you
must not do anything that they can say is wrong. Try
to shine as lights among the people of this world.*

PHILIPPIANS 2:14–15 CEV

Lindsey's parents were getting a divorce, and it felt like every time they talked, they argued about Lindsey and her brother, Austin. Where would the children spend holidays? How long should they be with each parent in the summer? Who had to pay for school expenses?

It made Lindsey feel guilty, and that made her grumpy. She seemed to get angry with Austin no matter what he did. One day when she lashed out, he said, "I wish you wouldn't be mad at me all the time. You're no fun anymore."

Instead of her usual fury, Lindsey started to cry. "I don't know what's wrong with me! I hate feeling this way. I'm sorry."

They sat down on the family room floor and talked about what was happening in their family. Lindsey realized her brother was hurting as much as she was. That made her want to protect him. "I'll try my best to be nicer, Austin. It's not your fault that I'm mad."

"I know. And it's not your fault Mom and Dad are getting a divorce," he said.

Dear Jesus, even when things go wrong and other people don't do what I like, help me not to grumble or argue. I want to be like a bright light that shines in dark places to help people see You.

GOD'S PROTECTION

The LORD is good. He protects those
who trust him in times of trouble.

NAHUM 1:7 CEV

Sydney was friendly with almost everyone at school, but one boy, Zach, seemed creepy. There was something about his eyes. He wasn't in any of her classes, so she only saw him in the hallways, but every time she noticed him, he seemed to be staring at her.

One day after school, Zach was standing by the door that Sydney went through. When she passed him, he followed her. She lived near the school and usually walked home alone. When she realized Zach was behind her, she went faster and pulled her phone from her pocket. Her hands were shaking. She didn't want her parents to freak out, but she was getting scared.

She punched in her dad's number. When he picked up, she whispered what was going on. Zach was still there, staying about half a block away. Her father tried to calm her down and told her he would pray for God to take care of her. He also said, "Stay on the line. I'll call for help from a different phone."

Within a few minutes, a police car drove by, slowly. Sydney glanced behind her and saw Zach turn around and run the other way. When the police got near him, one of the cops jumped out and ran to stop him. Sydney began to relax. She believed God showed her what to do and who to call.

. . . .

Heavenly Father, thank You that You promise to
protect me. I want to always trust You to watch
over me and keep me from being afraid.

TRUST IN THE LORD

You love him even though you have never seen him.
Though you do not see him now, you trust him; and you
rejoice with a glorious, inexpressible joy. The reward for
trusting him will be the salvation of your souls.

1 PETER 1:8–9 NLT

Have you ever heard someone say, "I'm a Christian," but they act hateful or say mean things? You may know other people who are really nice, but they don't claim to believe in Jesus.

So what is a Christian? Just thinking God is real or even that Jesus actually lived here on earth isn't enough. Christianity is so much more than how we behave or just believing He's real without faith that makes a difference in our actions. True believers ask Jesus Christ to forgive them and take control of everything. They know He died to take away their sins, and they are filled with joy because of His amazing love.

Christians aren't always super sweet and don't necessarily do everything right. Sometimes we really mess up and aren't proud of what we do, but we know Jesus loves us no matter what. Our actions don't make us Christians, but because people notice how we act, our lives should show that we belong to Him.

When we learn to trust Him, He gives us joy that's more than mere happiness. In today's verse, Peter calls it "glorious" and "inexpressible." And when we experience that kind of joy, people around us are going to see something special.

I love You, Jesus, and want people who are
with me to know You are in control of my life.

DON'T GRUMBLE—PRAY

Try to do good, not evil, so that you will live, and the LORD God All-Powerful will be with you just as you say he is.

AMOS 5:14 NCV

When elections are coming up, every time we turn on the TV, candidates tell us why they're the best. Signs about who is running for what are posted in yards and all along streets. It's hard to know who is telling the truth and who isn't. Even though you aren't old enough to vote, you may have an opinion. Do your parents talk about who they hope will win? Maybe you have an idea about the best candidates just from seeing the ads.

We're very fortunate to live in a free country where the people choose their leaders. Even though the ones we like might not always win elections, it's decided by the majority of the citizens. That's not true in a lot of nations.

The Bible tells us to pray for our leaders (1 Timothy 2:1–2) and to obey and honor them (1 Peter 2:13, 17). Unless a government forces people to do things that go against what the Bible teaches, we are to submit to elected officials. Sometimes we grumble and complain about our leaders, but that doesn't please God. If we want to do good and not evil, we need to have the right attitude about people in authority.

Lord Jesus, help me remember these things as I grow up. I want to understand how important it is to elect godly people and to honor those who are in office. Give me opportunities to show others that You are in control.

DIRECT MY HEART

Now may the Lord direct your hearts into the
love of God and into the patience of Christ.
2 THESSALONIANS 3:5 NKJV

What do you think of when you hear the word *direct*? Sometimes people direct traffic around construction sites. Musicians learn to pay close attention to their director so all the voices or instruments stay in harmony. Political leaders direct the government, teachers direct students, and parents direct their children.

So how does the Lord direct our hearts? He doesn't hold a big Stop sign or a conductor's wand, but He gets our attention. He is gentle, persistent, and always knows the best way to get us where we need to go. He'll direct us to avoid dangerous situations and take us straight into the heart of God's love.

Sometimes God uses a scripture from the Bible to speak to us and show us what we should do. Other times a preacher, teacher, or good friend tells us something, and we know it's the Lord. He has a wonderful imagination and will use whatever works best to show us what we need at that time.

When we listen to Him, we can feel safe and secure. Even then, sometimes it takes a long time to see where He's taking us. That's when we need the patience of Christ. It's really hard to wait patiently for anything. We want to see results quickly. But when we learn to wait on Him, we grow more like Jesus.

Lord, I really want to understand You more. I want You to lead my heart into Your love and teach me to be patient—like Jesus.

DISCIPLINE SHOWS LOVE

My dear child, don't shrug off God's discipline, but don't be crushed by it either. It's the child he loves that he disciplines; the child he embraces, he also corrects.

HEBREWS 12:5–6 MSG

Emma lived in a very small town and her cousin was visiting for a weekend from the city.

That night, Lauren said, "Let's do something fun."

"Like what?" Emma asked.

"Maybe go to a movie."

"How? We'd need a ride."

Lauren just said, "Watch."

After Emma's parents were in bed, Lauren tiptoed to the back door with Emma at her heels. They hurried to the highway, and Lauren stuck out her thumb when a car came along. The driver stopped to let the girls in.

"Where in the world are you two headed at this time of night?" the driver asked.

Oh no! Lauren started making up a story, but Emma stopped her. "Lauren, this is my teacher!"

Both girls scrunched down in their seats as Mrs. Maxwell headed toward Emma's house.

Emma's parents were upset and disappointed. They told Emma they'd have to decide what to do, but she knew she deserved to be punished. Before they all headed for bed, her parents hugged both girls and said, "We love you. We'll discuss this tomorrow."

Dear heavenly Father, thank You for parents who show their love through discipline as well as hugs.

HEROES

GOD's Message: "Don't let the wise brag of their wisdom. Don't let heroes brag of their exploits. Don't let the rich brag of their riches. If you brag, brag of this and this only: That you understand and know me. I'm GOD, and I act in loyal love."

JEREMIAH 9:23-24 MSG

Destiny's whole family waited at the airport for Justin's plane. She was so excited! He was coming home after a year in Afghanistan, just in time for Veterans Day. Her school had invited him to speak at a special assembly.

When Destiny spotted him, she jumped up and down like a little kid. And when he saw them all waiting, a huge grin spread across his face. The next few minutes were filled with hugs and laughter.

One of their uncles said, "Glad you came home in one piece." But at his words, something seemed to change in Justin.

Destiny didn't understand—until the next day at the school assembly. Justin talked about his friends who were real heroes. Some of them were badly injured or killed. He said, "I can't brag about anything I did over there. Every victory was God's doing, and He's the one who kept me alive. I got to know the Lord better than I ever had, and I experienced His love when I was scared and far from home."

Dear Lord, thank You for all the men and women who serve in the military to keep us free. Show each of them how much You love them. Let them really know You.

BE AN EXAMPLE

*Don't let anyone think less of you because you are young.
Be an example to all believers in what you say, in the way
you live, in your love, your faith, and your purity.*

1 TIMOTHY 4:12 NLT

Lexi was cute and perky—the one who said funny things to make her friends laugh. Even though she was smart, people who didn't really know her thought she was an airhead.

One day she overheard some girls at school and realized she was the topic of their conversation. "She's so ditzy! How has she been able to get this far?"

Lexi didn't want people to think she was dumb. She just liked to have fun and make others happy. After hearing the girls, she decided she'd better get serious. So she tried, but she had to work hard to hide her natural bubbly personality.

One of her close friends asked, "What's wrong? You always act like you're mad anymore."

"People think I'm stupid when I'm happy, so I have to change."

"Oh, stop! Your friends know how smart you are. You act goofy because you want us to feel good. Look at your grades—I'd like to be dumb like you and make straight As!"

"So what can I do?"

"Just be you! Don't try to change from the person God made you. You're a good example of how someone can be fun and still have faith and integrity. We all know you care about us."

. . . .

Lord Jesus, thank You for making me the person
I am. Let me enjoy life and show others You are
with me, keeping me pure and faithful.

GROWING UP

*But grow in the grace and knowledge of our Lord and Savior
Jesus Christ. To him be glory both now and forever! Amen.*
2 PETER 3:18 NIV

It's hard to imagine our parents, grandparents, or other adults when
they were children. Even if we see pictures and hear stories of things
they did, they'll always be older than us. Their lives are different.
They've experienced and learned from a lot of things that take time.

When we accept Jesus as our Savior, we're like babies all over
again. We need to grow up by talking to God and reading the
scriptures to learn more. That was even true for Jesus! Luke 2:52
(NIV) says that Jesus "grew in wisdom and stature." It's easy to imagine
Him as a baby in a manger, like we see at Christmas. And we know
about miracles and all the wonderful things He did when He was
an adult. But none of that came automatically. He grew from an
infant to a toddler to a teenager to an adult, just like everyone else.

Christians "grow up" by learning about Jesus, our Lord and Savior.
As we study the Bible and pray, His grace and love will show in our
own lives. We'll gain knowledge of what He is like and how He treats
people. Then whatever we do, we can imagine what He would do.
That doesn't make us proud or act like we're special. Actually, we
have to be humble to depend on Him.

Dear Jesus, I'm so glad You came to earth so we can picture
how You lived. Teach me how to glorify You by my life.

DAY 318

DON'T TAKE THE BAIT

Don't let me so much as dream of evil or thoughtlessly fall into bad company. And these people who only do wrong—don't let them lure me with their sweet talk!

PSALM 141:4 MSG

Leah watched a couple of girls on the bus. They wore lots of makeup and dressed in skimpy clothes—just barely within the school's dress code. They always seemed to be laughing. Leah was fascinated.

When she got home that afternoon, she tried some dark eyeliner, heavy mascara, and bright lipstick just to see what she looked like. She fiddled with her hair until it looked kind of sexy. Then she pinned up one of her skirts so it was shorter than anything she ever wore. She stood in front of the mirror, swishing this way and that.

Right then, she heard her mother at the front door and felt like she'd been caught doing something wrong. She ran to the bathroom to scrub her face but wasn't fast enough.

"Good grief, honey—what are you doing?"

"Just playing around with some makeup."

"You're much prettier without it, but I understand. I did the same thing when I was your age."

"Really? Some girls at school use lots of makeup, and all the boys watch them. I just wanted to see what I'd look like."

"That's okay, but don't be fooled by looks. Maybe that's the only way they know to get attention. Don't let them lure you away from what's right."

. . . .

Lord, I ask You to make me happy with the way I look. I trust You to keep me from getting involved with anything I shouldn't.

KEEP YOUR EYES CLEAR

*Your eyes are like a window for your body. When
they are good, you have all the light you need.*
MATTHEW 6:22 CEV

A pop-up appeared on Alyssa's screen while she checked out Facebook. It had a picture of a gorgeous guy and said, "Meet a hunk!" She was intrigued and clicked on the window. What came up was shocking. Men with almost no clothes on in all sorts of poses. Even though it was offensive, for some reason she kept scrolling through the photos.

Suddenly, she stopped herself and clicked off the site. Hardly thinking about what she was doing, she'd spent several minutes staring at those images. She felt dirty simply from looking at them. So why did she go there? It was really disgusting! She was at home by herself but looked around feeling guilty, glad no one saw her.

Alyssa realized how easy it is to get caught up in things without even trying. Fascinated by that little bit of temptation, she had taken a wrong step. Her pastor said being tempted isn't evil—even Jesus was tempted—but giving in to temptation was sin.

Alyssa had accepted Jesus as her Savior a few years earlier. She knew He loved her and would forgive her. She prayed right then but hated how simple it was to fall into something that made her feel so cruddy.

Dear Jesus, thank You for dying for me, erasing my
sin with Your blood. Forgive me any time I fall for the
stupid things that seem appealing when I see them.
Keep my eyes clear so Your light shines through me.

BE KIND, EVEN TO YOUR ENEMIES

*"But to you who are listening I say: Love your enemies,
do good to those who hate you, bless those who
curse you, pray for those who mistreat you."*

LUKE 6:27–28 NIV

"I hate those girls!" Alexis could hardly believe the words she read. "Why would anybody act so mean?" She just saw a post about Bailey, a new girl in her class who had moved from Texas. "She's shy and having a hard time making friends, but she seems really nice," Alexis said.

Some girls from her class made ugly comments about Bailey's drawl, and said, "She sounds like she belongs on a farm. Somebody should rope her like a cow and put her in a barn where she belongs."

Alexis started to type a reply, but her little sister, who heard her fume, said, "I'm glad you aren't mean. You treat everyone nice."

Alexis stopped. She realized the words she was about to write weren't nice. She wanted to blast those hateful girls, but hearing her sister made her feel uncomfortable. Her Sunday school teacher had just been talking about how God wants us to treat others—even our enemies. Firing back a hateful response wouldn't be right. In fact, it would probably make things worse.

Instead, she prayed for God to bless those girls and show them how to be kind.

. . . .

Dear Father in heaven, it's easy to get mad and say mean
things, but I ask You to keep me from just doing what's
easy. I want to make You happy by doing something
good for those who act hateful to me or to others.

GOD IS LOVE

*Beloved, let us love one another, for love is of God; and
everyone who loves is born of God and knows God. He
who does not love does not know God, for God is love.*

1 JOHN 4:7-8 NKJV

God isn't just loving. He *is* love. It's more than merely one of His
special traits—love defines who He is. And it's pretty scary to think
that if we don't show love to others, we don't really know God.
Not only that, but we don't get to choose who we love. It's not just
people who treat us special. We're to love everyone.

God sent Jesus to earth to show us what love looks like. We can
hardly imagine anyone loving so much He'd even forgive the people
who spit on Him and called Him names and jammed a thorny crown
on His head. He loved those who beat Him and drove spikes into
His hands and feet.

Because of His tremendous love, He can expect us to love those
in our lives. Most people will never experience anything as horrible
as Jesus did. We may know bullies and people who say mean things
but nothing like what Jesus suffered.

Can you love the people in your life? All of them? You can, if
you ask Jesus to give you the grace you need to be a loving person.
We have to depend on Him for everything—even the love we need
to show.

Dear Father, on my own, I can't love the way You want me
to. I ask for grace to let me love others the way You do.

TRUE LOVE

Love is kind and patient, never jealous, boastful,
proud, or rude. Love isn't selfish or quick tempered.
It doesn't keep a record of wrongs that others do.
1 CORINTHIANS 13:4–5 CEV

On their way home from church, Olivia thought about something the pastor said: *"God's kind of love involves emotions but isn't ruled by them."*

Later, while she and her older sister changed clothes, she asked Hailey, "So, do you love Jason the way Pastor Bradley talked about?"

Hailey giggled, "Probably not! We just have fun together."

"Do you think you're going to marry him?"

"I don't know. I don't think the pastor was talking about that kind of love. He meant the love we're supposed to have for everyone—not just boyfriends."

They were quiet for a while, then Hailey said, "You know, Jason does treat me like that scripture says. God probably wants us to love everyone that way, but I guess if I was dating somebody that was selfish and proud and impatient, I wouldn't like him very much."

"Maybe God means it for everyone, but especially for the people we spend the most time with. Even sisters," Olivia said, throwing her sock at Hailey.

"Stop it!"

"Remember, don't keep track of wrongs," Olivia teased.

Thank You, Lord, for showing us what true love is. Help me learn from You how to love others, even my family.

REAL PEACE COMES FROM JESUS

*Therefore, since we have been made right in God's
sight by faith, we have peace with God because
of what Jesus Christ our Lord has done for us.*

ROMANS 5:1 NLT

Whether people realize it or not, everyone needs to live in peace. That doesn't mean we're boring and don't ever do exciting things—even things that can be risky sometimes.

The word *peace* in the Bible is "shalom." That's still a greeting in Israel—instead of saying "Hello," people say, "Shalom." It's sort of like passing on a blessing.

When we have a close relationship with God, because of our faith in Jesus, we feel complete and peaceful. Shalom doesn't just mean there's no fighting or trouble. In fact, we can have the kind of peace God wants even in the midst of problems, if we know Jesus.

When angels announced to some shepherds that Jesus, the Savior, was born, they said, "Glory to God in highest heaven, and peace on earth to those with whom God is pleased" (Luke 2:14 NLT). Genuine peace only comes from God.

Hundreds of years earlier, Isaiah prophesied about the Messiah who would come. One of His titles was to be Prince of Peace. The prophet even said, "His government and its peace will never end" (Isaiah 9:7 NLT). Wars and huge problems have always been issues people have to deal with, but when we depend on Jesus, we can have peace even then. Isn't that awesome?

Dear Lord Jesus, I want to always experience the peace
You promise. I trust You to give me real peace no
matter what's happening around me. Thank You!

HUMILITY

*Now Moses was a very humble man, more humble
than anyone else on the face of the earth.*
NUMBERS 12:3 NIV

Do you know the story of Moses? When he was born, the Egyptian king was worried about the Hebrews in his country becoming too strong. So he did something horrible. He ordered the Hebrew women to kill their sons when they were born.

Moses' mother couldn't do anything that awful and hid her baby for a few months. Eventually she placed him in a watertight basket and Moses' sister took him to a place near the river where the king's daughter would find him. She was tenderhearted and raised Moses as her son.

When he grew up, Moses saw an Egyptian beating a Hebrew. Moses killed the Egyptian but realized he'd been seen. So he left town! Years later, when he was old, God called him back to rescue the Hebrews from slavery.

Can you imagine leading hundreds of thousands of people, along with lots and lots of livestock, through the wilderness? The people grumbled and complained and faced one problem after another for forty years. It would take an incredibly powerful leader to accomplish what Moses had to do. He was capable and strong, but most importantly, he was more humble than anyone else. God knew exactly what sort of man could do the job—and humility was one of the essential traits.

We probably won't lead a multitude, but whatever we do, humility is vital. And it takes strength to be humble.

Lord, I want to be humble. Please show me
how to be strong enough to live with humility.

BEAR DELICIOUS FRUIT

*"I am the vine, you are the branches. He who abides in Me, and
I in him, bears much fruit; for without Me you can do nothing."*

JOHN 15:5 NKJV

Autumn loved to visit her grandparents when grapes ripened in late summer. Plump purple grapes grew along a fence in their backyard. She helped her grandpa pick them and popped some in her mouth as she moved along. They were sweet and juicy, warm from the sunshine. Her mother would probably have said to wash them first, but her grandpa didn't worry about it. They carried baskets of grapes to the kitchen where her grandma was making jelly.

One day Autumn's grandpa said, "Do you know what would happen if I cut the vines down to the ground?"

"You wouldn't get any grapes," she said.

"Right. Even if I left branches dangling from the fence, without the vines, they would wither and die. The vine carries nutrients and water from the soil so the plants can thrive and bear grapes."

Grandpa went on to talk about how Jesus called Himself the vine and His followers the branches. "If we separate ourselves from Jesus," Grandpa said, "we won't produce a good crop of fruit."

God wants us to share good fruit with others—love, joy, peace, kindness, and other good traits—but without Jesus' life-giving power, we can't do it. The more time we spend with Him, the better our fruit will taste to others.

Dear Lord, I know I can't produce good fruit on my own. Show me every day how to stay connected to You so I bear good fruit.

WHAT GOD WANTS

But he's already made it plain how to live, what to do, what GOD is looking for in men and women. It's quite simple: Do what is fair and just to your neighbor, be compassionate and loyal in your love, and don't take yourself too seriously—take God seriously.

MICAH 6:8 MSG

Jessica was usually serious. She obeyed the rules, both at school and home. She did her homework and turned everything in on time. She kept her room neat and read her Bible most days. Her friend Jordan sometimes laughed at her. "Loosen up, Jess! Do you think the world would fall apart if you didn't do what you're supposed to once in a while?"

"What do you mean? I want God to like me."

Jordan gave her a strange look. "You think He won't like you if you relax?"

The girls went to the same church, but Jordan wasn't as disciplined as Jessica and didn't see anything wrong with the way she did things. "Look, I'm not saying to be bad, but you worry too much about whether you're doing things right. I don't think God's love depends on how we act. He just expects us to love Him and treat others the way we want to be treated. You make it too hard."

Jessica thought about it. "But I wouldn't be comfortable if I didn't do things the way I do."

"Okay, but remember you can't earn God's love by being strict with yourself. His rules are simple."

Dear heavenly Father, show me what matters to You. I don't want to expect more from myself than You do.

MOST IMPORTANT COMMANDMENT

"'You shall love the LORD your God with all your heart,
with all your soul, with all your mind, and with all
your strength.' This is the first commandment."

MARK 12:30 NKJV

What do you suppose the Bible means when it says we're to love the Lord with all our heart, soul, mind, and strength? When we commit our lives to Jesus, every part of us belongs to Him, but that doesn't explain what it means to love Him with our total being. The kind of love God has for us, and what He wants from us, doesn't have any edges—no boundaries.

If you stood (or sat) on a tiny life raft in the middle of an ocean, you could look all around and not notice anything that breaks the expanse of sky and sea. It's blended together endlessly.

The Bible says that God's love is endless like that, and higher than the heavens. Imagine floating in space and all you see is. . .space. That might feel scary, but think of that space being filled with God's love. His arms surround you. His strength protects you. His heart adores you. His love can't be measured. That's the kind of love He wants us to return to Him.

Boundless love frees us to trust God completely. We're willing to take risks when we know He is telling us to do something. We totally surrender to Him.

Dear Jesus, I want my love for You not to have any edges.
Keep me safe in Your loving embrace and overwhelm me with
a desire to give You everything, not holding anything back.

CELEBRATE WHAT GOD DOES

I trust your love, and I feel like celebrating because you rescued me. You have been good to me, LORD, and I will sing about you.

PSALM 13:5–6 CEV

It had been a tough year for Erin. She struggled in a couple of classes, a girl in the neighborhood bullied her, and she felt fat. It seemed like everything was going wrong.

School was out for Thanksgiving break, and her cousins were coming. Usually she loved that, but now she just wanted to be alone. Her mom yelled, "Erin, come on down and help. Our company will be here soon, and we have a lot to do."

She wanted to pretend she didn't hear but knew that wouldn't work, so she headed downstairs. Outside her bedroom, the aroma of turkey and something sweet brightened her attitude a little.

Suddenly the front door burst open, and her cousins and aunts and uncles spilled into the living room. Jade ran toward her and wrapped Erin in a huge hug. "I'm so glad to see you!" They both automatically headed toward the kitchen and started helping as they chattered about everything imaginable.

Everyone pitched in and the Thanksgiving feast was ready in no time. They sat down and followed their tradition of letting everyone tell something they were thankful for. When it was her turn, Erin realized she needed to stop concentrating on problems. "I'm thankful that God rescued me from feeling sorry for myself and showed me what a great family we have. He's so good!"

Dear Lord, help me to always celebrate Your goodness instead of letting negative thoughts drag me down.

STAY RIGHTEOUS

*"Yet the righteous will hold to his way, and he who
has clean hands will be stronger and stronger."*

JOB 17:9 NKJV

Today's verse is an amazing statement because it came from Job when he was in the pits. He was the richest man in town and the father of ten children. But in one day his life fell apart. Job's children died in a terrible storm while they were celebrating together. All his servants were killed, and his huge herd of livestock was stolen by an enemy.

Some people would have given up on God. But the first thing Job did was fall to his knees and worship the Lord.

Satan did his best to turn Job against God, but he didn't succeed. Job was covered with boils and sat among ashes, scraping the sores with shards of pottery. His wife put him down for clinging to God's promises. So-called friends said they knew he must be sinning for all that disastrous stuff to happen.

But through it all, Job's faith never failed. He spoke the words of this scripture even though his heart was breaking. In spite of everything, he knew he was righteous and believed he would grow stronger if he kept holding on.

Eventually, God honored Job for staying faithful. He became rich again and had more children. But the lesson for us is that he trusted God even when he couldn't see anything positive happening.

Almighty God, I don't ever want to go through horrible
things like Job, but I do want to stay strong and trust
in You to take care of all my needs, no matter what.

GUARD YOUR HEART

*Guard your heart above all else, for it
determines the course of your life.*
PROVERBS 4:23 NLT

Cheerleader tryouts were coming up, and even though Faith was good, she wasn't positive she could make it.

Walking to class one morning, a cute guy from the football team caught up with her. "Hey, you going out for cheerleader?"

Faith looked up at him. He seemed super friendly. She just nodded.

"I can make it happen if you're interested."

"What do you mean?"

"My mom is one of the judges. She'll make sure the girls I want are on the squad."

Faith was flattered to think he would do that for her, even though she felt a tug at her conscience. All she could think to say was, "That's nice of you."

"So, when can we go out?"

She didn't know a lot about guys, but her guard went up immediately. "My folks won't let me date yet."

"Oh, come on. You can figure out a way."

"Sorry. I'll figure out a way to do my best at the tryouts and not depend on your help."

Lord Jesus, please protect my heart from getting involved in any relationship or scheme that isn't what You want for me.

LIGHT IN SHADOWS

*"Feed the hungry, and help those in trouble. Then
your light will shine out from the darkness, and the
darkness around you will be as bright as noon."*
ISAIAH 58:10 NLT

Shelly was excited about going on a mission trip to Honduras with
her youth group. Her dad was a chaperone, so the idea of a foreign
country didn't seem scary. They went to a few classes to give them
an idea of what to expect and how to be a blessing to the people.
They would work with a church to help build a house for a needy
family and have Vacation Bible School for the children.

When the plane touched down, the pastor greeted them. They
climbed into his beat-up van for a bumpy ride to the church. Shelly
was stunned by what she saw along the way. Everything seemed
desolate and dirty. People lived in huts with grubby-looking children
playing outside. Even though she knew what to expect, actually
seeing it touched her heart. She blinked back tears.

After they dropped their bags in the church basement, the group
headed out to meet people. They had trinkets for the children, who
came running to them with expectant grins. The days zipped past
quickly, and Shelly loved everything they did for these people who
were so appreciative.

After ten days, they boarded the van to leave. Shelly's face
glowed with joy, even as tears streamed down her cheeks when the
kids ran for one last hug.

Heavenly Father, thank You for showing Your heart through
the joy we get from helping others. Give me a generous spirit.

GOD REIGNS

*How great are His signs, and how mighty His wonders!
His kingdom is an everlasting kingdom, and His
dominion is from generation to generation.*

DANIEL 4:3 NKJV

Today's scripture is powerful no matter what, but even more so because of who said it. Do you know? It was Nebuchadnezzar, king of Babylon. He loved to be praised by people and believed in multiple gods. . .until Shadrach, Meshach, and Abednego, Daniel's companions, survived a trip through the fire.

That happened after the king made a gold statue, about ninety feet tall. It was so huge, people couldn't miss it. And he ordered everyone to bow down to the statue at certain times. Shadrach, Meshach, and Abednego refused. That made the king furious. He watched as his servants tied them up and threw them into a furnace.

But what he saw astonished him. They were walking around in the flames, along with a fourth man who looked "like the Son of God" (Daniel 3:25 NKJV). Nebuchadnezzar called for them to come out, and when they did, they weren't burned and didn't even smell like smoke. The king was amazed by God's mighty wonders.

God honored Daniel's friends because they wouldn't worship things of this world. We probably won't be forced to bow down to a statue, but sometimes other things can get in the way of us worshipping the one true God. He blesses those who refuse to compromise their faith.

Heavenly Father, help me to always stay faithful to
You, no matter what might tempt me to turn away.

BE ONE WHO HONORS GOD

Just as water fills the sea, the land will be filled
with people who know and honor the LORD.
HABAKKUK 2:14 CEV

Taylor and her family were in the great room watching *Monday Night Football*. Their dad sat in his favorite recliner. Mom was on the couch, more interested in her magazine than men who got paid big bucks to run around a field.

Seats at the stadium were packed with screaming fans. When Taylor's mother glanced at the screen, she said, "Wow! Look at that crowd!"

"See, Mom, lots of people really love football," Taylor said.

Her mother got quiet again but wasn't really paying attention to her magazine. At halftime she headed to the kitchen and returned with popcorn and sodas. "Just imagine," she said, "what it would be like if Christians were that excited about God. What if we loved the Lord so much we packed stadiums all around the country every week to hear more about Jesus?"

Dad muted the sound. Somehow what she said made an impact on each of them, and they started talking about how awesome it would be. "Can you picture people screaming and yelling and cheering because they're so excited about their faith?" Taylor mused. "What if there were so many excited Christians that we spilled out of churches and even stadiums. Think of a sea of people who shout for joy because Jesus has saved them."

The game started again but wasn't quite as exciting.

Lord God, I want to join a sea of people who shout
praises to You because we're so thrilled to know You!

CLOTHED IN CHRIST

For you are all children of God through faith in Christ Jesus. And all who have been united with Christ in baptism have put on Christ, like putting on new clothes.
GALATIANS 3:26–27 NLT

Do you like to shop for new clothes? When we "put on Christ," we don't need to go to a fitting room and try various styles or sizes. He's a perfect fit for each of us as soon as we trust Him to be our Savior.

Jesus wants us to abide in Him, like we read in John 15. Then people will see Him when they are with us. They'll be aware of His amazing grace and love. Everywhere we go, we take Him—or maybe He takes us where He goes.

Do your friends see Jesus in you? Picture wearing garments that gleam from your love-filled words, sparkling as particles of joy shimmer in you, and feel velvety smooth with peace. Jesus' patience and kindness leave a sweet fragrance when you pass by. Traces of His goodness shine from you like diamonds.

When we go to heaven and stand before God, if we've given our lives to Jesus, we will be completely covered in Christ's glorious righteousness. The Father will be so pleased! When we're clothed in Jesus, our mistakes are all washed away, totally forgiven and forgotten. We are sparkling clean, completely pure—not because of who we are but because of who Jesus is.

Precious Jesus, I don't know the right words to tell You how much I love You. Thank You for what You've done for me that no one else could do.

HAVING DREAMS

"For I know the plans I have for you," declares
the Lord, *"plans to prosper you and not to harm
you, plans to give you hope and a future."*
JEREMIAH 29:11 NIV

Think really hard. In your heart of hearts, what is your deepest desire? Everyone has different hopes and dreams. Do you want to write a book one day? Be an engineer? Be a mother? Perhaps even President of the United States? People are naturally inquisitive and curious, so it should be no surprise that you have plenty of plans and goals for your life.

God has given you these dreams, and they are truly good and wonderful. God knows how the story of your life will play out, and He will guide you along the journey. He will hold your hand the entire way. Even if it seems like your plans will change, don't worry. God has the very best plan in mind for you. Just as you have the courage to follow your dreams, also have the courage to let God change them. You have a bright future! Trust in God, and you will accomplish great things.

Dear Lord, please give me the courage to chase my
dreams. Also give me the patience to wait on Your timing.
You have planned out all my days. Thank You for your
wisdom and for taking care of my every step. Amen.

YOUR WORTH IS IN CHRIST

[The Lord] said to me, "My grace is sufficient for you, for my power is made perfect in weakness." Therefore I will boast all the more gladly about my weaknesses, so that Christ's power may rest on me.
2 CORINTHIANS 12:9 NIV

It can seem like every day brings a new person to tell you that you are not good enough. You don't make the team. You don't get the grade. You don't look like the girls on television. No matter how hard you try, sometimes you just don't measure up to the pressures of being a modern girl. However, as long as you pull your worth from the world around you, you will always come up short. There will always be someone "better."

Fortunately, because you are loved by Christ, you have been made a new creation! In God's eyes, you are His child. He takes your weaknesses and turns them into opportunities to show His strength through you. It doesn't matter what people think about you. You are a child of God, and that is the most powerful identity there is. Whenever you feel like you aren't good enough, remember that the God of the universe loves you, and there is nothing greater than that.

Dear Lord, whenever I feel less than or inadequate, I will remember that I have been filled with Your power and love. Nothing can bring me down when I have You on my side! Amen.

MAYBE DON'T POST THAT...

*The Lord said to Samuel, "Do not consider his appearance
or his height, for I have rejected him. The Lord does not
look at the things people look at. People look at the
outward appearance, but the Lord looks at the heart."*
1 SAMUEL 16:7 NIV

Between Vine, Instagram, Twitter, Snapchat, and countless other social media sites, it seems like everyone is focused on documenting every single aspect of their day. It can be fun to post pictures of your friends, the occasional joke, or even a selfie online, but people are becoming more and more undiscerning with what they post.

Instead of just living life and letting things happen, people often act like if they don't Vine it, it didn't really happen. Also, people can very carefully control the image that they project through their social media. They can only post the amazing moments, the beautiful things. It is easy to forget that even though it looks like your friends and acquaintances have perfect lives, free from pain and frustration, that just isn't true. They have the same struggles and sadnesses that you do. Maybe instead of just following friends and liking their pictures, hang out with them in real life. Ask them how they're really doing and get to know them in a real and tangible way. This will be even better than that eleventh like on Instagram.

Dear Lord, help me remember that friendships call
for work and interaction. Show me how to be real
and vulnerable with those that I love. Amen.

THE DIFFERENCE BETWEEN HAPPINESS AND JOY

Then I will go to the altar of God, to God, my joy and my delight. I will praise you with the lyre, O God, my God.

PSALM 43:4 NIV

Think about your best day ever. The day where everything went your way and everything was beautiful. How did that day make you feel? Were you so happy that it felt like your heart would crack open to make more room for happiness? Did it stay that way? Probably not. Eventually, the sunshine went away or your friends went home or you broke your new toy. This is because happiness is a temporary feeling. It is impossible to be happy every moment of every day. However, this does not mean that you can't live a life of joy.

Joy is a little different than happiness. Happiness is a fleeting emotion in the moment, while joy refers more to living a lifestyle of contentment. If you have been given true joy in the Lord, you will still find reasons to rejoice, even when life is at its most bleak. Happiness won't stay, but true joy lasts a lifetime.

Dear Lord, thank You for making joy possible. Without Your loving-kindness, life would be a much gloomier thing. Remind me that even when I am not happy, I still have reason for joy. Amen.

BULLIES HURT

"Be strong and courageous. Do not be afraid or terrified because of them, for the LORD your God goes with you; he will never leave you nor forsake you."

DEUTERONOMY 31:6 NIV

You know that feeling. That feeling in the pit of your stomach when you see that person who goes out of their way to be cruel to you. Whether it is with mocking words or actual physical abuse, this person is a bully and you are their victim. It can be a truly hopeless feeling. Or maybe you aren't the one who is actually bullied, but some other kid in your class is. Maybe they are a little weird or different and that is why they have been made a target.

Being bullied is very hard, but it is important to remember that God is on your side. The key is being kind to everyone around you. If you see a kid in your class being bullied, invite them to sit with you and your friends at lunch. If you are the kid being bullied, don't let fear drive you to silence. Talk to your teacher, but remember to be forgiving. While bullies are awful, their cruelty often comes from a place of insecurity and fear. God calls us to love our enemies, even the bullies.

Dear Lord, give me the courage to stand up to the bullies of the world, but also give me the courage to forgive them. Amen.

MEMORIZING SCRIPTURE

"Keep this Book of the Law always on your lips; meditate on it day and night, so that you may be careful to do everything written in it. Then you will be prosperous and successful."

JOSHUA 1:8 NIV

On your way to school, your mom turns on the radio. As you are riding down the road, your favorite song comes on. You light up—this is your jam! You sing along at the top of your lungs, and you know every word. The next song comes on, and you still know all the words. You even know all the words to the songs that you don't like! Music is such a part of your life that your brain has stored endless lyrics away. Wouldn't it be wonderful if you knew scripture that well?

So often Christians don't even know what is inside their Bible. However, you are called to meditate on scripture day and night, never letting it depart from your lips. By reading the Bible every day, you will always have God's Word in the back of your mind. Consequently, it will be much easier to reference it as a guide for your life. Make it a goal to memorize scripture regularly as a part of your spiritual growth.

Dear Lord, Your Word is a lamp to guide my feet!
I will meditate on scripture daily so that I can
better understand Your plan for me. Amen.

THE IMPORTANCE OF FRIENDSHIP

One who has unreliable friends soon comes to ruin,
but there is a friend who sticks closer than a brother.

PROVERBS 18:24 NIV

Do you remember your first friend? Maybe you ran around outside and played with your dolls together, sharing secrets and watching movies. From an early age, humans are hardwired to seek out friends and build relationships. It is important to be discerning when you make friends, because while a good friend can build you up, a bad one can tear you down. While people all differ in how many friends they want, everyone needs a good friend to rely on. Whether you prefer to be friends with everyone or have a small, close-knit group on your side, friendship is truly one of God's greatest gifts.

With that in mind, be thankful every day for the friends that you have! Sometimes they will hurt you and you will hurt them, but a true friend apologizes, forgives, and works out their issues. Friendship is worth all the hard stuff. Good friends support you and help you become the best version of yourself, and you do the same for them. Friendship is a two-way street—make sure that it is a safe one.

Dear Lord, thank You for my friends! You have truly
blessed me with awesome people in my life. Help
me be the best friend that I can be! Amen.

BEING A BETTER SISTER

Be kind and compassionate to one another, forgiving each other, just as in Christ God forgave you.
EPHESIANS 4:32 NIV

You were just trying to get your homework done. You would think that you could get a little privacy in your own room, but no. You can hear the small hands scrabbling at the door. You roll your eyes and begin to scream. Either that or you are the younger sister. You know that your brother is hanging out with his friends, but you want to be the center of attention. You bang on the door until they open it, and then you run away cackling.

Sometimes it isn't easy being a sibling. Sometimes it even seems like it is just easier to be unkind and annoy your siblings instead of trying to build good relationships with them. However, patience and kindness can get you a long way. Being siblings is a truly special relationship, and you shouldn't let petty disagreements come between you. Instead, work together to keep these disagreements to a minimum. You may even become friends too instead of just siblings. Even if they still drive you a little bit crazy.

Dear Lord, thank You so much for my family.
Even if they can be frustrating and insane, I
know that they are always on my side. Amen.

YOUR PARENTS ARE SMARTER THAN YOU THINK

"Honor your father and your mother, so that you may live long in the land the LORD your God is giving you."

EXODUS 20:12 NIV

It happens to everyone: You get invited to your first teenage party. You desperately want to go, but your parents don't think it will be a safe environment for you. Because of their concerns, they tell you that you can't go. Because of this, your world is seemingly ending. You think they just don't understand you. How could they be so mean?

However, with a little age and experience, you start to realize that maybe your parents knew a little more than you thought. They have your best interests at heart and just want to help you flourish and be safe. So maybe you should cut them a little slack. Instead of fighting them on every choice, learn to accept their wisdom. This doesn't mean accepting it blindly—instead, try talking through your issues with your parents so you can fully understand each other's perspectives. Open communication and respect will help these relationships flourish! Your parents have so much love in their hearts for you, and you for them. Take some time to tell them.

Dear Lord, thank You for giving me great parents! I am so blessed to have such a supportive home! Thank You for this crazy bunch of people I call my family. Amen.

HARD WORK WILL GET YOU FAR

I can do all this through him who gives me strength.
PHILIPPIANS 4:13 NIV

It is good to have goals! Whether it is improving your grades, learning a new skill, or joining a sports team, all truly good things require work. You can't get As without studying. You can't learn a new piano piece if you don't practice. You can't score the winning goal without training with your team. If you really want to succeed, you have to put in the time. There is no shortcut to improvement.

Instead of just waiting around and slacking off, do the work. Even when it seems impossible, remember that God has given you the strength to succeed. However, you have to meet Him halfway. Good things come to those who try, and fail, and then try again. Even if it's hard, improving your skills and meeting your goals is great! Next time you are tempted to be lazy, think about what you could be doing instead. Success comes to those who put their talents to good use. Don't hide what God has given you under a basket!

Dear Lord, thank You for all the talents that You have given me! Keep me humble, but also give me the drive to set goals and work hard to meet them. Amen.

PUT DOWN YOUR PHONE!

When I consider your heavens, the work of your fingers, the moon and the stars, which you have set in place, what is mankind that you are mindful of them, human beings that you care for them?

PSALM 8:3–4 NIV

Modern technology is great. In a device that fits in the palm of your hand, you can call anyone you know or get endless information on any topic you want. With all that power at your disposal, it is easy to get drawn in and forget to engage in the world around you. It is great to be able to learn more about the world through your phone, but it is important not to forget to actually look at the beautiful world around you.

Put down your phone. Go outside. God has made a masterpiece with His creation, and you were made to care for it. Remember to spend some time out in nature and enjoy what God has given you. Look for ways that you can spend a little time outside. Help your mom in her garden or plant a tree with your dad. Don't get so caught up in the digital world that you forget the beauty of the natural one.

Dear Lord, thank You for creating such a beautiful world! You didn't have to have such wonderful variety in nature, and yet Your world is magnificent. Amen.

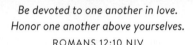

EVERYONE DESERVES RESPECT

Be devoted to one another in love.
Honor one another above yourselves.
ROMANS 12:10 NIV

It is easy to forget to think of others. You get so wrapped up in your own stuff: school, friends, sports, clubs. You start to think that your stuff is more important than anyone else's, that the sun orbits around you and your life. Because of this, you forget to treat the people around you with the respect that they deserve. Be understanding and realize that everyone has a lot going on, not just you. Their stuff is important as well, and you should treat them accordingly.

Everyone deserves respect. Everyone. From the teacher who runs your classroom to the kid down the street, it is important to treat others the way that you would like to be treated. Instead of just respecting the people who are in charge of you, try also to be compassionate to everyone, even those who can give you nothing. You may be surprised at how good you feel when you're kind to others. Everyone has been made in God's image, so everyone has value.

Dear Lord, help me be kind and respectful to others,
even if it isn't easy. Jesus cared for everyone He
met. Help me follow His example. Amen.

BE PATIENT

*My dear brothers and sisters, take note of this: Everyone should
be quick to listen, slow to speak and slow to become angry.*

JAMES 1:19 NIV

"Patience is a virtue!" Every time something goes wrong, your mom reminds you of this old adage. "Patience is a virtue." You know that this is true, but why do you have to wait so long? You're a pretty good person—why can't you get what you want when you want it? Unfortunately, that is not how the Christian life works. God's goal for our lives is not necessarily to be happy but to be made into a more perfect image of Himself. This often requires a lot of work and a lot of patience.

Instead of always chomping at the bit, try to practice being quiet or being still. Instead of always speaking first and loudly, work on your listening skills. God is molding you into a more beautiful creation every day, much like the blacksmith forges metal into a stronger, smoother shape. It may be painful, and sometimes even tedious, but having patience in the face of the Lord's molding will produce truly incredible results.

Dear Lord, give me the patience to be molded. You are
forming me into a being that reflects You in all things,
but that doesn't happen overnight. Teach me to be
patient and wait for Your steady hands. Amen.

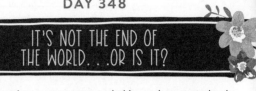

IT'S NOT THE END OF THE WORLD. . .OR IS IT?

*Therefore, since we are surrounded by such a great cloud
of witnesses, let us throw off everything that hinders
and the sin that so easily entangles. And let us run with
perseverance the race marked out for us, fixing our
eyes on Jesus, the pioneer and perfecter of faith.*

HEBREWS 12:1–2 NIV

When you're young, everything can feel like the end of the world.
If you don't get to see your favorite band on tour, your life is
meaningless. If you don't get to go to that party, everything is
terrible. If you make a bad grade, the universe is crumbling around
you. However, life still goes on. The band will come back, there will
be an even better party, and you can study harder for the next test.
By being patient, you will realize that not everything happens on
your timing but on God's.

Instead of getting upset and breaking down when things don't
go your way, focus on God's timing. He has a glorious plan for your
life; you just have to learn to wait on His plan. When it looks like
your plans won't pan out, the world is not ending. It is just shifting,
and you are shifting with it. When you learn to go where God's plan
leads you, you will experience true success.

Dear Lord, I am so excited to see the plan You have
for my life! I am ready for truly great things. Amen.

EVERYONE IS LONELY (SOMETIMES)

Cast all your anxiety on him because he cares for you.
1 PETER 5:7 NIV

Somehow, you can be surrounded by people but still be desperately lonely. Whether your friend group changes or your parents divorce, numerous factors can lead to you spending a lot of time on your own. You might feel inadequate or that it is somehow your fault. Anxiety and self-doubt plague your thoughts, and you withdraw deeper into a dark hole.

Everyone has felt "less than" at one point or another. But even when it feels like everyone you know has abandoned you, God hasn't. He is always there for you, no matter how alone you feel. He will carry you through these dark times of your life, even if you don't realize it at the time. Either through His Word or by putting people into your orbit to help you through the lonely times, God is always on your side. He cares for you and wants you to be surrounded by people who bring you joy and help you grow. He will never, ever abandon you, even when it seems that everyone else has. It is good to know that God's love for you will never waver.

Dear Lord, thank You for Your steadfast love. You are my rock in the difficult times. Thank You for helping me find my way out of the dark. Amen.

HONESTY IS THE BEST POLICY

"Then you will know the truth, and the truth will set you free."
JOHN 8:32 NIV

Well, it's happened. You've been caught in a lie. You didn't study for the pop quiz, and you tried to read the answers off of your best friend's paper. Your teacher caught you. She knows you cheated. You know you cheated, and yet you try to deny it. This only makes the deceit even more sticky. Now you not only lied on your quiz, but you also lied to your teacher's face. She is disappointed in you, and you are disappointed in yourself. A lying tongue is an affront to God.

In most situations, honesty is truly the best policy. By lying, you are distancing yourself from the people around you, building up walls on the foundation of lies. However, God doesn't stand for that. It is said that the truth will set you free, and the truth will always find you out. Instead of waiting for that terrible moment when you are caught in your lie, save yourself the stress and just tell the truth. Being transparent with your choices is a great way to live and grow in Christ.

Dear Lord, I am sorry for the lies that I have told, but thank You for always guiding me back to the truth. Amen.

JUST BE YOURSELF

I praise you because I am fearfully and wonderfully made; your works are wonderful, I know that full well.

PSALM 139:14 NIV

Sometimes it can feel like no one understands you. No one else loves your hobbies or they don't like to spend their time like you do. Sometimes it can feel like it is you against the world and no one around you gets what makes you tick. It's okay. Read your books. Listen to your music. Like what you like, and just be yourself. Eventually, you will find people who are filled with the same fire, and glorious friendships will be born.

Even if it seems like you'll never fit in or find people like you, God made you to be just who you are. There is not a hair out of place. He didn't make a mistake. Instead of wishing that God had made you differently, celebrate who you are! Work on becoming the best version of yourself, the best version of who God has made. There is a peace that comes with just being yourself, and everyone deserves to have that peace.

Dear Lord, thank You for creating me. Even when I feel weird or like the odd girl out, I know that I am a part of Your wonderful creation! Amen.

A WORLD IN WINTER

*There is a time for everything, and a season
for every activity under the heavens.*
ECCLESIASTES 3:1 NIV

In the wintertime it seems like the world is going into a deep sleep. Most plants are dormant, and many animals are going into hibernation. People stay home more to avoid the elements. While winter is nice for a while, it eventually begins to feel like spring will never come again. But every year spring does come again, gloriously alive.

In a similar way, many years ago, the world was waiting for a Savior. The hearts of men had grown cold and despondent. It felt like an endless spiritual winter, and it seemed as though the promised Child would never come. However, that Child did come, and His name was Jesus. This spiritual renewal was like spring popping up in the hearts of God's people. Now, many years on, it can feel again like a winter without Jesus. Fortunately, there is still the promise of a new spring when Jesus returns.

Dear Lord, thank You for the promise of spring.
When I am stuck in the bleakness of winter, all I have
to do is remember that You will always bring back the
warmth and sunshine. You are faithful. Amen.

IT IS OKAY TO NOT BE COOL

For we are God's handiwork, created in Christ Jesus to do
good works, which God prepared in advance for us to do.
EPHESIANS 2:10 NIV

Being cool is hard. It takes a lot of work to stay on top, and what is considered "cool" is always changing. New music becomes popular every day. New clothing styles come into fashion as quickly as they go out. Staying hip requires an extraordinary amount of time. Is it worth it?

Instead of focusing on how to be popular, focus on how you can become a greater vessel for God's love. Show people kindness instead of just showing off designer jeans. It is okay to not be cool. That's not why you were created. You were created to do good works, to show Christ's love to the world. It is easy to get caught up in a popularity contest, but remember, that isn't what life is about. Jesus hung out with the lepers, tax collectors, and other people with the least amount of power in society. He didn't worry about being cool; He worried about being kind and about loving others well.

Dear Lord, I am sorry that I have gotten so wrapped up in wanting to be popular. That isn't what life is about. Instead, help me reach out to people with kindness. Amen.

BEING A BETTER DAUGHTER

*But the fruit of the Spirit is love, joy, peace, forbearance,
kindness, goodness, faithfulness, gentleness and
self-control. Against such things there is no law.*
GALATIANS 5:22–23 NIV

You have pretty great parents, right? They work hard every single day to provide a safe and loving home for their children, never asking for anything in return. How often do you thank them? Every day? On Sundays? On your birthday? Because it is such a natural thing, you often forget how much your parents sacrifice to provide for you.

There are many ways that you can show your gratitude. First of all, remembering to say "Thank you" is a very simple place to start. This pair of small words can go a long way when combined with a sincere attitude. You can also help out with different things around your house without complaint. Bonus points if you do the task before you are even asked. Also, your general attitude can be either beneficial or detrimental to letting your parents know you care. Instead of emulating the teens on TV and being surly and insulting to adults, try to let your thankfulness show in an outpouring of good humor. This isn't always possible, but making a conscious effort is a step in the right direction.

Dear Lord, thank You for my loving parents. They provide
so much for me that I don't even know where to begin
to thank them. Show me how to be a good daughter and
grow in a spirit of thankfulness and respect. Amen.

GOSSIP HELPS NO ONE

Keep your tongue from evil and your lips from telling lies.
PSALM 34:13 NIV

Whether you have started a rumor, shared a rumor, or had a rumor spread about you, you have definitely been exposed to gossip. When you hear a new secret, it can be a bit of a thrill. You hold the information that could make or break a person, and with that comes the feeling of power. However, it is only hollow. Instead of encouraging and building up the people around you, gossip only tears down. Gossip is often the product of someone trying to feel better about themselves by making another person feel worse. However, in the long run, making someone feel worse will not make you feel any better.

While it is sometimes quite difficult, it is important to take a stand against gossip. Don't gossip and encourage your friends to do the same. Instead of spreading malice, focus on encouraging the people around you. A kind word can go a long way. Gossip often does irreparable harm, and it is not how God would want you to spend your time.

. . . .

Dear Lord, let the words that come out of my mouth
only be words of encouragement. Help me as I endeavor
to build up my friends and classmates instead of
tearing them down with hateful words. Amen.

WORRY WASTES TIME

*Now may the Lord of peace himself give you peace at
all times and in every way. The Lord be with all of you.*
2 THESSALONIANS 3:16 NIV

It is hard not being in control. You can plan out every step of your
life, but there is no way to really know what will happen down the
line. This worry can cause a great deal of inner turmoil and anxiety.
*What if I don't have any friends? What if I don't do well in school? What
if something happens to my family?* Worrying can be truly toxic and
can have a crippling effect on your life. If you are so worried about
every outcome, how will you ever actually make a choice?

Instead of worrying, trust God. He has promised countless times
in the Bible that He will always take care of His people. It isn't always
easy to do, but your life will be better for it. Instead of worrying
about what can happen, look forward to what will happen. God has a
great plan for you! Whatever He has in mind is infinitely more
awesome than anything that you can come up with.

Dear Lord, I am so excited to see the plans that You
have for me! Please ease my worried mind and remind
me to wait on Your timing, not my own. Amen.

FACING TEMPTATION

*"Watch and pray so that you will not fall into temptation.
The spirit is willing, but the flesh is weak."*

MATTHEW 26:41 NIV

You are faced with temptation every single day. You can be tempted to be unkind to your little sister or disrespectful to your parents. You may be tempted to cheat on a test or send a tweet making fun of your teacher. You may even have started being tempted into going too far with boys. Unfortunately, the constant allure of temptation never goes away. Staying on the straight and narrow path never gets easier. Every day the devil will try to tempt God's people to stray.

Luckily, you serve a God who can handle the pressure. He will give you all the strength and tools that you need to stand up in the face of temptation. You only need to call on Him for help. By constantly being in God's Word and filling your mind with His teachings, you will have everything you need to resist temptation. Never give up! Always keep fighting! The righteous path is never easy, but it always reaps the greatest rewards in the end.

Dear Lord, I look to You for guidance. Even though
it is hard to resist the temptations of the world, the
flesh, and the devil, I know that with You on my side,
I can stand strong against anything. Amen.

DAY 358

ANTICIPATING THE SAVIOR

For to us a child is born, to us a son is given, and the government
will be on his shoulders. And he will be called Wonderful
Counselor, Mighty God, Everlasting Father, Prince of Peace.

ISAIAH 9:6 NIV

We sometimes forget that big, beautiful, amazing things often come in small packages. Chocolates come in a small package. Even the Savior of the whole world came in a small package—as a baby! Jesus came down into a sinful world as an innocent baby and saved the world while sacrificing His life. He brought with Him the promise of peace, freedom, and eternal life.

When you are tempted to measure your life by the amount of stuff you have in your closet or by how many activities are on your calendar, remember life is best lived treasuring the simple things. Count Jesus as your number one friend, asset, and the purpose of your whole life.

Dear Lord, help me remember that life isn't about the superficial things, it is about the Savior. You sent Your only Son to save the world, and because of that, my relationship with You has been restored. Amen.

THE ULTIMATE GIFT

But the angel said to them, "Do not be afraid. I bring you good
news that will cause great joy for all the people. Today in the town
of David a Savior has been born to you; he is the Messiah, the Lord."
LUKE 2:10–11 NIV

Possibly the most exciting time of a birthday or Christmas celebration is the time dedicated to gift-giving! Everyone is smiling and content, getting exactly what they wanted. But still you wonder: *Is this it? Is this what I have been waiting all year for?* There is still a bit of emptiness, because ultimately, these gifts are just things.

There is only one present that can bring true contentment: the gift of salvation. God looked down on a weak and weary world, and instead of leaving us to our own sinful devices, He sent His only Son to free the world from the bonds of sin and death and to rebuild the communion between God and man. This is truly the greatest gift that you have ever been given.

Dear Lord, thank You for giving the world the gift of
Your Son! You are truly merciful, and You have filled
us with gladness and tidings of great joy! Amen.

REAL FREEDOM

"So if the Son sets you free, you will be free indeed."
JOHN 8:36 NIV

When you're young, you are always waiting on someone else. Waiting for your mom to get your little brother into the car so you can make it to your soccer game. Waiting for your teacher to let your class out at the end of the day. Waiting for your friend to come over so you can hang out. Waiting, waiting, waiting. You can't wait to be older and to be able to live by your own time and to be free to live your life. However, even then, you won't truly be "free." With this newfound freedom, you will also find yourself with a new, long list of responsibilities.

The only real freedom comes from putting your life in God's hands. It may seem wrong to hand over control of your life to experience true freedom. However, the only way to be free from the worries of the world is to trust in God. Trusting in God on earth will also prepare you for the ultimate freedom: freedom in heaven to worship Christ endlessly.

Dear Lord, You alone provide real freedom! I will focus on the help that You provide instead of looking for fleeting forms of freedom. Thank You for removing the shackles of sin and death from my ankles. Amen.

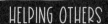

HELPING OTHERS

"In the same way, let your light shine before others, that they may see your good deeds and glorify your Father in heaven."
MATTHEW 5:16 NIV

As you get older, you start to get busier and busier. Instead of just playing with your friends all day, you go to school, you go to clubs, you join teams, you make more friends. Slowly but surely, your life is incredibly full, and it is easy to lose sight of the people who need you. You get wrapped up in your own busyness and you forget that it isn't all about you. Life with Christ is about helping others.

You can start out with small steps. Offer to help your mom take care of the house, or at least do your chores without her having to ask twice. Help your dad do some yard work on Saturday morning. Help your little sister build that fort that's been collapsing on her all week. You can even think beyond the walls of your home. Talk to your youth leader about getting your youth group involved with local organizations that help those who really need it, like the Red Cross or Habitat for Humanity. When you are filled with the love of Christ, there is no limit to how much you can help!

Dear Lord, You have poured out so much love into me that it is overflowing into the hearts of others! Thank You for helping me cultivate a compassionate spirit. Give me opportunities to help in every situation. Amen.

BEING GRATEFUL

Enter his gates with thanksgiving and his courts with praise; give thanks to him and praise his name. For the LORD is good and his love endures forever; his faithfulness continues through all generations.

PSALM 100:4–5 NIV

Sometimes you don't get what you want. You don't get the latest and greatest smartphone for your birthday. You don't get to hang out with your friends on Friday night. You have to share a room with your sister, and you may even have to wear some of her hand-me-down clothes. In such a consumerist culture, it is easy to get bogged down in what you don't have. "Life would be easier if I just had. . ." is often a common refrain. But would your life really be easier if you had more stuff?

No, it wouldn't. There is always that next new, cool thing that you just have to have. If your life becomes just one endless quest for what's next, you will only end up exhausted and grouchy. Instead of focusing on what you don't have, look at all the wonderful things God has given you! A loving family, a roof over your head, your good health—these are all gifts from God! His grace truly abounds.

Dear Lord, You have given me so much more
than I deserve! Thank You for all the treasures
of Your grace! I am so very grateful. Amen.

PRAY, PRAY, PRAY!

The LORD is near to all who call on him,
to all who call on him in truth.
PSALM 145:18 NIV

Think about how often you talk to your best friend. Between cell phones, the internet, and actual face-to-face time, it is possible to talk to your best friend constantly throughout the day. You can tell them a joke that you just heard or talk about your bad day to a willing ear. It is great to have someone to talk to all the time. Now, imagine if you treated your relationship with God like your relationship with your best friend.

God is always listening. If you bring your troubles and praises to Him daily, imagine how much your relationship will flourish! People get so caught up with trying to live a Christian life that they forget the relational aspect. God doesn't want you to just read and obey; He wants you to talk to Him like a child talks to their father. While it may feel a little weird at first, try to create an attitude of continuous prayer. You may be surprised by the results.

Dear Lord, thank You for always lending a willing ear. You truly care about my life and desire that I approach You as a Father and Friend. Even with all the universe at Your command, You still want to hear from me. Thank You for this beautiful gift. Amen.

BEING A BETTER FRIEND

Two are better than one, because they have a good return for their labor: if either of them falls down, one can help the other up. But pity anyone who falls and has no one to help them up.

ECCLESIASTES 4:9-10 NIV

Have you ever let a friend down? It's a terrible feeling, isn't it? A friend should always be there to help, but you missed your opportunity. You got caught up in your own life and forgot to ask them about theirs. Being a friend means putting others first, but selfishness is a weed that can often choke out the blossom of friendship. Instead of focusing on what a friend can do for you, set some concrete goals to strengthen your friendships.

For example, instead of just unloading all your drama after a hard day, ask them how they are doing first. And don't just ask without engagement. Really listen to what they have to say. Also, a big part of being a good friend is just showing up. If they are having a bad day, bake some cookies with your mom and bring them over to cheer them up. If they have a big game, cheer them on from the stands. If their grandparent is in the hospital, visit with them. By putting their needs above your own, you will prove yourself to be a really stellar friend.

Dear Lord, thank You for all my wonderful friends! You have truly blessed me with a great group of people. Help me strive to be the best friend I can be, always looking for what I can contribute instead of what I can gain. Amen.

DAY 365

LOOKING AHEAD

*Therefore, if anyone is in Christ, the new creation
has come: The old has gone, the new is here!*
2 CORINTHIANS 5:17 NIV

Over this past year, you have truly become the new creation that God has called you to be. You have continued to scrape off the old, sinful self while pulling on the new robes of righteousness that God has given you. The new year also presents a great opportunity to cast off lingering bad habits. How can you keep this up next year?

The main thing to remember is to stay in the Word. Set a goal to read through the Bible in a year! It may seem daunting when you look at it all in one giant book, but by breaking it down into small goals, it is a totally manageable ambition. Maybe encourage your entire family to take part. Also, as you approach the new year, remember to be thankful. You have been given the gift of life. What a blessing!

Dear Lord, thank You for a great year. It has truly been a time of growth, and I have been blessed beyond measure. Give me the strength to continue to follow You in the coming days. Amen.

CONTRIBUTOR INDEX

Emily Marsh lives in Virginia with her husband, Seth, and their various pit bull foster puppies. She works at a downtown real estate firm as a client care coordinator and also teaches ballet in her spare time. Emily wrote days 1–31.

Carol Hill is a Southern country girl who leans tightly on Jesus. She loves hot biscuits, BBQ, the Bible, writing, teaching, her husband of over 40 years, their 5 children, and 3 grandchildren. Just not in that order. Carol wrote days 32–59.

Shana Schutte is an author and speaker. She is the author of several books including *30 Days of Hope*. You can learn more about Shana by visiting shanaschutte.com. Shana wrote days 60–90.

Lydia Mindling's writing is inspired by three things: *God's love, Christ's sacrifice, and creation*. When not writing, Lydia enjoys horseback riding, hikes, and attempts at baking the world's best brownies. Lydia wrote days 91–120

Karon Phillips of Alabama is an inspiration to the tens of thousands of women who've read her books *You're Late Again, Lord!*; *Grab a Broom, Lord. . .*; and *You Still Here, Lord?* She has also written for many magazines, including *Woman's Day* and *Writer's Digest*. Karon wrote days 121–151.

Shelley R. Lee is the author of *Before I Knew You*, *Mat Madness*, numerous magazine and newspaper articles, contributor to *2014 Daily Wisdom for Women*, and several other Barbour projects. She resides in northwest Ohio with her husband of 29 years, David, and their four grown sons. Shelley wrote days 152–181.

Karin Dahl Silver is a former Air Force kid, voracious reader, and rock climbing novice (getting braver!). She and her husband, Scott, live in Colorado Springs, Colorado. Karin wrote days 182–212.

MariLee Parrish lives in Ohio with her husband, Eric, and young children. She's a freelance musician and writer who desires to paint a picture of God with her life, talents, and ministries. MariLee wrote days 213–243.

Shanna D. Gregor is a freelance writer, editor, and product developer who has served various ministries and publishers. The mother of two young men, Shanna and her husband reside in Tucson, Arizona. Shanna wrote days 244–273.

Renae Brumbaugh lives in Texas with her two noisy children and two dogs. She's authored four books in Barbour's Camp Club Girls series, *Morning Coffee with James* (Chalice Press), and has contributed to several anthologies. Her humor column and articles have appeared in publications across the country. Renae wrote days 274–304.

Ardythe Kolb writes articles and devotions for various publications and is currently working on her third book. She serves on the advisory board of a writers' network and edits their newsletter. Ardythe wrote days 305–334.

Alyssa Fikse lives and works in Philadelphia while continuing her education at Drexel University with a graduate degree in Library and Information Science. Alyssa wrote days 335–365.

SCRIPTURE INDEX

OLD TESTAMENT

Genesis
1:27 . . . . Day 13, 182, 213
2:18 . . . . Day 43
8:21–22 . . . . Day 99
40:23 . . . . Day 150
50:19–20 . . . . Day 206

Exodus
2:2–4 . . . . Day 128
17:11–12 . . . . Day 104
20:12 . . . . Day 343

Numbers
12:3 . . . . Day 324
30:1–2 . . . . Day 271

Deuteronomy
4:2 . . . . Day 294
11:1 . . . . Day 36, 274
11:8–9 . . . . Day 275
31:6 . . . . Day 260, 339
31:8 . . . . Day 193, 241

Joshua
1:8 . . . . Day 6, 340
1:9 . . . . Day 234

Ruth
3:5 . . . . Day 129
4:14 . . . . Day 120

1 Samuel
15:22 . . . . Day 49
16:7 . . . . Day 17, 153, 307, 337

2 Samuel
1:11 . . . . Day 267
22:32 . . . . Day 38

1 Chronicles
16:11 . . . . Day 77
28:20 . . . . Day 92
29:15 . . . . Day 179

Esther
1:11–12 . . . . Day 141

Job
17:9 . . . . Day 329

Psalms
4:8 . . . . Day 27
5:1–3 . . . . Day 142
8:3–4 . . . . Day 345
9:1–2 . . . . Day 91
13:5–6 . . . . Day 328
16:11 . . . . Day 196
18:28 . . . . Day 2
18:35 . . . . Day 61
19:7–8 . . . . Day 186, 227
27:14 . . . . Day 85
31:9 . . . . Day 217
31:19–20 . . . . Day 297

31:21–22 . . . . Day 298
31:23–24 . . . . Day 299
34:13 . . . . Day 355
37:3–5 . . . . Day 235
37:23–24 . . . . . . Day 155, 210
39:4 . . . . Day 28
43:4 . . . . Day 338
45:13–14 . . . . Day 103
46:1–2 . . . . Day 7
46:1–3 . . . . Day 181
46:5 . . . . Day 110
46:10 . . . . Day 34
56:3–4 . . . . Day 4
62:11–12 . . . . Day 284
63:7–8 . . . . Day 285
73:23–24 . . . . Day 22
73:23–26 . . . . Day 219
73:28 . . . . Day 107
74:13–14 . . . . Day 222
90:12 . . . . Day 207
96:7–9 . . . . Day 229
100:4–5 . . . . Day 362
101:3 . . . . Day 33
112:6–7 . . . . Day 233
118:6 . . . . Day 11
118:14–15 . . . . Day 202
118:24 . . . . Day 90
119:11 . . . . Day 46
119:105 . . . . Day 81
119:111 . . . . Day 89
121:1–4 . . . . Day 14
125:2 . . . . Day 208

130:6–7 . . . . Day 105
139:1–5 . . . . Day 45
139:5–6 . . . . Day 243
139:13–14 . . . . .Day 74
139:14 . . . . Day 351
139:14, 16–17 . . . . . . Day 180
141:3–4 . . . . Day 52
141:4 . . . . Day 318
145:18 . . . . Day 363
145:18–21 . . . . Day 116
150:6 . . . . Day 25

Proverbs
2:6 . . . . Day 136
3:5–6 . . . . Day 65
4:23 . . . . Day 87, 330
12:22 . . . . Day 53
13:4 . . . . Day 249
13:17 . . . . Day 269
16:3 . . . . Day 211
16:23–24 . . . . Day 119
16:28 . . . . . . Day 80, 194, 245
17:9 . . . . Day 224
18:10 . . . . Day 51
18:21 . . . . Day 47, 59
18:24 . . . . Day 223, 341
20:6 . . . . Day 203
20:27 . . . . Day 199
25:28 . . . . Day 173
26:2 . . . . Day 195
27:17 . . . . Day 50
31:30 . . . . Day 230

Ecclesiastes
2:11, 13 .... Day 174
3:1 .... Day 306, 352
3:14–15.............. Day 101
4:4, 8 .... Day 253
4:9–10 .... Day 364
4:9–10, 12 .... Day 242

Isaiah
1:17 .... Day 18
9:6............ Day 118, 358
26:4 ....Day 3
35:3–4.............Day 102
40:8 ....Day 97
40:10–11............ Day 98
40:26............. Day 282
40:31 .... Day 84
41:10 .... Day 66
41:13 .... Day 236
43:1................. Day 31
43:1–2, 4 .... Day 151
43:1–4 ....Day 106
43:2 .... Day 278
43:2–3.............Day 167
43:18–19 .... Day 279
44:2–3............. Day 276
45:5–6............. Day 295
45:7–8............. Day 296
46:9 .... Day 117
49:9 ....Day 185
49:16 .... Day 26
49:23 ....Day 277

54:10 .... Day 280
55:9 ....Day 164
55:12.............. Day 281
58:10 ....Day 331

Jeremiah
1:6 ....Day 126
9:23–24.... Day 21, 246, 315
15:16 .... Day 171
29:11 .... Day 335
29:12–13............. Day 172
29:12–14. .... Day 209
29:13.........Day 63, 283
31:3 ....Day 212

Lamentations
3:22–23............. Day 20
3:55–57............ Day 93

Daniel
2:20–22............. Day 96
4:3 .... Day 332

Hosea
2:14................. Day 114
6:3.................. Day 94
14:5–7.............. Day 115
Joel
2:11 .... Day 300

Amos
5:14................. Day 312

Micah
6:8 . . . . .Day 112, 326

Nahum
1:7 . . . . .Day 310

Habakkuk
2:14. . . . . Day 338

Zephaniah
3:14–15. . . . . Day 113
3:17 . . . . Day 225

Haggai
2:5. . . . . Day 140

NEW TESTAMENT
Matthew
5:16. . . . . .Day 361
5:23–24. . . . . Day 71, 163
5:44 . . . . Day 70
5:48 . . . . Day 248
6:6. . . . . Day 144
6:19–21. . . . . .Day 192
6:22 . . . . .Day 319
6:25–26 . . . . Day 64
6:26 . . . . .Day 170
7:7–8 . . . . Day 286
7:24–25 . . . . Day 287
9:36 . . . . Day 69
10:19 . . . . .Day 76
10:20 . . . . .Day 145

11:28–30 . . . . Day 240
13:3–8 . . . . .Day 183
13:15–16 . . . . Day 265
14:27–31. . . . . Day 131
14:28–31 . . . . Day 266
14:29–30 . . . . Day 226
14:30–31 . . . . Day 16
22:35–40 . . . . Day 121
22:37–39. . . . . .Day 216
23:4–5 . . . . .Day 135
26:41. . . . . Day 357

Mark
11:25 . . . . Day 258
12:30. . . . . Day 327
12:43–44. . . . . Day 108

Luke
2:10–11 . . . . Day 359
2:51. . . . . Day 305
6:27–28 . . . . Day 320
6:45 . . . . Day 270
6:48 . . . . Day 24
7:47. . . . . .Day 124
9:23 . . . . Day 244
10:27. . . . . .Day 41
11:9–10 . . . . Day 200
12:48 . . . . .Day 37
16:10 . . . . .Day 178

John
2:5. . . . . .Day 125

3:16 . . . . .Day 79
3:30 . . . . .Day 9
5:6–9 . . . . .Day 139
6:19–21. . . . . .Day 130
8:29 . . . . Day 257
8:32 . . . . Day 350
8:36 . . . . Day 360
10:27–28 . . . . .Day 19
12:42–43. . . . . Day 268
13:34. . . . . Day 40
14:13–14. . . . . .Day 261
15:5 . . . . Day 325
15:10 . . . . Day 228
16:33. . . . . .Day 111
20:16 . . . . Day 127

Acts
5:8–10 . . . . .Day 146
12:6. . . . . .Day 132
12:12–14. . . . . .Day 133
17:26–29 . . . . Day 137

Romans
1:20. . . . . .Day 214
5:1 . . . . Day 323
6:23 . . . . Day 86
8:1. . . . . .Day 198
8:5, 12. . . . . Day 252
8:6 . . . . Day 232
8:26–27. . . . . Day 303
8:31. . . . . Day 62
10:12 . . . . .Day 148

12:2 . . . . .Day 154
12:10 . . . . Day 346
12:16–17 . . . . .Day 301
12:17 . . . . Day 56
12:21 . . . . .Day 67
13:10 . . . . Day 254
15:13 . . . . Day 302
16:19–20 . . . . Day 304

1 Corinthians
3:16–17 . . . . Day 264
6:19. . . . . .Day 189
9:24–25. . . . . Day 1
10:13 . . . . Day 176, 237
10:31 . . . . Day 250
12:4–8 . . . . .Day 147
13:4–5 . . . . Day 322
15:33. . . . . .Day 143
16:13–14 . . . . .Day 123

2 Corinthians
1:9 . . . . .Day 138
5:17 . . . . Day 218, 365
10:4–5 . . . . .Day 162
12:9 . . . . Day 336

Galatians
3:26–27 . . . . Day 334
5:22–23 . . . . Day 78, 354
6:14. . . . . Day 95

Ephesians
2:4–5 . . . . .Day 166
2:8–9 . . . . Day 30
2:10 . . . . Day 35, 54, 149,
273, 353
3:17–19 . . . . .Day 187
3:20 . . . . Day 55
4:2–3 . . . . .Day 169
4:16 . . . . Day 204
4:29 . . . . Day 10, 83
4:32 . . . . Day 342
5:1–2 . . . . .Day 57

Philippians
1:6 . . . . . . .Day 156, 188, 205
2:12–13 . . . . Day 272
2:14–15 . . . . Day 309
4:6–7 . . . . Day 60
4:8 . . . . Day 12, 184, 239
4:8–9 . . . . .Day 175
4:13 . . . . Day 344

Colossians
3:12 . . . . Day 177

3:23–24 . . . . .Day 5
4:6 . . . . Day 308

1 Thessalonians
5:16–18 . . . . Day 191
5:19–22 . . . . Day 42

2 Thessalonians
3:5 . . . . .Day 313
3:16 . . . . Day 356

1 Timothy
4:12 . . . . . Day 23, 32, 161, 316

2 Timothy
1:7 . . . . .Day 157
2:15 . . . . Day 289
2:16 . . . . Day 290
2:20–21 . . . . Day 293
2:22 . . . . Day 44, 291
2:22–26 . . . . .Day 134
2:23–24 . . . . Day 292

Titus
2:4–5 . . . . .Day 168
2:14 . . . . .Day 197
3:10 . . . . Day 288

Hebrews
2:17–18 . . . . Day 238
4:12–13 . . . . Day 255
10:23–25 . . . . Day 100
10:24–25 . . . . Day 263
10:35–36 . . . . Day 247
11:1 . . . . .Day 109, 231
11:6 . . . . Day 48
12:1–2 . . . . Day 348
12:5–6 . . . . .Day 314
13:8 . . . . Day 8, 58

James

1:5 . . . . Day 75, 221
1:17 . . . . .Day 201
1:19 . . . . Day 347
2:9. . . . . Day 259
5:16. . . . . Day 262

1 Peter

1:8-9. . . . . Day 311
1:16 . . . . Day 39
2:9-10 . . . . .Day 251
3:3-4 . . . . Day 160, 256
3:12. . . . . .Day 73
4:10. . . . . Day 82
5:7. . . . . Day 72, 349
5:8 . . . . .Day 159

2 Peter

3:17 . . . . .Day 158
3:18. . . . . Day 317

1 John

1:8-9. . . . . Day 220
1:9 . . . . Day 68
3:1 . . . . Day 15
4:7-8 . . . . .Day 321
4:8 . . . . .Day 215
4:10. . . . . Day 29
4:15-16. . . . . .Day 190
4:19. . . . . .Day 122

2 John

4:18. . . . . Day 88

Revelation

2:3-4 . . . . .Day 152
22:17 . . . . .Day 165

INSPIRATION AND ENCOURAGEMENT FOR GIRLS LIKE YOU!

MORE THAN COURAGEOUS

180 encouraging readings and inspiring prayers, rooted in biblical truth, challenge you to be courageous, kind, wise, honest, loving, loyal, hard-working, and so much more! In each devotional reading, you will discover your value and purpose, while coming to understand God's plan for your life.

Paperback / 978-1-63609-255-3 / $12.99

QUIET-TIME PRAYERS FOR A GIRL'S HEART

Here you'll find 180 just-right-sized, devotional-like prayers just for you. Whether you're feeling anxious or courageous and confident, you'll encounter just the inspiration and encouragement you need to strengthen your faith.

Paperback / 978-1-63609-280-5 / $4.99